# Prentice Hall
# LITERATURE
## *Timeless Voices, Timeless Themes*

# Adapted Reader's Companion
# Teacher's Edition

## GOLD LEVEL

Prentice
Hall

Upper Saddle River, New Jersey
Glenview, Illinois
Needham, Massachusetts

ISBN 0-13-063680-0

3 4 5 6 7 8 9 10    06 05 04 03 02

# Acknowledgments

Grateful acknowledgment is made to the following for permission to reprint copyrighted material:

**The Estate of Margaret Walker Alexander**
"Memory" from *For My People* by Margaret Walker, copyright 1942 Yale University Press.

**Susan Bergholz Literary Services**
From "A Celebration of Grandfathers." Copyright © 1983 by Rudolfo Anaya. First published in *New Mexico Magazine*, March 1983. All rights reserved.

**Brandt & Hochman Literary Agents, Inc.**
"The Most Dangerous Game" by Richard Connell. Copyright, 1924 by Richard Connell. Copyright renewed © 1952 by Louise Fox Connell.

**Doubleday, a division of Random House, Inc.**
"The Machine That Won the War," copyright © 1961 by Mercury Press, Inc., from *Isaac Asimov: The Complete Stories, Vol. I* by Isaac Asimov. "The Gift of the Magi," from *The Complete Works of O. Henry* by O. Henry. Published by Press Publications Company.

**Harcourt, Inc.**
"A Lincoln Preface," copyright 1953 by Carl Sandburg and renewed 1981 by Margaret Sandburg, Janet Sandburg, and Helga Sandburg Crile.

**Rosemary Thurber and The Barbara Hogenson Agency, Inc.**
"The Secret Life of Walter Mitty" from *My World— And Welcome To It* copyright © 1942 by James Thurber; copyright renewed © 1971 by James Thurber. All rights reserved.

**Houghton Mifflin Company**
Excerpt from *Silent Spring* (pp. 1–3) by Rachel Carson. Copyright © 1962 by Rachel L. Carson, renewed 1990 by Roger Christie. All rights reserved.

**James R. Hurst**
"The Scarlet Ibis" by James Hurst, published in *The Atlantic Monthly*, July 1960. Copyright © 1988 by James Hurst.

**International Creative Management, Inc.**
"Single Room, Earth View" by Sally Ride, published in the April/May 1986 issue of *Air & Space/Smithsonian Magazine*, published by The Smithsonian Institution.

**The Heirs to the Estate of Martin Luther King, Jr. c/o Writer's House**
"I Have a Dream" from *The Words of Martin Luther King, Jr.* Copyright 1963 by Martin Luther King, Jr., copyright renewed 1991 by Coretta Scott King.

**Andrew MacAndrew**
"The Necklace" from *Boule de Suif and Selected Stories* by Guy de Maupassant, translated by Andrew MacAndrew. Translation copyright © 1964 by Andrew MacAndrew.

**New American Library, a division of Penguin Putnam, Inc.**
From *The Tragedy of Romeo and Juliet* by William Shakespeare, edited by J. A. Bryant, Jr. Published by New American Library, a division of Penguin Putnam, Inc.

**The New York Times**
"Woman's Work" by Julia Alvarez, published in *The New York Times*, September 5, 1994. Copyright © 1994 by The New York Times Co.

**Orchard Books, an imprint of Scholastic, Inc.**
"Checkouts" from *A Couple of Kooks and Other Stories About Love* by Cynthia Rylant. Published by Orchard Books, an imprint of Scholastic, Inc. Copyright © 1990 by Cynthia Rylant.

**G.P. Putnam's Sons, a division of Penguin Putnam, Inc.**
From "Rules of the Game" from *The Joy Luck Club* by Amy Tan, copyright © 1989 by Amy Tan. "Go Deep to the Sewer" from *Childhood* by Bill Cosby. Copyright © 1991 by William H. Cosby, Jr.

**University Press of New England**
Gary Soto, "The Talk", from *A Summer Life* © 1990 by University Press of New England.

**Viking Penguin, a division of Penguin Putnam, Inc.**
From *The Road Ahead* by Bill Gates. Copyright © 1995 by William H. Gates III. "Old Man of the Temple", from *Under The Banyan Tree* by R. K. Narayan, copyright © 1985 by R. K. Narayan. "The Interlopers" from *The Complete Short Stories of Saki* by Saki (H. H. Munro). Published by The Viking Press.

**Vintage Anchor Publishing**
Excerpts from the *Odyssey* by Homer, translated by R. Fitzgerald. Copyright © 1961, 1963 by Robert Fitzgerald and renewed 1989 by Benedict R. C. Fitzgerald.

**Note: Every effort has been made to locate the copyright owner of material reprinted in this book. Omissions brought to our attention will be corrected in subsequent editions.**

# Contents

## Unit 3: Moments of Discovery

## Unit 4: The Lighter Side

## Unit 5: Visions of the Future

## Unit 6: Short Stories

## Unit 7: Nonfiction

## Unit 8: Drama

## Unit 9: Poetry

## Unit 10: The Epic

# To the Teacher

As you face the challenge of heterogeneous classes, you will find a wide variety of abilities and strengths among your students. This book is aimed at special education students who have difficulty with their grade-level text-books. You can use it to keep your classes reading the same selections, but getting the instruction and reading support at the appropriate level. This book provides extended support for those students who need more guidance with reading strategies, literary analysis, and critical thinking skills.

## Factors That Affect Reading Success

There are four key factors that influence students' ability to achieve reading success. These factors, alone and in combination, determine how well a student will learn, grow, and succeed as a reader. To understand the students in your classroom, consider these factors:

(a) **Kinds of Learners** Consider each student's background, previous learning experiences, and special needs. In addition to students who read fluently at grade level, you may find a mix of the following learning characteristics in your classroom:

- *Students who speak a language other than English at home* Unlike their fully fluent counterparts, these students often speak English only at school. This situation leaves them limited hours in which to learn the grammar, vocabulary, idioms, and other intricacies of English.

- *Students who have recently moved to this country* These students may be highly capable students without the specific language skills to function academically in English.

- *Students with learning disabilities* These students may have cognitive, behavioral, social, or physical challenges that make reading more difficult.

(b) **Kinds of Skills and Instruction** Students' reading ability is influenced by the skills they bring to the task. Students must master the skills of decoding, activating and building prior knowledge, and making connections among experiences and new information. Other factors include a student's knowledge of the English language and vocabulary, and a student's ability to apply reading comprehension strategies.

Active reading, including the practice of summarizing, questioning, setting a purpose, and self-monitoring, is key to successful reading. For those students who have not yet developed such skills, your classroom instruction is critical. You should model such skills and encourage students to practice them.

Through practice, students should be able to internalize the strategies of active reading.

(c) **Kinds of Texts** Just as students and their backgrounds and skills vary, so do the texts presented in a language arts curriculum. The grade-level language arts classroom curriculum traditionally addresses fiction, nonfiction, poetry, and drama. Each of these forms presents unique challenges to students. Each writer and selection also presents challenges in the difficulty of the concepts addressed or in the coherence of the writing. For example, you may find that students are more comfortable with narratives than with expository writing. Focused reading strategies that you model and reinforce can help students tackle texts that are more dense or difficult for them to master.

(d) **Classroom Environment** The classroom environment affects everything and everyone within it. Research suggests that students learn best in a friendly, respectful setting categorized by these criteria:

- Students feel a sense of safety and order.
- They feel comfortable taking risks.
- They understand the purpose and value of the tasks presented.
- Students have high expectations and goals for learning.
- They feel accepted by their teachers and peers.

Students performing below grade level may be especially self-conscious. Therefore, these criteria are key to helping students take full advantage of the opportunities the classroom affords. Set up your classroom as a caring yet on-purpose environment that helps students achieve.

Researchers encourage teachers to be truthful with students about the work it will take to build and master abilities in the language arts. Tell your students that improving reading, writing, speaking, and listening takes a great deal of practice. You need to be prepared to provide direct instruction, guided practice, specific feedback, coaching, and more. Then, encourage your students to understand their responsibilities as active, self-directed learners as well.

## The Special Education or Special Needs Student

Most likely, your classroom has a number of special education or special needs students—young people who begin the year three or more years below grade level and yet do not qualify for special education services. Special education and special needs students have difficulty in organizing and categorizing new information during instruction. They may have trouble in the following areas:

### Memory

- ordering or arranging information

- classifying information

- grasping a main idea or "big picture"

- using long-term memory to make meaningful connections or connecting to prior knowledge

### Attention

- focusing attention on the most important elements of a presentation or a selection

By presenting specific focused strategies and interactive review and extension activities, you can provide these students with full access to the language arts curriculum.

Another category of deficiency in special education readers is the ability to apply learning strategies to a variety of situations. Special education and special needs students often have these weaknesses:

### Learning Strategies

- a lack of effective or efficient strategies for completing academic tasks such as taking notes, responding to literature, or writing a focused paragraph

- a limited set of learning strategies from which to draw

- difficulty in self-monitoring—they often don't know which strategies to use or when a strategy is not working

Many of these students are underprepared; their deficiencies are generally based on their lack of experience, not on any biological difference. When these students learn effective strategies, they can improve their academic performance. Teachers need to provide direct instruction to explicitly show them how, when, and why to use each strategy.

## Overview of Components for Universal Access

The *Prentice Hall Literature: Timeless Voices, Timeless Themes* program includes an array of products to provide universal access. Fully integrated, these materials help teachers identify student needs or deficiencies and teach to the varying levels in a classroom, while providing the quality that literature teachers expect.

As your main resource, the *Annotated Teacher's Edition* provides a lesson plan for every selection or selection grouping. In addition to teaching notes and suggestions, it also includes cross-references to ancillary materials. Customize for Universal Access notes help teachers direct lessons to the following groups of students: special needs students, less proficient readers, English learners, gifted and talented students, and advanced readers. In addition to teaching notes and suggestions, it also includes cross-references to ancillary material such as the *Reader's Companion*, the *Adapted Reader's Companion*, and the *English Learner's Companion*.

The **Teaching Guidebook for Universal Access** gives you proven strategies for providing universal access to all students. In addition to its general teaching strategies and classroom management techniques, this component explains how the parts of the Prentice Hall program work together to ensure reading success for all student populations.

The **Reading Diagnostic and Improvement Plan**—part of the Reading Achievement System—provides comprehensive diagnostic tests that assess students' mastery of reading skills. The book also includes charts that help you map out improvement plans based on students' performance on the diagnostics.

You can use the **Basic Reading Skills: Comprehensive Lessons for Improvement Plan**—also part of the Reading Achievement System—to give instruction and practice that bring students up to grade level, enabling them to master the skills in which they are deficient. For each skill covered, you'll find the following materials:

- lesson plan with direct instruction
- teaching transparency
- blackline master for student application and practice

The **Reader's Companion** and **Reader's Companion Teacher's Edition** are consumable components of the Reading Achievement System. The books contain the full text of approximately half of the selections from the student book. Questions prompt students to interact with the text by circling, underlining, or marking key details. Write-on lines in the margins also allow for students to answer questions. You can use this book in place of the student book to help students read interactively. In addition, a summary and a reading-skill worksheet support every selection grouping in the student book.

The **Adapted Reader's Companion** and **Adapted Reader's Companion Teacher's Edition** are another set of consumable components of the Reading Achievement System. These books use the same format and contain the same selections as the *Reader's Companion*. However, the selections are abridged and appear in a larger font size. The questions are targeted toward special education students. You can use this book as a supplement to or in place of the student book for certain selections to enable special education students to experience the same literature and master the same skills as on-level students. These components also contain a summary and a reading-skill worksheet to support every selection grouping in the student book.

The **English Learner's Companion** and **English Learner's Companion Teacher's Edition** are a third set of consumable components of the Reading Achievement System. These books use the same format and contain the same selections as the *Reader's Companion*. Again, the selections are abridged and appear in a larger font size. The questions are targeted toward English learners. You can use this book as a supplement to or in place of the student book for certain selections to enable English learners to experience the same literature and master the same skills as students who are native English speakers. These components also contain summaries in English and Spanish, along with a reading-skill worksheet to support every selection grouping in the student book.

**Listening to Literature Audiotapes and CDs** These components feature professional recordings of every selection in the student book. To support student reading, you can play the selections, in part or in full, before students read them.

**Spanish/English Summaries Audio CD** Audio summaries in both English and Spanish are provided for every selection. You can play these selection summaries for struggling readers, special education students, and English learners before they read the actual texts.

**Basic Language Skills: Reteaching Masters** With the reteaching masters, you can provide basic-level instruction and practice on grammar and language skills.

**Interest Grabber Videos** These videos are an optional enrichment resource designed to provide background for a selection or otherwise motivate students to read the selection. There is a video segment for every selection or selection grouping in the student book.

## About the Adapted Reader's Companion

The *Adapted Reader's Companion* is designed to support your special education or special needs students. Its two parts offer different levels of support.

### Part 1: Selection Adaptations with Excerpts of Authentic Text

Part 1 will guide special education or special needs students as they interact with half the selections from *Prentice Hall Literature: Timeless Voices, Timeless Themes.* This range of selections includes the more challenging selections, the most frequently taught selections, and many examples of narrative and expository writing. Part 1 provides pre-reading instruction, larger print summaries of literature selections with passages from the selection, and post-reading questions and activities.

The **Preview** page will help your students get the general idea of the selection and therefore be better equipped to understand it. Both written and visual summaries preview the selections before students read the adapted versions.

The **Prepare to Read** page is based on its parallel in *Prentice Hall Literature: Timeless Voices, Timeless Themes.* It introduces the same literary element and reading strategy addressed in the textbook and provides a graphic organizer to make the information more accessible.

The **selection** pages present the text in a larger font size. Interspersed among blocks of authentic text, the companion also provides summaries of episodes or paragraphs to make the selections more accessible to your students.

The **side notes** make active reading strategies explicit, asking students to look closely at the text to analyze it in a variety of ways. Notes with a *Mark the Text* icon prompt students to underline, circle, or otherwise note key words, phrases, or details in the selection. Notes with write-on lines offer students an opportunity to respond in the margin to questions or ideas. These notes offer focused support in a variety of areas:

> **Literary Analysis** notes provide point-of-use instruction to reinforce the literary element introduced on the Preview page. By pointing out details or events in the text in which the literary element applies, these notes give students the opportunity to revisit and reinforce their understanding of literature.

> **Reading Strategy** notes help students practice the skill introduced on the Preview page. These notes guide students to understand when, how, and why a strategy is helpful.

> **Stop to Reflect** notes ask students to reflect on the selection or on a skill they are using. By encouraging students to solidify their own thinking, these notes help to develop active reading skills.

**Reading Check** notes help students confirm their comprehension of a selection. These notes help to make explicit a critical strategy of active reading.

**Read Fluently** notes provide students with concrete, limited practice reading passages aloud with fluency.

**Background** notes provide further explanation of a concept or detail to support students' understanding.

The ***Review and Assess*** questions following the selection ensure students' comprehension of the selection. Written in simple language, they assess students' understanding of the literary element and the reading strategy. In addition, they offer a scaffolded guide to support students in an extension activity based on either a writing or a listening and speaking activity in the *Student Edition* of the grade-level textbook.

### Part 2: Selection Summaries with Alternative Reading Strategies

Part 2 contains summaries of all selections in *Prentice Hall Literature: Timeless Voices, Timeless Themes*. These summaries can help students prepare for reading the selections. Alternatively, the summaries may serve as a review tool.

This section also includes alternative reading strategies to guide students as they read selections. The strategies may be useful for reviewing selection events and ideas or to reinforce specific reading strategies for students.

## How to Use the *Adapted Reader's Companion*

When you are planning lessons for heterogeneous classes, this companion reader offers you an opportunity to keep all the students in your class reading the same selection and studying the same vocabulary, literary element, and reading strategy but getting the support they need to succeed. Here are some planning suggestions for using the book in tandem with the grade-level volume of *Prentice Hall Literature: Timeless Voices, Timeless Themes.*

Use the *Annotated Teacher's Edition* and the *Student Edition* of the grade-level textbook as the central text in your classroom. The *Annotated Teacher's Edition* includes *Customize for Universal Access* notes throughout each selection. In addition, it identifies when use of the *Adapted Reader's Companion* is appropriate.

## TEACHING SELECTIONS INCLUDED IN PART ONE

### PRE-TEACH with the Full Class

***Consider presenting the* Interest Grabber *video segment.*** This optional technology product can provide background and build motivation.

***Preview the selection.*** To help students see the organization of a selection, or to help them get a general idea of the text, lead a quick text pre-reading or "text tour" using the textbook. Focus student attention on the selection title, the art accompanying the text, and any unusual text characteristics. To build connections for students, ask them to identify links between the selection and other works you have presented in class, or to find connections to themes, activities, or other related concepts.

***Build background.*** Use the Background information provided in the *Student Edition.* Whether explaining a historical time period, a scientific concept, or details about an idea that may be unfamiliar to students, this instruction presents useful information to help all students place the literature in context.

***Focus vocabulary development.*** The *Student Edition* includes a list of vocabulary words included in the selection or selection grouping. Instead of attempting to cover all of the vocabulary words you anticipate your students will not know, identify the vocabulary that is most critical to talking and learning about the central concepts. However, for the words you do choose to teach, work to provide more than synonyms and definitions. Using the vocabulary notes in the *Annotated Teacher's Edition,* introduce the essential words in more meaningful contexts: for example, through simple sentences drawing on familiar issues, people, scenarios, and vocabulary. Guide students in internalizing the meanings of key terms through these familiar contexts and ask them to write the definitions in their own words. Look at these examples of guided vocabulary instruction:

Point out the word *serene* and explain that it means "calm or peaceful." Then, provide the following scenarios and ask students to determine whether the situations are *serene* or not: an empty beach at sunset *(yes)*; a playground at recess *(no)*. You might also ask students to provide their own examples of *serene* situations.

Point out the word *interval* and explain that it means "the period of time between two events or point of time." Ask students to identify the interval between Monday and Wednesday *(two days)* and the interval between one Monday and the next Monday *(one week)*.

You might also take the opportunity to teach the prefix *inter-*, meaning "between." Then, discuss with students the following group of words:

> *interview* (a meeting between two or more people);
> *interstate* (between two or more states);
> *international* (between nations);
> *intervene* (to come between two sides in a dispute).

**Introduce skills.** Introduce the *Literary Analysis* and *Reading Strategy,* using the instruction in the *Student Edition* and the teaching support in the *Annotated Teacher's Edition.*

**Separate the class.** As average-level students begin reading the selection in the *Student Edition,* have special education and special needs students put their textbooks aside. Direct these students to the *Adapted Reader's Companion* for further pre-teaching.

**PRE-TEACH for Special Education or Special Needs Students Using the *Adapted Reader's Companion***

**Reinforce the general idea.** Use the selection and visual summaries presented on the first page of every selection in the *Adapted Reader's Companion.* These summaries will give students a framework to follow for understanding the selection. Use these tools to build familiarity, but do not use them as a replacement for reading.

**Present audio summaries.** The *Spanish/English Summaries Audio CD* can reinforce the main idea of a selection.

**Reinforce skills instruction.** Next, use the *Prepare to Read* page to reinforce the *Literary Analysis* and *Reading Strategy* concepts. Written in simpler language and in basic sentence structures, the instruction will help students better grasp these ideas.

**Provide decoding practice.** Because many special education students lack strategies for decoding bigger words, give them guided practice with the vocabulary words for the selection. Using the list, model a strategy for decoding polysyllabic words. First, show students how to break the word into parts and then put the parts back together to make a word.

> For the word *mimic*, ask students to draw a loop under each word part as they pronounce it.
>
> *mim ic*        *fright en ing*

Using this strategy, you can encourage students to look for familiar word parts and then break the rest of the word down into its consonant and vowel sounds. By building this routine regularly into your pre-teaching instruction, you reinforce a key reading skill for your students.

***Prepare for lesson structure.*** To build students' ability to complete classroom activities, examine your lesson to see what types of language functions students will need to participate. Look at these examples:

> If students are being asked to make predictions about upcoming paragraph content in an essay, review the power of transition words that act as signals to meaning. Rather than teaching all transitions, limit your instruction to the ones in the passages. Identify the key transition words and point out their meaning. In addition, teach students some basic sentence patterns and verbs to express opinions. Model for students statement patterns such as:
>
> *I predict that . . .*
>
> *Based on this transition word, I conclude that . . .*

## TEACH Using the *Adapted Reader's Companion*

As average-achieving students in your class read the selection in the textbook, allow special education and special needs students to read the adapted version in the *Adapted Reader's Companion*. Whenever possible, give these students individualized attention by pairing them with aides, parent volunteers, or student peers.

***Set purposes and limits.*** To keep students focused and motivated, and to prevent them from becoming overwhelmed as they read a selection, clearly establish a reading purpose for students before assigning a manageable amount of text. Once you identify a focus question or a purpose, revisit the question occasionally as students read. You can do this with a brief whole-group dialogue or by encouraging students in pairs to remember the question. In addition, your effective modeling will also provide the scaffolding for students to begin internalizing these strategies for effective reading.

***Model your thinking.*** Describe and model strategies for navigating different kinds of text. Use the questions raised in the side notes as a starting point.

Then, explain how you arrive at an answer. Alternatively, ask a student to explain his or her responses to classmates.

**Reinforce new vocabulary.** Present key words when they occur within the context of the reading selection. Review the definition as it appears on the page. Then, make the words as concrete as possible by linking each to an object, photo, or idea.

**Build interactivity.** The side notes in the *Adapted Reader's Companion* are an excellent way to encourage student interactivity with the selections. To build students' ability to use these notes, model several examples with each selection. These are not busy work; they are activities that build fluency and provide the scaffolding necessary for student success.

Whenever possible, get students physically involved with the page, using *Mark the Text* icons as an invitation to use highlighters or colored pencils to circle, underline, or number key information. In addition, some students may find that using a small piece of cardboard or heavy construction paper helps to focus and guide their reading from one paragraph or page to the next.

**Vary modes of instruction.** To maintain student attention and interest, monitor and alternate the mode of instruction or activity. For example, alternate between teacher-facilitated and student-dominated reading activities. Assign brief amounts of text at a time, and alternate between oral, paired, and silent reading.

**Monitor students' comprehension.** As students use the side notes in the margins of the *Adapted Reader's Companion,* build in opportunities to ensure that students are on purpose and understanding. Consider structured brief conversations for students to share, compare, or explain their thinking. Then, use these conversations to praise the correct use of strategies or to redirect students who need further support. In addition, this is an excellent chance for you to demonstrate your note-taking process and provide models of effective study notes for students to emulate.

**Reinforce the reading experience.** When students read the selection for the first time, they may be working on the decoding level. If time allows, students should read the selection twice to achieve a greater fluency and comfort level.

**REVIEW AND ASSESS Using the *Adapted Reader's Companion***

**Reinforce writing and reading skills.** Assign students the extension activity in the *Adapted Reader's Companion.* Based on an activity presented in the grade-level text, the version in the *Adapted Reader's Companion* provides guided, step-by-step support for students. By giving students the opportunities to show their reading comprehension and writing skills, you maintain reasonable expectations for their developing academic competence.

**Model expectations.** Make sure that students understand your assessment criteria in advance. Provide models of student work, whenever possible, for them to emulate, along with a non-model that fails to meet the specified assessment criteria. Do not provide exemplars that are clearly outside of their developmental range. Save student work that can later serve as a model for students with different levels of academic preparation.

**Lead students to closure.** To achieve closure, ask students to end the class session by writing three to five outcome statements about their experience in the day's lesson, expressing both new understandings and needs for clarification.

**Encourage self-monitoring and self-assessment.** Remember to provide safe opportunities for students to alert you to any learning challenges they are experiencing. Consider having students submit anonymous written questions (formulated either independently or with a partner) about confusing lesson content and process. Later, you can follow up on these points of confusion at the end of class or in the subsequent class session.

### EXTEND Using the *Student Edition*

**Present the unabridged selection.** Build in opportunities for students to read the full selection in the grade-level textbook. This will allow them to apply familiar concepts and vocabulary and stretch their literacy muscles.

**Play an audio reading of the unabridged selection.** Use the *Listening to Literature Audiotapes* or *CDs*. Students may benefit from reading along while listening to a professional recording of the selection. Encourage students to use their fingertips to follow the words as they are read.

**Invite reader response.** When students have finished reviewing the selection—whether in the companion or in the grade-level textbook—include all students in your class in post-reading analysis. To guide an initial discussion, use the Respond question in the *Thinking About the Selection* in the textbook. You will find that questions such as the following examples will provide strong springboards for classroom interaction:

> **Respond :** What advice would you have given the mother and daughter? Why?

> **Respond:** What questions would you like to ask the writer about his experience?

> **Respond:** Do you find the boy's actions courageous, touching, or silly? Explain your answer.

Encourage students to explain their answers to these questions by supporting their ideas with evidence from the text or their own lives. In addition, invite students to respond to classmates' ideas. These questions will lead students from simply getting the gist of a selection to establishing a personal connection to the lesson content.

***Direct student analysis with scaffolded questions.*** When you are ready to move students into the Review and Assess questions, let your average-achieving students use the instruction and questions in the grade-level textbook. At the same time, encourage special education and special needs students to use the questions in the *Adapted Reader's Companion*.

- Questions in the companion, written in more simple language and providing more explicit support, will be more accessible to these students. Students will be applying concepts and practicing strategies at their own level.

- Some special education or special needs students may be prepared to answer questions in the grade-level text. The two-part questions in the *Thinking About the Selection* section are written to build and support student analysis. First, students use lower-level thinking skills to identify information or to recall important details in a selection. For the second part, students use a higher-level thinking skill based on the answer to the first part.

Look at these examples of scaffolded questions from the grade-level textbook:

**(a) Recall:** Why does the boy tell his father to leave the sickroom?
**(b) Infer:** What does this reveal about the boy?

**(a) Recall:** Why does the boy think he will die?
**(b) Infer:** What is the meaning of the title?

***Revisit and reinforce strategies.*** Recycle pre- and post-reading tasks regularly, so students can become more familiar with the task process and improve their performance. If they are constantly facing curricular novelty, special education and special needs students never have the opportunity to refine their skills and demonstrate improved competence. For example, if you ask them to identify a personality trait of an essential character in a story and then support this observation with relevant details in an expository paragraph, it would make sense to have them write an identical paragraph in the near future about another character.

***Show students how to transfer skills.*** Consider ways in which students can transfer knowledge and skills gleaned from one assignment/lesson to a subsequent lesson. For example, discuss with students the ways in which they can apply new vocabulary and language strategies outside of the classroom. In addition, demonstrate the applicability of new reading and writing strategies to real-world literacy tasks. Include periodic writing tasks for an authentic audience other than the teacher: another class, fellow classmates, local businesses, family, etc.

***Offer praise and encourage growth.*** Praise students' efforts to experiment with new language in class, both in writing and in speaking.

## USING PART TWO

For selections that are not presented as adaptations in Part One, use the summaries and activities in Part Two to support your special education or special needs students.

## PRE-TEACH

In addition to the pre-teaching strategies listed on page xvii, consider these strategies to accommodate special education or special needs students:

***Provide students with a "running start."*** Use the selection summaries provided in the *Adapted Reader's Companion*. These summaries will give students a framework for understanding the selection to follow.

***Build interest.*** To take full advantage of the summaries, ask students to write one or two questions that the summaries raise in their minds. Share these questions in a discussion before reading the full text.

## TEACH

As your students read the full selection in the textbook, provide special education and special needs students with support and individualized attention by pairing them with aides, parent volunteers, or student peers. In addition to the suggestions on page xviii, consider these additional strategies.

***Model your thinking for side-column questions.*** To help these students practice the *Literary Analysis* skill and the *Reading Strategy,* use the questions raised in the side notes as a starting point. If students have difficulty answering the questions, review the concept for students and model your thinking process. Look at these examples of modeling explicit thinking:

> ### Reading Strategy: Making Inferences
> Remind students that, in a work of fiction, a writer expects readers to make connections with what they already know or have read in an earlier passage. Show students how to make inferences based on the side-column question and the appropriate text. Look at this passage from a selection as an example:
>
>> "Mary, you oughta write David and tell him somebody done opened his letter and stole that ten dollars he sent," she said.
>>
>> "No mama. David's got enough on his mind. Besides, there's enough garden foods so we won't go hungry."
>
> Then, use language like this to model your thinking process:
>
> *I'm not sure who the characters are talking about. There hasn't been any David mentioned in the story. What's this about a letter? First, I ask myself what information there is in the passage. Mama sounds like she cares about this person; it's probably a*

*friend or a family member. David sends money to the family, so he must be in another place. I'll ask myself what I know from what I've already read. Do I know anything about characters who live far away? Earlier, Mama said the father worked in Louisiana so that he could support the family. Could David be the father? I think so! He probably sends his wages back to Mississippi. That's the part about the letter! Somebody opened up one of the letters and took the money.*

### Reading Strategy: Interpreting Poetic Language

In poetry, writers may describe an event in very different language from what they might use in writing an essay. Students can increase their understanding of poetry by learning to interpret poetic language. To help them, use the side notes and any marked texts to model your thinking process. Look at this example based on the following poetic lines:

> You crash over the trees,
> you crack the live branch—
> the branch is white,
> the green crushed,

Then, use language like this to model your thinking process:

*I am not sure exactly what is being described in the last two lines. What do the colors mean? Why is the branch white? What is the author referring to by "green crushed"? I'll start by figuring out what I do know. This poem is about a storm. From the second line, I can figure out that lightning or wind has struck the tree and cracked a branch. Green is the color of leaves. When a storm cracks a branch, it may fall to the ground. The leaves are crushed by the fall; this must be "the green crushed." But branches aren't white; they're brown or gray. However, if they're cracked open, the wood inside is white. The storm has cracked the branch and exposed its white insides.*

*Use the* **Reading Check** *questions in the* **Student Edition.** Consider pairing students, working with small groups, or setting brief instructional time for *Reading Check* questions that appear with every selection. These recall-level questions can be answered based on information in the text. Ask students to point to their answers in the selection before returning to reading.

### REVIEW AND ASSESS

In addition to the suggestions on page xix, consider these additional strategies:

***Build tests using the computer test bank.*** The computer test bank allows you to sort questions by difficulty level. Use this feature to generate tests appropriate to special education and special needs students.

# Part 1

## Selection Adaptations With Excerpts of Authentic Text

Part 1 will guide and support you as you interact with selections from *Prentice Hall Literature: Timeless Voices, Timeless Themes.* Part 1 provides summaries of literature selections with passages from the selection.

- Begin with the Preview page in the *Adapted Reader's Companion.* Use the written and visual summaries to preview the selections before you read.

- Then study the Prepare to Read page. This page introduces skills that you will apply as you read selections in the *Adapted Reader's Companion.*

- Now read the selection in the *Adapted Reader's Companion.*

- Respond to all the questions along the sides as you read. They will guide you in understanding the selection and in applying the skills. Write in the *Adapted Reader's Companion*—really! Circle things that interest you. Underline things that puzzle you. Number ideas or events to help you keep track of them. Look for the **Mark the Text** logo for help with active reading.

- Use the Review and Assess questions at the end of each selection to review what you have read and to check your understanding.

- Finally, do the Writing or the Speaking and Listening activity to extend your understanding and practice your skills.

# Interacting With the Text

As you read, use the information and notes to guide you in interacting with the selection. The examples on these pages show you how to use the notes as a companion when you read. They will guide you in applying reading and literary skills and in thinking about the selections. When you read other texts, you can practice the thinking skills and strategies found here.

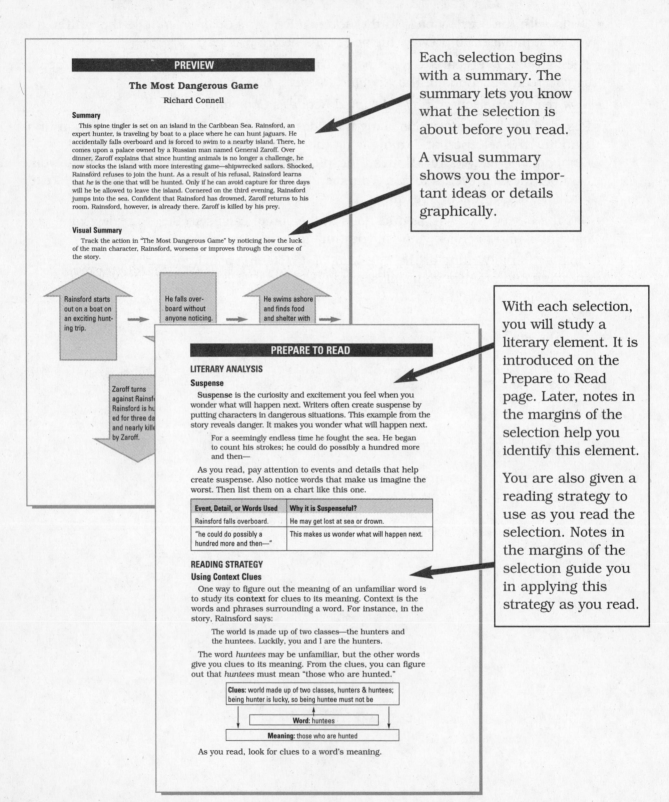

Each selection begins with a summary. The summary lets you know what the selection is about before you read.

A visual summary shows you the important ideas or details graphically.

With each selection, you will study a literary element. It is introduced on the Prepare to Read page. Later, notes in the margins of the selection help you identify this element.

You are also given a reading strategy to use as you read the selection. Notes in the margins of the selection guide you in applying this strategy as you read.

---

**PREVIEW**

### The Most Dangerous Game
#### Richard Connell

**Summary**

This spine tingler is set on an island in the Caribbean Sea. Rainsford, an expert hunter, is traveling by boat to a place where he can hunt jaguars. He accidentally falls overboard and is forced to swim to a nearby island. There, he comes upon a palace owned by a Russian man named General Zaroff. Over dinner, Zaroff explains that since hunting animals is no longer a challenge, he now stocks the island with more interesting game—shipwrecked sailors. Shocked, Rainsford refuses to join the hunt. As a result of his refusal, Rainsford learns that *he* is the one that will be hunted. Only if he can avoid capture for three days will he be allowed to leave the island. Cornered on the third evening, Rainsford jumps into the sea. Confident that Rainsford has drowned, Zaroff returns to his room. Rainsford, however, is already there. Zaroff is killed by his prey.

**Visual Summary**

Track the action in "The Most Dangerous Game" by noticing how the luck of the main character, Rainsford, worsens or improves through the course of the story.

Rainsford starts out on a boat on an exciting hunting trip.

He falls overboard without anyone noticing.

He swims ashore and finds food and shelter with

Zaroff turns against Rainsf... Rainsford is hu... ed for three da... and nearly kille... by Zaroff.

---

**PREPARE TO READ**

**LITERARY ANALYSIS**

**Suspense**

Suspense is the curiosity and excitement you feel when you wonder what will happen next. Writers often create suspense by putting characters in dangerous situations. This example from the story reveals danger. It makes you wonder what will happen next.

> For a seemingly endless time he fought the sea. He began to count his strokes; he could do possibly a hundred more and then—

As you read, pay attention to events and details that help create suspense. Also notice words that make us imagine the worst. Then list them on a chart like this one.

| Event, Detail, or Words Used | Why it is Suspenseful? |
|---|---|
| Rainsford falls overboard. | He may get lost at sea or drown. |
| "he could do possibly a hundred more and then—" | This makes us wonder what will happen next. |

**READING STRATEGY**

**Using Context Clues**

One way to figure out the meaning of an unfamiliar word is to study its **context** for clues to its meaning. Context is the words and phrases surrounding a word. For instance, in the story, Rainsford says:

> The world is made up of two classes—the hunters and the huntees. Luckily, you and I are the hunters.

The word *huntees* may be unfamiliar, but the other words give you clues to its meaning. From the clues, you can figure out that *huntees* must mean "those who are hunted."

| **Clues:** world made up of two classes, hunters & huntees; being hunter is lucky, so being huntee must not be |
|---|
| **Word:** huntees |
| **Meaning:** those who are hunted |

As you read, look for clues to a word's meaning.

---

## ◆ Reading Strategy

What does *strokes* mean here? Study the **context**, and circle any clues to the word's meaning. Then, circle the letter of its meaning below.

(a) pats in a soothing way
(b) swimmer's movements
(c) deep breaths
(d) uses a paintbrush

**Mark the Text**

## ◆ Literary Analysis

Circle three words that help build **suspense** in the bracketed paragraph above. Who or what might be in danger? Write your answer on this line.

_____
_____

**Mark the Text**

## ◆ Read Fluently

Try saying General Zaroff's remarks out loud. Say them as you think he might say them. Think about your first impression of the general. Write two words you would use to describe him:

_____
_____

For a seemingly endless time he fought the sea. He began to count his <u>strokes</u>; he could do possibly a hundred more and then—
Rainsford heard a sound. It came out of the darkness, a high screaming sound, the sound of an animal in an extremity of <u>anguish</u> and terror. He did not recognize the animal that made the sound; he did not try to; with fresh <u>vitality</u> he swam toward the sound. He heard it again; then it was cut short.

♦ ♦ ♦

Rainsford swims to shore with difficulty. Then, he falls asleep. The next day, he can see that a large animal was recently hunted nearby. He follows the hunter's trail through the jungle. He comes to a mansion. At the [ ]or, a large and dangerous-looking servant points a gun at him. His name is Ivan. Then, another man appears.

♦ ♦ ♦

"It is a very great pleasure to welcome Mr. Sanger Rainsford, the <u>celebrated</u> hunter, to my home."
Automatically Rainsford shook the man's hand.
"I've read your book about hunting snow leopards in Tibet, you see," explained the man. "I am General Z[ ]

♦ ♦ ♦

Zaroff is a nobleman and a Cossack² who left Russia after the revolution[ ] After giving Rainsford a comfortabl[ ]

### Vocabulary Development

**anguish** (AN gwish) *n.* painful suffering
**vitality** (VI tal uh tee) *n.* energy
**celebrated** (SELL uh brayt id) *adj.* famous

2. **Cossack** (KAHS ik) member of a people from southern famous for their fierceness.
3. **revolution of 1917** this russian Revolution was a defeat[ ] class Russians like Zaroff.

---

## REVIEW AND ASSESS

1. Circle three words that best describe General Zaroff.

   kind   competitive   rich   cruel   lazy   uneducated

2. The word "game" can mean "animals hunted for sport." What is "the most dangerous game" in this story? Explain the double meaning on the lines below.
   Meaning 1: _____
   Meaning 2: _____

3. What happens in the end? Circle the letter of the best answer.
   (a) Rainsford drowns trying to escape Zaroff's dogs.
   (b) Rainsford and Zaroff fight, then shake hands and go to sleep.
   (c) Rainsford kills Zaroff and sleeps comfortably in his bed.
   (d) Rainsford kills Zaroff and then has trouble falling asleep.
   Write the words from the story that gave you this answer.
   _____
   _____

4. In the beginning, what is Rainsford's attitude toward the animals he hunts? What lessons do you think he has learned since the hunt with Zaroff? Finish the sentences below.
   Before the hunt with Zaroff, Rainsford thought _____
   _____
   After the hunt with Zaroff, Rainsford probably feels _____
   _____

5. **Literary Analysis:** List three events in the story where the author creates suspense by placing a character in great danger.

| Event | Character(s) in Danger |
|---|---|
| _____ | _____ |
| _____ | _____ |
| _____ | _____ |

# The Cask of Amontillado

## Edgar Allan Poe

## Summary

This story takes place long ago in Italy. It is carnival season, a time of parties and parades, when people wear costumes and masks. Montresor is a man from an important family. He feels that his friend Fortunato has insulted him. He wants revenge. In fact, his desire for revenge has made him crazy, and he plans a horrible death for Fortunato. But he keeps pretending that he is Fortunato's good friend.

Fortunato is proud of his knowledge of wine. Montresor uses this to lure Fortunato to the family palace to judge a cask of Amontillado sherry (an elegant Spanish wine). The men descend to caves, where wine is stored and people have been buried. Montresor gets Fortunato drunk. Far into the caves, they come to a small room. Montresor chains Fortunato to the wall. He then begins to brick up the entrance. As the wall rises, Fortunato begs, screams, and finally tries to get Montresor to admit that he is only playing a prank. Montresor ignores Fortunato. As he puts the last stone in place, he hears only the bells jingling on Fortunato's costume.

## Visual Summary

| Characters | Montresor | Fortunato |
|---|---|---|

| Problem | Montresor feels that he has been insulted by Fortunato. |
|---|---|

| Events | 1. Montresor meets Fortunato and mentions the cask of Amontillado.<br>2. Fortunato goes with Montresor to Montresor's palace. They descend winding stairways and wander through caves filled with wine bottles and bones.<br>3. Montresor acts as if he is Fortunato's friend, getting Fortunato drunk as he leads him deeper into the caves.<br>4. Montresor chains Fortunato in a small room far into the caves. He then walls up the room, as Fortunato screams and begs for mercy. |
|---|---|

| Conclusion | Montresor notes that it has been fifty years since these events occurred. |
|---|---|

## LITERARY ANALYSIS

### Mood

The **mood** of a story is the feeling the story gives you. The author chooses words to create a feeling. The author also includes specific details to create a feeling. For example, words like "loud and shrill screams" and "bursting suddenly" might make you feel nervous and afraid. Picture in your mind the following sentence from the story:

The drops of moisture trickle among the bones.

Wet bones might make you think of a cemetery or a lonely place. Notice how the author's words and story details make you feel as you read the story.

## READING STRATEGY

### Breaking Down Confusing Sentences

Some story sentences are hard to understand. Sometimes, you may need to **break down confusing sentences**. It helps to stop or slow down your reading when you do not understand a sentence. Then use these tips to help you understand the sentence:

- Find out who or what is the subject of the sentence. (The subject tells what the sentence is about.)
- Find out what the subject has done.
- Change the words around to make the sentence clearer.
- You can also take out some words to make it clearer.

Notice how this part of the first sentence of "The Cask of Amontillado" breaks down in the chart:

". . . when he ventured upon insult I vowed revenge."

| Who or what is the subject? | I |
| --- | --- |
| What has the subject done? | vowed revenge |
| Change confusing words around. | I vowed revenge when he insulted me. |

# The Cask of Amontillado
## Edgar Allan Poe

As the story opens, the narrator,
Montresor, reveals his feelings toward
Fortunato. He explains that Fortunato has
greatly insulted him. So, Montresor is
determined to get <u>revenge</u> on him.
Montresor acts friendly toward Fortunato
when he meets him at the carnival.
Fortunato is dressed in a costume. He has a
cap of bells on his head. He is also very
friendly. Montresor and Fortunato are very
knowledgeable about wine.

Montresor tells Fortunato that he has
bought a pipe[1] of very good wine. The wine
is Amontillado[2]. He tells Fortunato that he
needs an <u>expert</u> opinion. He says he is not
sure if it truly is Amontillado. He says he
does not wish to bother Fortunato, but
instead he will ask another man, Luchesi.
Fortunato is eager to try the Amontillado. He
wants to give his opinion. He tells Montresor
not to ask Luchesi. He is eager to go to
Montresor's wine <u>cellar</u> to taste the wine.

◆ ◆ ◆

"Come, let us go."

"Whither?"

"To your <u>vaults</u>."

"My friend, no; I will not impose upon
your good nature. I perceive you have an
engagement. Luchesi—"

---

### Vocabulary Development

**revenge** (reh VENJ) *n.* harm done in return for an insult

**expert** (X pert) *n.* a person who knows a lot about
something

**cellar** (SEL er) *n.* a room that is underground

**vault** (VAWLT) *n.* a room that is underground

---

1. **pipe** (PĪP) *n.* large barrel. A pipe holds about 126 gallons.
2. **Amontillado** (uh MON tee ya do) *n.* a light-colored, not sweet wine.

"I have no engagement—come."

"My friend, no. It is not the engagement, but the severe cold with which I perceive you are afflicted. The vaults are insufferably <u>damp</u>. They are encrusted with niter."[3]

"Let us go, nevertheless. The cold is merely nothing. Amontillado!"

◆　◆　◆

Montresor's house is empty. The servants are at the carnival. Montresor takes two torches. He leads Fortunato through the house. They come to an archway. It leads down to the underground vaults. They walk down a long stairway to the family catacombs.[4] Fortunato asks about the white cobwebby chemical on the walls.

◆　◆　◆

"Niter?" he asked, at length.

"Niter," I replied. "How long have you had that cough?"

"Ugh! ugh! ugh!—ugh! ugh! ugh!—ugh! ugh! ugh!—ugh! ugh! ugh!—ugh! ugh! ugh!"

My poor friend found it impossible to reply for many minutes.

"It is nothing," he said, at last.

"Come," I said, with decision, "<u>we will go back; your health is precious</u>. You are rich, respected, admired, beloved; you are happy, as once I was. You are a man to be missed. For me it is no matter. We will go back; you will be ill, and I cannot be responsible. Besides, there is Luchesi—"

"Enough," he said; "the cough is a mere nothing; it will not kill me. I shall not die of a cough."

---

### Vocabulary Development

**damp** (DAMP) *adj.* slightly wet, moist

---

3. **niter** (NĪ ter) potassium nitrate, a white salt found in soil and covering rocks.

4. **catacombs** (CAT uh cohms) network of underground burial places.

◆ **Stop to Reflect**

Catacombs are underground burial places. Would you be nervous walking through catacombs? Circle your answer.

yes　　　　no

Explain why or why not.

_____

_____

_____

◆ **Read for Fluency**

Read aloud the dialogue in the brackets. Underline the words that Fortunato says. Then read the dialogue again. Use a different voice for each character.

◆ **Stop to Reflect**

Do you think Montresor is serious when he says "your health is precious."?

_____

Why or why not?

_____

_____

_____

◆ **Literary Analysis**

Write two ideas from the bracketed passage that create an eerie mood.

1. _____

_____

_____

2. _____

_____

_____

◆ **Reading Check**

What happens at one of the niches? Finish each sentence.

First, Fortunato tries to see

_____

Next, the narrator tells Fortunato

to _____

Then, the narrator chains

_____

Then, the narrator moves

_____

Finally, the narrator builds

_____

"True—true," I replied; "and, indeed, I had no intention of alarming you unnecessarily—but you should use all proper caution. A draft[5] of this Medoc will defend us from the damps."

◆ ◆ ◆

They go deeper into the catacombs. The walls of the catacombs are lined with skeletons. There are also barrels of wine among the skeletons.

◆ ◆ ◆

"The niter!" I said; "see, it increases. It hangs like moss upon the vaults. We are below the river's bed. The drops of moisture trickle among the bones. Come, we will go back ere it is too late. Your cough—"

"It is nothing," he said; "let us go on."

◆ ◆ ◆

They go deeper into the burial vaults. The air is foul. Their torches are dull and do not show much light. Piles of human bones line the walls.

At one of the niches, Fortunato tries to see into it. The light from his torch is too weak. He cannot see the back wall. Montresor tells him to go in. He tells him the Amontillado is in there. Fortunato goes in. Montresor quickly chains Fortunato to the back wall. Then, Montresor moves a pile of bones. Under the bones were bricks and mortar. He begins to build a wall.

◆ ◆ ◆

I had scarcely laid the first tier of the masonry when I discovered that the intoxication of Fortunato had in a great measure worn

---

**Vocabulary Development**

**niche** (NICH) *n.*  a hollow place in a wall
**tier** (TEER) *n.*  one row of many rows that are one above the other

---

5. **draft** (DRAFT) amount of drink taken in one swallow.

off. The earliest indication I had of this was a low moaning cry from the depth of the recess. It was not the cry of a drunken man. There was then a long and obstinate silence. I laid the second tier, and the third, and the fourth; and then I heard the furious vibrations of the chain. The noise lasted for several minutes, during which, that I might hearken to it with the more satisfaction, I ceased my labors and sat down upon the bones. When at last the clanking subsided, I resumed the trowel, and finished without interruption the fifth, the sixth, and the seventh tier. The wall was now nearly upon a level with my breast. I again paused, and holding the flambeaux[6] over the masonwork, threw a few feeble rays upon the figure within.

A succession of loud and shrill screams, bursting suddenly from the throat of the chained form, seemed to thrust me violently back. For a brief moment I hesitated, I trembled.

◆ ◆ ◆

Montresor also begins to scream. He screams even louder than Fortunato, and Fortunato becomes quiet. By midnight, Montresor has made a wall of 11 rows of bricks. Fortunato is nearly sealed into the small room. Montresor says that one more brick will complete the wall.

◆ ◆ ◆

I struggled with its weight; I placed it partially in its destined position. But now there came from out the niche a low laugh that erected the hairs upon my head. It was succeeded by a sad voice, which I had difficulty in recognizing as that of the noble Fortunato. The voice said—

◆ **Reading Check**

Before laying the second tier, what does Montresor hear from the recess of the wall?

_____

Finish this sentence.

First he heard _____

_____

and then there was a long

_____.

◆ **Literary Analysis**

Write three words from the bracketed passage that create a mood of horror.

_____

_____

_____

◆ **Reading Strategy**

Reread the underlined sentence. Circle the word that tells you what made the narrator scared. Then, rewrite the sentence to make this sentence clear.

_____

_____

_____

6. **flambeaux** (flam BO) a flaming torch.

Did anyone find Fortunato alive in the underground vault? Circle your answer.

        yes   no

Use words from the story to explain how you know.

_____

_____

_____

"Ha! ha! ha!—he! he! he!—a very good joke, indeed—an excellent jest. We will have many a rich laugh about it at the palazzo—he! he! he!—over our wine—he! he! he!"

"The Amontillado!" I said.

"He! he! he!—he! he! he!—yes, the Amontillado. But is it not getting late? Will not they be awaiting us at the palazzo, the Lady Fortunato and the rest? Let us be gone."

"Yes," I said, "let us be gone."

"*For the love of God, Montresor!*"

"Yes," I said, "for the love of God!

♦ ♦ ♦

Fortunato is quiet. Montresor puts the last stone in place. Then he hides the new wall with a pile of old bones.

♦ ♦ ♦

For the half of a century no mortal has disturbed them. *In pace requiescat!*[7]

---

7. **In pace requiescat!** Latin for "May he rest in peace!"

1. Read this definition.

   **revenge** (reh VENJ) *n.* harm done in return for an insult

   Write a sentence about the story that uses the word revenge.

   _____

   _____

2. How did Montresor get Fortunato to go to the cellar with him?

   _____

3. Reread page 9, the part of the story where Montresor builds the wall by tiers, or row by row. Tell what Fortunato does as each tier of the wall is built.

   Tier one: _____

   Tiers two, three, and four: _____

   Tiers five, six, and seven: _____

4. **Literary Analysis:** Circle three words that best describe the mood of the story.

   scary   funny   disturbing   suspenseful   helpful   quiet   cheerful

   Find one detail from the story that demonstrates one of the words you circled.

   _____

   _____

5. **Reading Strategy:** Use the chart to break down the following sentence from the story:

   "I again paused, and holding the flambeaux over the masonwork, threw a few feeble rays upon the figure within."

   | Who or what is the subject? | |
   |---|---|
   | What has the subject done? | |

# Writing Activity

## Description of a Set

Think about filming "The Cask of Amontillado" as a movie. To describe the set of a movie, you need to describe the way the scenes in the movie look. Write a paragraph that describes the set of one scene of the story. Start by answering these questions.

1. Write a sentence to describe how you think the carnival looks.

_____

_____

2. Write a sentence to describe how you think the entrance to the catacomb looks.

_____

_____

3. Write a sentence to describe how you think the small room where Fortunato is buried looks.

_____

_____

Choose one of the three places you described above to write your description of a set. On a separate piece of paper, draw a picture of what that place would look like in the movie. Label your drawing with words that describe it, such as "a mossy wall." Then, use your labels to help you write a paragraph that describes your movie set.

_____

_____

_____

_____

_____

# The Most Dangerous Game
## Richard Connell

## Summary

This spine tingler is set on an island in the Caribbean Sea. Rainsford, an expert hunter, is traveling by boat to a place where he can hunt jaguars. He accidentally falls overboard and is forced to swim to a nearby island. There, he comes upon a palace owned by a Russian man named General Zaroff. Over dinner, Zaroff explains that since hunting animals is no longer a challenge, he now stocks the island with more interesting game—shipwrecked sailors. Shocked, Rainsford refuses to join the hunt. As a result of his refusal, Rainsford learns that *he* is the one that will be hunted. Only if he can avoid capture for three days will he be allowed to leave the island. Cornered on the third evening, Rainsford jumps into the sea. Confident that Rainsford has drowned, Zaroff returns to his room. Rainsford, however, is already there. Zaroff is killed by his prey.

## Visual Summary

Track the action in "The Most Dangerous Game" by noticing how the luck of the main character, Rainsford, worsens or improves through the course of the story.

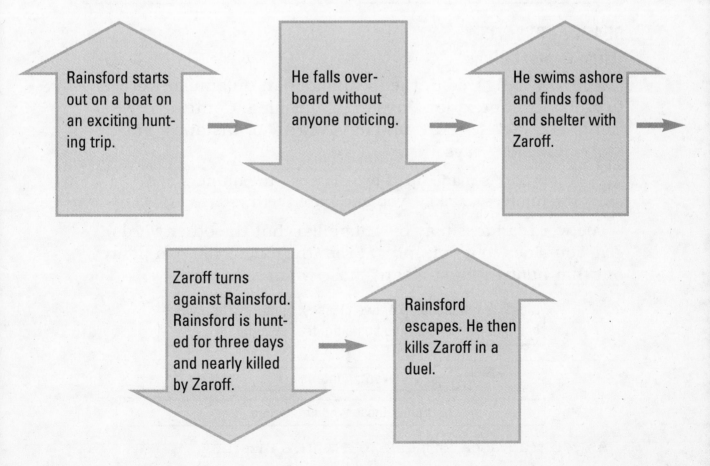

Rainsford starts out on a boat on an exciting hunting trip.

He falls overboard without anyone noticing.

He swims ashore and finds food and shelter with Zaroff.

Zaroff turns against Rainsford. Rainsford is hunted for three days and nearly killed by Zaroff.

Rainsford escapes. He then kills Zaroff in a duel.

## LITERARY ANALYSIS

### Suspense

**Suspense** is the curiosity and excitement you feel when you wonder what will happen next. Writers often create suspense by putting characters in dangerous situations. This example from the story reveals danger. It makes you wonder what will happen next.

> For a seemingly endless time he fought the sea. He began to count his strokes; he could do possibly a hundred more and then—

As you read, pay attention to events and details that help create suspense. Also notice words that make us imagine the worst. Then list them on a chart like this one.

| Event, Detail, or Words Used | Why it is Suspenseful? |
|---|---|
| Rainsford falls overboard. | He may get lost at sea or drown. |
| "he could do possibly a hundred more and then—" | This makes us wonder what will happen next. |

## READING STRATEGY

### Using Context Clues

One way to figure out the meaning of an unfamiliar word is to study its **context** for clues to its meaning. Context is the words and phrases surrounding a word. For instance, in the story, Rainsford says:

> The world is made up of two classes—the hunters and the huntees. Luckily, you and I are the hunters.

The word *huntees* may be unfamiliar, but the other words give you clues to its meaning. From the clues, you can figure out that *huntees* must mean "those who are hunted."

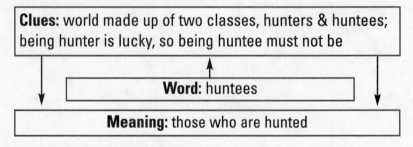

As you read, look for clues to a word's meaning.

# The Most Dangerous Game
## Richard Connell

Sanger Rainsford is a famous hunter of big game, or large animals. He and another hunter named Whitney are sailing from the U.S. to South America. They will hunt large cats called jaguars in South America. Whitney surprises Rainsford by showing sympathy for the jaguars.

◆ ◆ ◆

"Don't talk rot,[1] Whitney," said Rainsford. "You're a big-game hunter, not a <u>philosopher</u>. Who cares how a jaguar feels?"

"Perhaps the jaguar does," observed Whitney.

"Bah! They've no understanding."

"Even so, I rather think they understand one thing—fear. The fear of pain and the fear of death."

"Nonsense," laughed Rainsford. "This hot weather is making you soft, Whitney. Be a <u>realist</u>. The world is made up of two classes—the hunters and the huntees. Luckily, you and I are the hunters."

◆ ◆ ◆

They pass Ship-Trap Island. Whitney tells Rainsford that all the sailors fear the place. Whitney goes to bed. Then, Rainsford hears gunshots from the island. He goes to the ship's rail to see better. It is dark. He strains to get a good view of the island. Then a rope knocks his pipe from his mouth. He tries to catch it, but he falls into the sea.

◆ ◆ ◆

---

### Vocabulary Development

**philosopher** (fuh LAHS uh fer) *n.* a deep thinker

**realist** (REEL ist) *n.* someone who sees the world as it really is

---

1. **rot** nonsense.

---

◆ **Reading Check**

What are Rainsford and Whitney going to do in South America?

_____

_____

◆ **Read Fluently**

Read aloud Rainsford's remarks about the jaguars he hunts. What seems to be his attitude toward them? Circle the letter of the best answer below.

(a) sympathy  (c) unconcern

(b) respect    (d) rage

◆ **Think Ahead**

Circle the two classes that Rainsford says make up the world. What kind does he say he is? Label it "Rainsford." Then, on the lines below, predict what you think may happen to change his views.

_____

_____

_____

_____

_____

For a seemingly endless time he fought the sea. He began to count his <u>strokes</u>; he could do possibly a hundred more and then—

Rainsford heard a sound. It came out of the darkness, a high screaming sound, the sound of an animal in an extremity of <u>anguish</u> and terror.

He did not recognize the animal that made the sound; he did not try to; with fresh <u>vitality</u> he swam toward the sound. He heard it again; then it was cut short.

◆ ◆ ◆

Rainsford swims to shore with difficulty. Then, he falls asleep. The next day, he can see that a large animal was recently hunted nearby. He follows the hunter's trail through the jungle. He comes to a mansion. At the door, a large and dangerous-looking servant points a gun at him. His name is Ivan. Then, another man appears.

◆ ◆ ◆

"It is a very great pleasure to welcome Mr. Sanger Rainsford, the <u>celebrated</u> hunter, to my home."

Automatically Rainsford shook the man's hand.

"I've read your book about hunting snow leopards in Tibet, you see," explained the man. "I am General Zaroff."

◆ ◆ ◆

Zaroff is a nobleman and a Cossack[2] who left Russia after the revolution of 1917[3]. After giving Rainsford a comfortable room,

---

**Vocabulary Development**

**anguish** (AN gwish) *n.* painful suffering
**vitality** (VI tal uh tee) *n.* energy
**celebrated** (SELL uh brayt id) *adj.* famous

---

2. **Cossack** (KAHS ik) member of a people from southern Russia, famous for their fierceness.
3. **revolution of 1917** this russian Revolution was a defeat for upper-class Russians like Zaroff.

he and Rainsford eat together. He reveals that he is a lifelong hunter. He says he grew bored because the animals he hunted no longer had a chance against him.

◆ ◆ ◆

"I needed a new animal. I found one. So I bought this island, built this house, and here I do my hunting. The island is perfect for my purpose—there are jungles with a maze of trails in them, hills, swamps—"

"But the animal, General Zaroff?"

◆ ◆ ◆

Rainsford does not immediately realize that Zaroff hunts people. Zaroff says his ideal quarry must be able to reason. Rainsford is shocked when he realizes Zaroff's ideal <u>quarry</u> is a person.

◆ ◆ ◆

"I can't believe you are serious, General Zaroff. . . ."

"Why should I not be serious? I am speaking of hunting."

"Hunting? General Zaroff, what you speak of is murder."

◆ ◆ ◆

Zaroff says that he considers the men he hunts to be <u>lowly</u> men, not even as valuable as a good horse or dog.

◆ ◆ ◆

"But they are men," said Rainsford hotly.

"Precisely," said the general. "That is why I use them. It gives me pleasure. They can reason, after a fashion.[4] So they are dangerous."

◆ ◆ ◆

© Pearson Education, Inc.

---

**Vocabulary Development**

**lowly** (LO lee) *adv.* of a low position

---

◆ **Stop to Reflect**

Which detail in the bracketed passage suggests that Zaroff is rich? Circle the detail.

◆ **Reading Strategy**

What does *quarry* mean here? Study the **context**, and circle clues to the word's meaning. Then, circle the letter of its meaning below.

(a) something hunted

(b) a place where rock is dug up

(c) to dig for rock

(d) a dog who is a good hunter

◆ **Read Fluently**

Read Zaroff's words in the bracketed section in the way you think he would say them. How do you think Rainsford feels while he listens to Zaroff's words?

_____

_____

_____

◆ **Stop to Reflect**

What is the new animal that Zaroff hunts?

_____

What is your opinion of Zaroff now?

_____

_____

_____

◆ **Reading Check**

In the bracketed passage, circle the two things Zaroff gives the man he is hunting.

What does the man have to do to win the "game"? Underline the answer.

◆ **Literary Analysis**

Explain what is suspenseful about the underlined passage.

_____

_____

_____

_____

Zaroff tells Rainsford that the men he hunts come from ships wrecked off the island. They often come with the help of the lights he uses to trick them onto the rocks. Rainsford is shocked by what he is hearing from Zaroff.

Zaroff explains that he sends a man out with food and a knife. If he connot find the man in three days, then the man wins. If Zaroff finds the man during the three days, he kills him. If they choose not to hunt, he turns them over to Ivan.

◆   ◆   ◆

"Suppose he refuses to be hunted?"

"Oh," said the general, "I give him his option, of course. He need not play the game if he doesn't wish to. If he does not wish to hunt, I turn him over to Ivan. Ivan once had the honor of serving as official knouter[5] to the Great White Czar, and he has his own ideas of sport. Invariably, Mr. Rainsford, invariably they choose the hunt."

"And if they win?"

<u>The smile on the general's face widened. "To date I have not lost," he said.</u>

◆   ◆   ◆

Rainsford refuses to join Zaroff in hunting a sailor that night. The next day he demands to leave. But Zaroff has other plans. He wants to hunt Rainsford.

◆   ◆   ◆

"Tonight," said the general, "we will hunt—you and I."

Rainsford shook his head. "No, general," he said. "I will not hunt."

The general shrugged his shoulders and delicately ate a hothouse grape. "As you wish, my friend," he said. "The choice rests entirely

---

4. **after a fashion** in their way.
5. **knouter** (nout er) *n.* someone who beats criminals with a leather whip.

with you. But may I not venture to suggest that you will find my idea of sport more diverting than Ivan's?"

He nodded toward the corner to where the giant stood, scowling, his thick arms crossed on his hogshead of chest.

"You don't mean—" cried Rainsford.

◆　◆　◆

Rainsford is forced to agree. He takes his knife and food and heads into the jungle. There he creates a twisted trail that he believes no one could follow. He then sleeps up in a tree. He is careful to leave no trace below. But later that night Zaroff appears. He is clearly able to follow the trail. He stops below the tree, looks up. Then he leaves.

Heading into the woods, Rainsford spots a dead tree leaning against a smaller tree. He uses his knife to build a trap. He wants the trap to cause a tree to crash down on Zaroff. Soon, Zaroff appears, following Rainsford's trail. However, Zaroff sees the trap in time. He escapes with only an injured shoulder. He calls out to Rainsford telling him he will be back.

Rainsford continues to try to get away. He comes to a swamp filled with quicksand. He digs a deep hole for another trap. Then, he hears Zaroff coming toward the trap. Again Zaroff escapes, but his dog falls into the quicksand pit.

◆　◆　◆

"Again you score, I think, Mr. Rainsford", called the general. "I'll see what you can do against my whole pack. I'm going home for a rest now. Thank you for a most amusing evening."

◆　◆　◆

◆ Reading Check

What will happen to Rainsford if he does not agree to hunt with Zaroff?

_____

_____

_____

◆ Literary Analysis

Circle a sentence in the bracketed passage that helps build **suspense**. Which character is in the most danger?

_____

◆ Literary Analysis

The author builds **suspense** by describing three traps that Rainsford builds to try to stop Zaroff. What does Rainsford hope the tree will do?

_____

_____

◆ Reading Check

What does Rainsford decide to do when he realizes Zaroff is getting closer to him?

_____

_____

_____

◆ Think Ahead

Which man do you think will win? Why? Answer on the lines below.

_____

_____

_____

◆ Reading Check

Who wins the final matchup? Write the winner on the line below, and circle the sentence that shows you the answer.

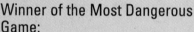

Winner of the Most Dangerous Game:

_____

At sunrise, Zaroff returns with Ivan and the dog pack. Rainsford tries one last trick that he learned in Uganda. He ties his knife to a young tree that will serve as a spring when someone comes by. But the trap kills only Ivan. As Zaroff and the dogs continue to close in, Rainsford can do nothing but jump into the sea. Zaroff arrives at the place where Rainsford jumped. He shrugs and heads for home.

After dinner that night, Zaroff goes up to bed. When he switches on his light, Rainsford is standing in his room. Zaroff asks him how he got there. Rainsford says he swam.

◆ ◆ ◆

The general sucked in his breath and smiled. "I congratulate you," he said. "You have won the game."

Rainsford did not smile. "I am still a beast at bay,"[6] he said, in a low hoarse voice. "Get ready, General Zaroff."

The general made one of his deepest bows. "I see," he said. "Splendid! One of us is to furnish a repast for the hounds.[7] The other will sleep in this very excellent bed. On guard, Rainsford. . . ."

He had never slept in a better bed, Rainsford decided.

---

6. **at bay** Cornered and forced to fight.
7. **repast** (ri PAST) for the hounds: meal for the dogs.

1. Circle three words that best describe General Zaroff.

   kind   competitive   rich   cruel   lazy   uneducated

2. The word "game" can mean "animals hunted for sport." What is "the most dangerous game" in this story? Explain the double meaning on the lines below.

   Meaning 1: _____

   Meaning 2: _____

3. What happens in the end? Circle the letter of the best answer.

   (a) Rainsford drowns trying to escape Zaroff's dogs.

   (b) Rainsford and Zaroff fight, then shake hands and go to sleep.

   (c) Rainsford kills Zaroff and sleeps comfortably in his bed.

   (d) Rainsford kills Zaroff and then has trouble falling asleep.

   Write the words from the story that gave you this answer.

   _____

   _____

4. In the beginning, what is Rainsford's attitude toward the animals he hunts? What lessons do you think he has learned since the hunt with Zaroff? Finish the sentences below.

   Before the hunt with Zaroff, Rainsford thought _____

   _____

   After the hunt with Zaroff, Rainsford probably feels _____

   _____

5. **Literary Analysis:** List three events in the story where the author creates suspense by placing a character in great danger.

| Event | Character(s) in Danger |
|---|---|
| _____ | _____ |
| _____ | _____ |
| _____ | _____ |

6. **Reading Strategy:** Study the **context** for clues to the meaning of each word in italics. Then, on the line, write the meaning of the word.

(a) Rainsford soon realizes that Zaroff hunts people. Zaroff says his ideal *quarry* is a person because of a person's ability to reason.

quarry: _____

(b) If the man being hunted *eludes* Zaroff for three days, then the man wins. However, if Zaroff finds the man during the three days, then the man loses.

eludes: _____

# Writing

## Survival Manual

Imagine that Rainsford is writing a survival manual, or a book, telling others how to survive in wild places.

List three things that Rainsford does to survive in this story.

1. _____

_____

2. _____

_____

3. _____

_____

List the equipment Rainsford uses to survive.

_____

_____

_____

On a separate sheet of paper, write the instructions Rainsford might have written about how to survive in the wild. Include at least five steps. Use some or all of the information you listed above.

# Casey at the Bat

## Ernest Lawrence Thayer

## Summary

As the poem opens, a baseball game is entering its ninth inning. The score is four to two, and the Mudville baseball team seems sure to lose. Two men are out; then two batters get on base. That brings star player Casey up to bat as the crowd cheers. A cocky Casey entertains the fans and sneers at the pitcher. Casey lets the first two pitches go by. The fans object to the umpire calling them strikes, but Casey signals to the crowd that he does not object, and they become quiet. At the third pitch, Casey finally makes a mighty swing—and strikes out.

## Visual Summary

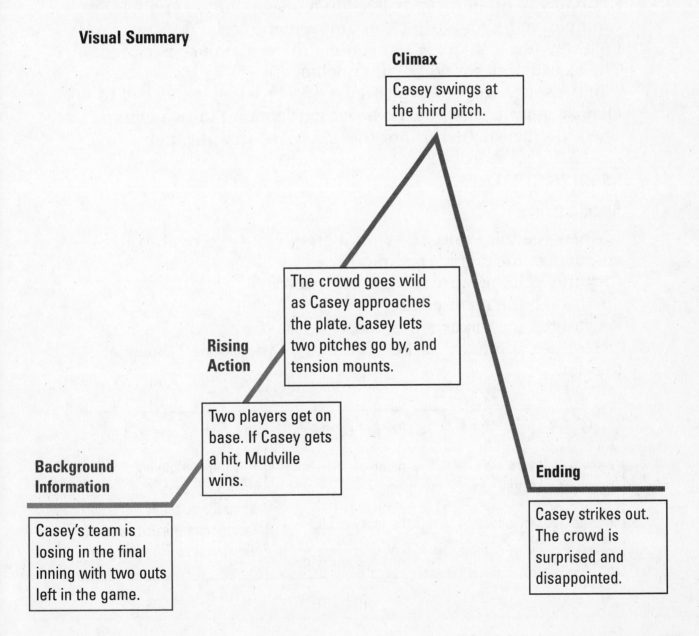

**Climax**

Casey swings at the third pitch.

**Rising Action**

The crowd goes wild as Casey approaches the plate. Casey lets two pitches go by, and tension mounts.

Two players get on base. If Casey gets a hit, Mudville wins.

**Background Information**

Casey's team is losing in the final inning with two outs left in the game.

**Ending**

Casey strikes out. The crowd is surprised and disappointed.

## LITERARY ANALYSIS

### Climax and Anticlimax

The **climax** is the biggest moment in the story. It is when the reader learns how the story will turn out. For example, imagine you plan a trip to an amusement park. You travel a long way to get there. You stand in line for tickets. Then, you go inside and ride the roller coaster. The roller coaster ride would be the climax.

The **anticlimax** is when what you expected to happen does not happen. An anticlimax is often a disappointing ending. For example, you plan a trip to an amusement park. You travel a long way to get there. When you get there, the park is closed. The closed park would be an anticlimax.

In "Casey at the Bat," the events of a baseball game lead to a climax. As you read, notice how the events build to a climax. Then, decide whether or not the story has an anticlimax.

## READING STRATEGY

### Summarizing

When you tell someone about a story you have read, you summarize the story. To summarize,

- you retell the story in your own words.
- you tell the main points.
- you tell the important details.

Here is a summary of the beginning of the poem, "Casey at the Bat."

| Main Points | Details | Summary |
|---|---|---|
| Baseball players are playing a baseball game.<br><br>The hometeam is losing. | The losing team is from Mudville.<br><br>It is the last inning.<br><br>The fans are worried. | It is the last inning of the baseball game. The hometeam, Mudville, is losing, and the fans are worried. |

# Casey at the Bat
## Ernest Lawrence Thayer

It is the last inning of the baseball game. The score is two to four. The hometeam, Mudville, is losing. The fans are worried that their team will not win the game. Some fans are going home. Yet some fans are hopeful that their team will win. They hope the great baseball player, Casey, will have a turn at bat. Two players bat before Casey. They are Flynn and Blakey. They are not strong players. There is little chance that Casey will get a turn to hit the ball.

◆　◆　◆

But Flynn let drive a "single," to the wonderment
    of all.
And the much-despised Blakey "tore the cover
    off the ball."[1]
And when the dust had lifted, and they saw
    what had occurred,
There was Blakey safe at second, and Flynn
    a-huggin' third.

◆　◆　◆

The two players get hits. Both are on base. The fans are surprised. Now Casey will come to bat. Casey has a chance to win the game for Mudville.

◆　◆　◆

There was ease in Casey's manner as he
    stepped into his place,
There was pride in Casey's bearing and a smile
    on Casey's face;

---

### Vocabulary Development

**single** (SING guhl) *n.* a hit of the ball that lets the batter go to first base

---

◆ **Reading Check**

What inning of the baseball game is described in the poem?

_____

◆ **Reading Strategy**

Summarize the action of the baseball game so far.

The score is _____

The Mudville players, Flynn and Blakey have just batted.

Flynn is _____ .

Blakey is _____ .

◆ **Stop to Reflect**

Do you think Casey will help the team win? Why, or why not?

_____

_____

_____

---

1. **tore the cover off the ball** hit the baseball very hard with the bat so that the ball traveled a long way.

## ◆ Stop to Reflect

Underline the words in the first bracketed passage that help describe how Casey responds to the crowd.

Then, circle two of the following words that describe how Casey feels.

nervous   proud   confident

afraid   shy   lazy

## ◆ Literary Analysis

Reread the second bracketed lines of the poem. Write the two events and the climax that happens here.

Event: _____

_____

Event: _____

_____

Climax: _____

_____

## ◆ Literary Analysis

Circle the words that explain the anticlimax of the poem.

And when responding to the cheers he lightly
    doffed his hat,[2]
No stranger in the crowd could doubt 'twas
    Casey at the bat.

◆  ◆  ◆

All the fans watch Casey. They cheer. The pitcher gets ready to throw the ball. Casey gets ready to hit the ball. The pitcher throws the ball, but Casey does not swing at it. The umpire calls, "Strike one." The fans do not like the call. Casey raises his hand. The jeering crowd becomes quiet.

The pitcher throws the ball again. Casey does not swing at it. The umpire calls, "Strike two." The fans do not like the call. Casey looks at the crowd. Again, they become quiet. Casey gets ready for the next pitch.

◆  ◆  ◆

The <u>sneer</u> is gone from Casey's lips, his teeth
    are clenched in hate.
He pounds with cruel vengeance his bat upon
    the plate:
And now the pitcher holds the ball, and now
    he lets it go,
And now the air is shattered by the force of
    Casey's blow.

Oh, somewhere in this favored land the sun is
    shining bright,
The band is playing somewhere, and somewhere
    hearts are light:
And somewhere men are laughing, and
    somewhere children shout,
But there is no joy in Mudville: Mighty Casey
    has struck out.

---

### Vocabulary Development

**sneer** (SNEER) *adj.*  a look of scorn and belittlement

---

2. **doffed his hat** (DAWFT) lifted, raised in a friendly greeting

1. Why are the Mudville fans worried at the beginning of the poem?

_____

_____

2. (a) Where on the baseball diamond are these three players when Casey comes to bat? Circle the correct answer for each player.

Blakey:   1st   2nd   3rd   home plate

Flynn:    1st   2nd   3rd   home plate

Casey:    1st   2nd   3rd   home plate

(b) Write the three players' names on your drawing to show where they are.

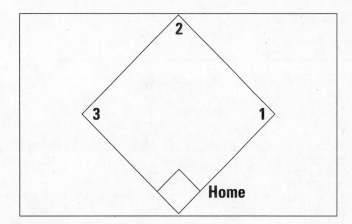

3. Describe what Casey looks like.

_____

_____

Circle all of the words that you think describe Casey as a player.

(a) proud       (b) lazy       (c) strong       (d) talented

4. How many times does the pitcher throw the ball when Casey is at bat?

_____

5. **Literary Analysis:** Casey's turn at bat provides a climax and an anti-climax in this poem.

What is the biggest moment when Casey is at bat?

_____

What is the lowest, or most disappointing, moment in the poem?

_____

6. **Reading Strategy:** Reread the last two stanzas of the poem. How would you retell this part of the poem in your own words? Use the chart to record the main points and details. Then, write your summary.

| Main Points | Details | Summary |
|---|---|---|
|  |  |  |

# Writing

**Sportscast**

Imagine you were a sportscaster at the ballpark when Casey came to bat. Write a story that tells what happened.

1. List five words about baseball, such as *base* and *strike*.

_____  _____  _____  _____  _____

2. Picture in your mind what happened when it was Casey's turn at bat. Write three sentences to describe what you saw. Try to use some of the baseball terms above.

_____

_____

_____

Using the information above, write a story about Casey's experience. Make sure it sounds lively and exciting.

## *from* A Lincoln Preface
### Carl Sandburg

## Summary

   This selection is a profile of the sixteenth U.S. president, Abraham Lincoln. Carl Sandburg, the profile's author, begins by describing Lincoln's assassination. Next, he describes Lincoln's role in the Civil War. Sandburg shows how Lincoln stubbornly supported the cause of the Union despite tremendous loss of life and property. In the final section, Sandburg explores the conflicting sides of Lincoln's personality. He tells stories that show how Lincoln could be cunning and ill-tempered. But he also shows Lincoln as a man who was often humorous, patient, and generous. In his essay, Sandburg crafts a portrait of a complex man who was determined to save the Union at any cost.

## Visual Summary

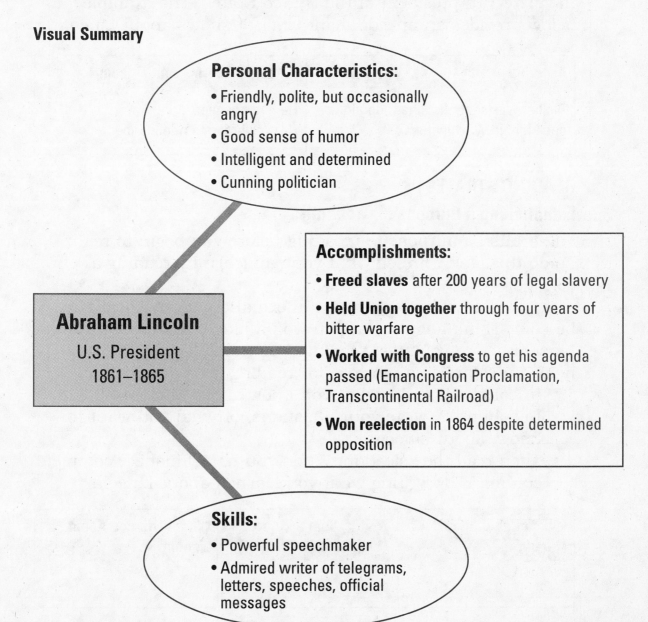

**Personal Characteristics:**
- Friendly, polite, but occasionally angry
- Good sense of humor
- Intelligent and determined
- Cunning politician

**Abraham Lincoln**
U.S. President
1861–1865

**Accomplishments:**
- **Freed slaves** after 200 years of legal slavery
- **Held Union together** through four years of bitter warfare
- **Worked with Congress** to get his agenda passed (Emancipation Proclamation, Transcontinental Railroad)
- **Won reelection** in 1864 despite determined opposition

**Skills:**
- Powerful speechmaker
- Admired writer of telegrams, letters, speeches, official messages

## LITERARY ANALYSIS

### Anecdote

An **anecdote**
- is a very short story about a person.
- tells about an interesting or amusing event.
- helps the reader better understand an idea.

Anecdotes might be written or told. Carl Sandburg uses anecdotes in his biography of Abraham Lincoln. His anecdotes help readers to better understand Abraham Lincoln.

As you read, think about what each anecdote tells you about the sixteenth president of the United States. The example below provides an anecdote and what it shows about Lincoln.

| Anecdote About Lincoln | What You Learn About Lincoln |
| --- | --- |
| His hat was shot off as he rode alone one night in Washington . . ." | He had enemies.<br>He was brave to ride alone. |

## READING STRATEGY

### Establishing a Purpose for Reading

**Establish a purpose for reading** before you begin to read. To do this, ask yourself what you can learn by reading a selection.

"A Lincoln Preface" gives you information about Abraham Lincoln. Think about what you would like to learn about Lincoln before you start reading. Use the following chart to help you establish a purpose for reading.
- In column 1, write what you know about Lincoln.
- In column 2, write your questions, or what you want to know, about Lincoln.
- Then read the selection. When you have finished, complete column 3 by writing what you learned about Lincoln.

| What I Know About Lincoln | What I Want to Know About Lincoln | What I Learned About Lincoln |
| --- | --- | --- |
| | | |

# *from* A Lincoln Preface
## Carl Sandburg

President Abraham Lincoln was shot and killed in April 1865. The people of the nation were deeply saddened. Lincoln was president of the United States for four years before he died. He was a powerful president. He was the head of the Union army of the North during the American Civil War.[1]

❖ ❖ ❖

When the woman who wrote *Uncle Tom's Cabin*[2] came to see him in the White House, he greeted her, "So you're the little woman who wrote the book that made this <u>great war</u>," and as they seated themselves at a fireplace, "I do love an open fire: I always had one at home." As they were finishing their talk of the days of blood, he said, "I shan't last long after it's over."

❖ ❖ ❖

Lincoln was elected president when our country was greatly troubled. A <u>Congressman</u> told Lincoln he was surprised that a small-town man like Lincoln could be elected president. Lincoln said he couldn't believe it either. He said he just tried to do his best each day.

❖ ❖ ❖

---

### Vocabulary Development

**congressman** (KAHN gres man) *n.* a person who serves in the lawmaking body called Congress

---

1. **American Civil War** *n.* war between the northern and southern states between 1861 and 1865.
2. **Uncle Tom's Cabin** *n.* a novel by Harriet Beecher Stowe. This book caused many people to have opinions against slavery.

❖ **Reading Strategy**

To set a purpose for reading, write two questions that you would like answered about Abraham Lincoln.

1. _____

_____

2. _____

_____

❖ **Reading Strategy**

Write one thing you learned about Lincoln in the first paragraph.

_____

_____

_____

❖ **Literary Analysis**

The author uses an anecdote to tell you something about Lincoln. In the bracketed section above, underline what Lincoln says about an open fire. Do you think Lincoln liked his home?

_____

Circle the word that helped you know how he felt.

*Mark the Text*

Lincoln said that both sides in the Civil War did not follow the laws of the Constitution.

1. According to Lincoln, who was destroying the Union? Underline the answer.

2. According to Lincoln, who would save the Union? Draw a box around the answer.

Lincoln calls the Constitution a "sacred instrument." He says he is guarding the Constitution "with great care."

Circle the answer that tells Lincoln's opinion of the Constitution.

(a) He thinks it is of no use to anyone.

(b) He thinks it is important.

(c) He thinks it is not important.

(d) He thinks it causes too much trouble.

What type of transportation does Lincoln write about?

_____

Circle the words in the bracketed text that tell you that Lincoln thought this transportation was important for the United States.

"I don't intend precisely to throw the Constitution overboard, but I will stick it in a hole if I can," he told a Cabinet officer.[3] The enemy was violating the Constitution to destroy the Union, he argued, and therefore, "I will violate the Constitution, if necessary, to save the Union." He instructed a messenger to the Secretary of the Treasury, "Tell him not to bother himself about the Constitution. Say that I have that sacred instrument here at the White House, and I am guarding it with great care."

◆   ◆   ◆

Lincoln ran for reelection in 1864. There were powerful people in the North who were against his reelection. They said Lincoln had made mistakes. They said Lincoln had committed crimes. Some of these people supported the South.

◆   ◆   ◆

While propagandas raged, and the war winds howled, he sat in the White House, the Stubborn Man of History, writing that the Mississippi was one river and could not belong to two countries, that the plans for railroad connection from coast to coast must be pushed through and the Union Pacific[4] realized.

◆   ◆   ◆

### Vocabulary Development

**Constitution** (KAHN stuh too shuhn) *n.* the written document that tells how the United States is governed

**propaganda** (PRAHP uh gan duh) *n.* opinions and beliefs that are spread purposefully

---

3. **Cabinet** (KAB i nit) *n.* group of people who advise the president.
4. **Union Pacific** *n.* railroad built across the United States.

Lincoln had a sense of humor and a unique way of describing people. For example, he compared one man to an old worn-out shoe that is so rotten it cannot be mended.

Lincoln held the Union army together. He found generals who won battles for the Union.

♦  ♦  ♦

His own speeches, letters, telegrams and official messages during that war form the most significant and enduring document from any one man on why the war began, why it went on, and the dangers beyond its end. He mentioned "the politicians," over and again "the politicians," with scorn and blame. As the platoons filed before him at a review of an army corps, he asked, "What is to become of these boys when the war is over?"

♦  ♦  ♦

Lincoln was greatly troubled by the Civil War. Because of the war, he hardly slept and he sometimes cried. He seemed to cry at appropriate times.

Lincoln had many accidents during his life. Once his hat was shot off his head. His thumb was nearly cut off by an ax when he was a boy. His eye was scarred when he was hit by a robber on a flatboat.

Lincoln's family was very important to him. One of his sons died before he did. One son was brilliant but had a deformed palate and a speech impediment. Lincoln defended his wife when she was accused of betrayal.

♦ **Reading Check**

What four types of communication did Lincoln use during the war?

1. _____

2. _____

3. _____

4. _____

♦ **Reading Strategy**

Which information in the bracketed section did you already know about Lincoln?

_____

_____

_____

_____

_____

Which idea in the bracketed section is the most interesting point you learned about Lincoln?

_____

_____

_____

_____

Lincoln was a clever politician. He made appointments without Cabinet approval. He helped Nevada become a state so that Nevada's votes could help him free the slaves. He made deals with Congressmen to gain their votes for laws he wanted passed. When receiving gifts from foreign kings, he could be as grand as they were.

◆ ◆ ◆

While the war drums beat, he liked best of all the stories told of him, one of two Quakeresses[5] heard talking in a railway car. "I think that Jefferson[6] will succeed." "Why does thee think so?" "Because Jefferson is a praying man." "And so is Abraham a praying man." "Yes, but the Lord will think Abraham is joking."

An Indiana man at the White House heard him say, "Voorhees, don't it seem strange to you that I, who could never so much as cut off the head of a chicken, should be elected, or selected, into the midst of all this blood?"

A party of American citizens, standing in the ruins of the Forum in Rome, Italy, heard there the news of the first assassination of the first American dictator, and took it as a sign of the growing up and the aging of the civilization on the North American continent. Far out in Coles

---

Circle the words that tell how Lincoln felt about the Quakeresses story. What do these words tell you about Lincoln?

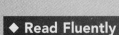

_____

_____

_____

_____

_____

Read the bracketed anecdote aloud. Use a voice that expresses the feelings Lincoln probably had.

What is Lincoln saying about himself in this anecdote?

_____

_____

_____

_____

_____

County, Illinois, a beautiful, gaunt old woman[7] in a log cabin said, "I knowed he'd never come back."

◆ ◆ ◆

Lincoln was praised by his enemies. He was admired by people who worked for him. He was a friend to many. He lived to be 56 years old, and his life was <u>rich and full</u>.

Lincoln was able to be funny and odd. He had a sense of humor and knew what was fun and what was silly. Even so, he wrote many speeches and letters that were important to the nation even after his death. In fact, when you read them, you will see snippets of wisdom, teasing, and subtle meanings.

Lincoln's legacy is known the world over. He is known as an important American. His fame rose because he was a strong communicator and a good neighbor. In addition, he is known for being a friend to people he did not even know.

◆ Stop to Reflect

Give one reason why Lincoln's life could be considered "rich and full."

_____

_____

_____

◆ Reading Strategy

Write one thing you learned about Lincoln in the bracketed passage.

_____

_____

_____

7. **beautiful, gaunt old woman** refers to Lincoln's stepmother, Sarah. She and Lincoln were very close. When he became president, she predicted that he would be killed.

1. Circle the letter of the choice that best completes the following statement: Lincoln believed that the Mississippi River should belong to

   (a) two countries     (c) Illinois

   (b) one country      (d) Mississippi

   Why do you think he felt this way?

   _____

   _____

2. Circle three phrases that you learned about Lincoln from reading Sandburg's preface.

   He enjoyed war.
   He had a perfect family.
   He defended the United States.
   He could tell a funny story.
   He was a powerful president.
   He was afraid of his enemies.

3. **Literary Analysis:** Circle the letter of the answer that tells the meaning of the following anecdote.

   An Indiana man at the White house heard him say, "Voorhees, don't it seem strange to you that I, who could never so much as cut off the head of a chicken, should be elected, or selected, into the midst of all this blood?"

   (a) Lincoln liked chickens.
   (b) Lincoln was a chicken farmer.
   (c) Lincoln did not like violence.
   (d) Lincoln liked being in the war.

4. **Reading Strategy:** Write three things you learned about Lincoln from reading this selection.

   1. _____

   2. _____

   3. _____

# Writing

## Character Profile

A character profile uses words to draw a picture of a character. The words show what the character is like. Write your own character profile of Abraham Lincoln. Before you begin, gather details from the selection using the chart below.

In the first column of the chart, read the sentences from "A Lincoln Preface." Write a word or phrase from the box to complete each sentence in the chart. The first sentence is done for you.

| one United States | war |
| determined | the soldiers |

| Carl Sandburg's Words about Lincoln | What Abraham Lincoln Was Like |
|---|---|
| 1. "I will violate the Constitution, if necessary, to save the Union." | Lincoln was <u>determined</u>. |
| 2. . . . he sat in the White House, the Stubborn Man of History, writing that the Mississippi was one river and could not belong to two countries, . . . | Lincoln believed in _____. |
| 3. As the platoons filed before him at a review of an army corps, he asked, "What is to become of these boys when the war is over?" | Lincoln was worried about _____. |
| 4. An Indiana man at the White House heard him say, "Voorhees, don't it seem strange to you that I, who could never so much as cut off the head of a chicken, should be elected, or selected, into the midst of all this blood?" | Lincoln did not like _____. |

Use the ideas in the second column of the chart to help you write your profile.

## "I Have a Dream"
### Martin Luther King, Jr.

### Summary

In this famous speech, Dr. Martin Luther King, Jr., presents his vision of what America would be like if racism and inequality did not exist. He quotes from the Declaration of Independence and the Bible in order to illustrate his idea of freedom. King begins the speech by identifying what he wants to see happen. This is done in a series of word pictures, all of which begin with the phrase "I have a dream." Then he states that it is through faith that these changes can occur. He closes with an encouragement to all who are listening to "let freedom ring" throughout the country.

### Visual Summary

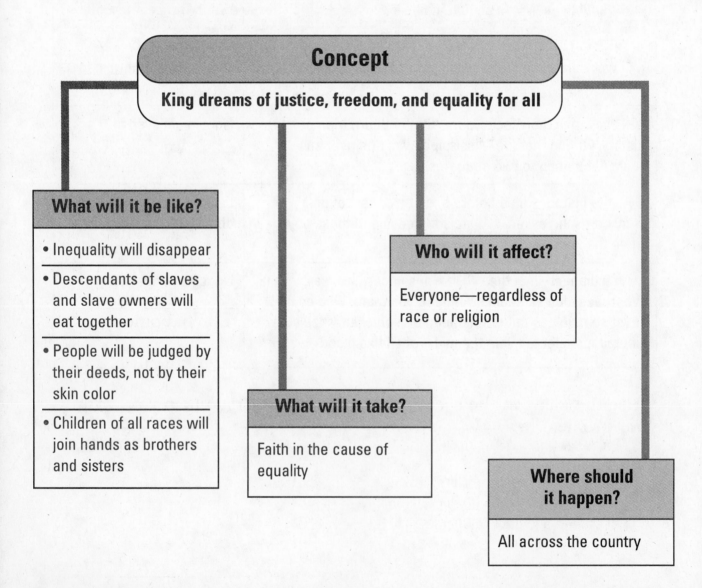

**Concept**

King dreams of justice, freedom, and equality for all

**What will it be like?**

- Inequality will disappear
- Descendants of slaves and slave owners will eat together
- People will be judged by their deeds, not by their skin color
- Children of all races will join hands as brothers and sisters

**What will it take?**

Faith in the cause of equality

**Who will it affect?**

Everyone—regardless of race or religion

**Where should it happen?**

All across the country

## LITERARY ANALYSIS
### Author's Purpose

An author has a reason for writing. This reason is called the **author's purpose**. The author's purpose might be
- to entertain you.
- to give you information.
- to persuade you to think a certain way.

Martin Luther King had a purpose when he wrote his speech "I Have a Dream." He wanted to persuade or convince his audience to accept all people as equal. The following example from the speech shows how King used words from the Declaration of Independence to persuade his audience:

> I have a dream that one day this nation will rise up and live out the true meaning of its creed: "We hold these truths to be self-evident; that all men are created equal."

Think about the author's purpose when you read.

## READING STRATEGY
### Responding

Sometimes a story or article causes you to **respond**. This means you react or have feelings about the words and ideas. You might feel happy, angry, or excited when you read. When you read, notice which words or ideas make you feel a particular way. For example, reading the words "our great high school team won the state championship" in your school newspaper might make you happy. Your feeling of happiness is your response.

Notice how you feel as you read. Use a chart like this to write your responses.

| From the Text | My Response |
| --- | --- |
| King dreams that his children will one day be judged by the content of their character and not by the color of their skin. | I feel hopeful |

Why do you think so many people came to the March on Washington?

_____

_____

_____

In the bracketed text, read Dr. King's dream for his four children.

Write in your own words what this dream is.

_____

_____

_____

_____

How do you feel when you read the words "my four little children" in the bracketed paragraph?

_____

_____

Why do you think you respond in this way?

_____

_____

_____

# I Have a Dream
## Martin Luther King, Jr.

This speech was given by Martin Luther King, Jr., on August 28, 1963 as part of the March on Washington. He spoke to more than 250,000 people in Washington, D.C. The people came to Washington to show their support for the American civil rights movement.[1]

In his speech, King tells the people that he has a dream for a better America.

King dreams that all people will have the freedom stated in the Declaration of Independence.

King hopes that the sons of slaves and the sons of slaveholders will someday be equal.

King dreams that even the state of Mississippi will be a land of freedom and justice for everyone.

◆　◆　◆

I have a dream that my four little children will one day live in a nation where they will not be judged by the color of their skin but by the content of their character.

◆　◆　◆

---

1. **American civil rights movement** a movement by people in the 1950s and 1960s that challenged the laws that treated people unequally.

King continues his speech by expressing his hope and dream. He uses a reference from the Bible to help express his dream of a peaceful world where all people are treated equally. He says faith will bring brotherhood and freedom to America.

◆ ◆ ◆

This will be the day when all of God's children will be able to sing with new meaning "My country 'tis of thee, sweet land of liberty, of thee I sing. Land where my fathers died, land of the pilgrim's pride, from every mountainside, let freedom ring."[2]

And if America is to be a great nation this must become true. So let freedom ring from the prodigious hilltops of New Hampshire. Let freedom ring from the mighty mountains of New York. Let freedom ring from the heightening Alleghenies of Pennsylvania!

Let freedom ring from the snowcapped Rockies of Colorado!

◆ ◆ ◆

King dreams of freedom in all parts of our country, from the east coast to the west coast, and from north to south.

King says, in closing, that when America lets freedom ring everywhere, then all people will be truly free.

◆ Read Fluently

Practice reading the bracketed passage aloud. Speak slowly and strongly, as if you are speaking to a very large crowd.

Which words will you say strongly when you read aloud? Write the words here.

_____

_____

_____

◆ Literary Analysis

Underline each time Dr. King uses the words "let freedom ring."

Circle the letter of Dr. King's **purpose** in repeating this phrase.

(a) to entertain

(b) to inform

(c) to persuade

---

**Vocabulary Development**

**prodigious** (PRO dij us) *adj.* wonderful; of great size

---

2. **My country 'tis of thee . . . freedom ring** these are words from a popular song written in 1830.

1. (a) Name four states mentioned in the speech.

1. _____

2. _____

3. _____

4. _____

(b) Why do you think King mentions so many states in his speech?

_____

_____

2. King has a dream that his children will live in a world where they "will not be judged by the color of their skin but by the content of their character." What is the meaning of the phrase "the content of their character"?

_____

_____

_____

3. **Literary Analysis:** Read the following passage from King's speech, in which he uses words from the Declaration of Independence.

   I have a dream that one day this nation will rise up and live out the true meaning of its creed: "We hold these truths to be self-evident; that all men are created equal."

What is the **author's purpose** in this passage? Circle the letter of the best answer.

(a) to entertain      (b) to inform      (c) to persuade

Explain why you chose this answer.

_____

_____

4. **Reading Strategy:** Using the chart below, explain how you **respond** when you read the words in the first column.

| Words from the Text | My Response |
|---|---|
| an oasis of freedom and justice | |
| let freedom ring | |

## Listening and Speaking

### Radio News Report

**Radio news reports** often give on-the-spot coverage of an important event. Write a paragraph of a radio news report about King's speech that you will read to your class. Fill in these sentence-starters to help you before you write.

1. The civil rights movement is _____

_____

_____

_____

2. King's dream for America is _____

_____

_____

_____

3. The most memorable part of King's speech is _____

_____

_____

_____

4. The crowd reacted to King's speech by _____

_____

_____

After you have written your paragraph, practice reading it aloud. If possible, tape-record yourself while reading. Listen to your recording to make sure you capture the feelings of the event. Then, read it to your class.

# Old Man of the Temple

## R. K. Narayan

## Summary

This work of fantasy is set in India. As the story opens, the narrator, called The Talkative Man, is explaining events that happened "some years ago." He and his driver were driving down a lonely country road at night. Doss, the driver, suddenly swerved the car, shouting at an old man. The narrator, however, saw no one. Doss claimed to have seen an old man come out the door of the nearby temple. The narrator is confused, because the temple is in ruins. Doss passes out. When Doss wakes up, he speaks in the voice of an old man. He claims to be Krishna Battar, the builder of the temple. The narrator tells Battar that he is dead and that he should join his deceased wife, Seetha. Battar thinks about his dead wife, then sees her coming. He falls to the ground. When Doss awakens, he is his old self. The narrator learns that strange knocking has disturbed village residents and animals for years. After this incident, however, the knocking stops and the animals are no longer afraid.

## Visual Summary

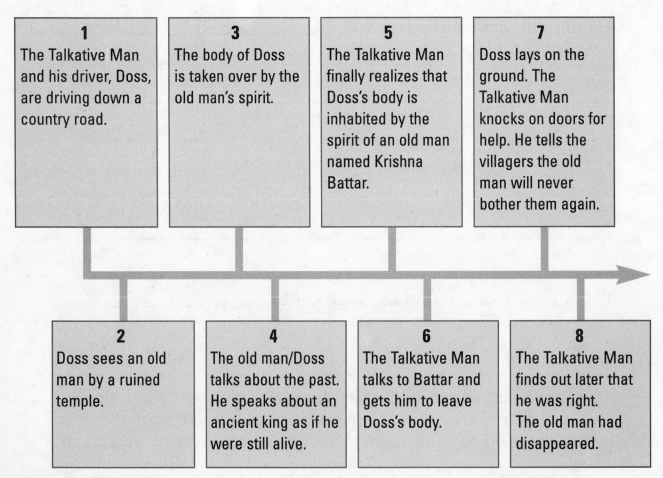

**1**
The Talkative Man and his driver, Doss, are driving down a country road.

**3**
The body of Doss is taken over by the old man's spirit.

**5**
The Talkative Man finally realizes that Doss's body is inhabited by the spirit of an old man named Krishna Battar.

**7**
Doss lays on the ground. The Talkative Man knocks on doors for help. He tells the villagers the old man will never bother them again.

**2**
Doss sees an old man by a ruined temple.

**4**
The old man/Doss talks about the past. He speaks about an ancient king as if he were still alive.

**6**
The Talkative Man talks to Battar and gets him to leave Doss's body.

**8**
The Talkative Man finds out later that he was right. The old man had disappeared.

## LITERARY ANALYSIS
### Fantasy

In literature, things that could happen are called real. Things that could not happen are called **fantasy**. Characters, places, or events in a fantasy story do not appear in the real world. They could not truly happen. Yet, fantasies always contain some realistic elements. For example, this passage from "Old Man of the Temple" has fantastic events and characters. It also has real events and characters.

> "Listen to me," I said. "You ought not to be here any more."
>
> "What do you mean?" he asked, drawing himself up, proudly.
>
> "Don't feel hurt; I say you shouldn't be here any more because you are dead."
>
> "Dead! Dead!" he said. "Don't talk nonsense. How can I be dead when you see me before you now?"

The two men talking to each other could be a real event. But one of the men is a dead man. That is fantasy.

## READING STRATEGY
### Distinguishing Fantasy from Reality

When you distinguish between two things you see the difference between them. Sometimes it is difficult to **distinguish fantasy from reality**. This story includes some events based on reality. They are events that could happen. It also has some events based on fantasy. They are events that could not happen.

- If you feel confused by something you are reading, pause and think about what you have just read. Then, go back and reread the section.
- Decide which events in the passage could happen. Then decide which events could not happen.

Use a chart like this as you read the story to help you distinguish fantasy from reality.

| Reality | Fantasy |
|---|---|
| Two men talking | A dead man who talks |

# Old Man of the Temple
## R. K. Narayan

◆ **Reading Check**

Who are the two characters in the beginning of the story?

The Talkative Man is the narrator of this story. He talks about the time he met a strange old man. The Talkative Man was riding in a taxi. He was going to Kumbum, a town fifty miles from Malgudi.[1] His driver's name was Doss.[2] It was late at night when the Talkative Man and Doss drove through a village.

Doss suddenly swerves the car and shouts at an old man. The narrator does not see anyone and asks what is the matter.

◆ ◆ ◆

Doss stopped the car and said, "You see that old fellow, sir. He is trying to kill himself. I can't understand what he is up to."

I looked in the direction he pointed and asked, "Which old man?"

"There, there. He is coming towards us again. As soon as I saw him open that temple door and come out I had a feeling, somehow, that I must keep an eye on him."

◆ ◆ ◆

◆ **Literary Analysis**

Which sentence is an example of **fantasy** in this story? Circle the letter of your answer.

(a) An old temple stands next to the road.

(b) An old man comes out of locked doors.

(c) The narrator steps out of the taxi.

(d) Doss returns to the taxi.

The narrator steps out of the taxi. He sees no one. He only sees an old temple next to the road. The temple is falling down, and its doors are locked. But Doss says he sees an old man coming out of the temple doors. The narrator wants to go on, so he and Doss

---

### Vocabulary Development

**temple** (TEM puhl) *n.* building used for worship

---

1. **Malgudi** (mahl GOO dee) *n.* a fantasy city that often appears in this author's stories.
2. **Doss** (DAHS) *n.* the name of the taxi driver.

return to the taxi. Then Doss asks if the man may join them in the taxi.

♦ ♦ ♦

"Which fellow?" I asked.

Doss indicated the space next to him.

"What is the matter with you, Doss? Have you had a drop of drink[3] or something?"

"I have never tasted any drink in my life, sir," he said, and added, "Get down, old boy. Master says he can't take you."

"Are you talking to yourself?"

"After all, I think we needn't care for these unknown fellows on the road," he said.

"Doss," I pleaded. "Do you feel confident you can drive? If you feel dizzy don't drive."

♦ ♦ ♦

Doss admits that he is not feeling well and seems to fall asleep.

When the narrator wakes him, Doss is like an old man. His hands shake. His voice is thin and high. Doss says he is eighty years old. The narrator asks Doss to drive the taxi. But now Doss says he is unable to drive a car. He says he only knows how to drive an ox cart. The narrator is confused by Doss's behavior. Then Doss asks a strange question.

♦ ♦ ♦

"Where is everybody?"

"Who?"

"Lots of people I knew are not to be seen at all. All sorts of new fellows everywhere, and nobody seems to care. Not a soul comes near the temple. All sorts of people go about but not one who cares to stop and talk. Why doesn't the king ever come this way? He used to go this way at least once a year before."

"Which king?" I asked.

♦ ♦ ♦

3. **drink** *n.* alcoholic beverage, such as wine, whiskey, or beer.

---

**♦ Reading Strategy**

**Distinguish fantasy from reality** in the first bracketed passage below. What is one example of fantasy?

_____

_____

What is one example of reality?

_____

_____

**♦ Stop to Reflect**

How has Doss changed?

How do you think this makes the narrator feel?

_____

_____

_____

_____

**♦ Read Fluently**

Practice reading aloud the second bracketed passage to help you answer these questions:

1. Who is speaking here?

_____

2. Circle two words below that tell how the speaker feels.

lonely         happy

busy          confused

Read to convey the speaker's feelings.

Write three things the old man says that give the Talkative Man an idea.

1. _____

_____

2. _____

_____

3. _____

_____

The **reality** in this bracketed passage is that two men are talking. What is the **fantasy**?

_____

_____

Which of the following is an example of **fantasy** in this story? Circle your answer here.

(a) The old man is 500 years old.

(b) A man was robbed and stabbed in the jungle.

Doss is angry because the narrator does not know what he is talking about. Doss walks toward the temple. He walks like a very old man. When the narrator asks him his name, he says, "Krishna Battar."[4] He says everyone knows him. He says he is the one who built the temple. Then the old man says the name of the king. The narrator admits he never heard of this king. These strange events give the Talkative Man an idea.

◆ ◆ ◆

"Listen to me," I said. "You ought not to be here any more."

"What do you mean?" he asked, drawing himself up, proudly.

"Don't feel hurt; I say you shouldn't be here any more because you are dead."

"Dead! Dead!" he said. "Don't talk nonsense. How can I be dead when you see me before you now? If I am dead how can I be saying this and that?"

◆ ◆ ◆

The narrator tells the old man if he built the temple, then he must be 500 years old. The man thinks about this. Then he tells his story. He says he was robbed and stabbed in the jungle. He says the robbers left him for dead, but that he returned to the temple. He says he has been at the temple ever since.

The narrator addresses the old man as Krishna Battar and tells him he is dead. The old man is puzzled.

◆ ◆ ◆

"Where am I to go? Where am I to go?"

"Have you no one who cares for you?" I asked.

"None except my wife. I loved her very much."

"You can go to her."

---

4. **Krishna Battar** (KRISH nuh buh TAR) *n.* the name of the old man.

"Oh, no. She died four years ago." He was clearly without any sense of time.

◆   ◆   ◆

The narrator suggests that the old man think about his dead wife. The old man thinks about her for a while. Suddenly the old man screams. He says his wife is there. He says he will go with her. He stands up tall, but then falls down in the road. Doss lays on the ground. He is breathing, but will not open his eyes. The narrator knocks on the door of a nearby cottage. The people inside do not answer his knock. He shouts out who he is and where he is from. His call goes unanswered.

When he sounds the car horn, a family emerges from the cottage and explains that they thought they heard the usual knocking.

◆   ◆   ◆

"When was this knocking first heard?" I asked.

"We can't say," said one. "The first time I heard it was when my grandfather was living; he used to say he had even seen it once or twice. It doesn't harm anyone, as far as I know. The only thing it does is bother the bullock[5] carts passing the temple and knock on the doors at night . . ."

◆   ◆   ◆

The narrator tells the family that they would not be troubled by the knocking anymore. This seems to be true. The next time the narrator travels through the village he is told there has been no more knocking on doors. It seems the old man went away with his wife.

---

5. **bullock** (BOOL ek) *n.* ox; steer.

**◆ Background**

The followers of the Hindu religion believe that the soul of a person gives up worldly life to move to another level. The old man's soul has not given up his old life. He is trapped between life and death. How does the Talkative Man help the old man?

_____

_____

**◆ Reading Check**

What does the narrator have to do to get the people in the cottage to come to their door?

_____

_____

_____

**◆ Reading Check**

Who do you think was bothering the villagers?

_____

Why has the knocking stopped at the end of the story?

_____

_____

1. Write the numbers 1, 2, 3, 4 to show the order of events in this story.

   ____ The Talkative Man tells the old man he is dead.

   ____ Doss changes into an old man.

   ____ The people in the village do not hear knocking anymore.

   ____ The old man sees his dead wife.

2. List three changes that happen to Doss after he awakens from his sleep.

   1. _____

   2. _____

   3. _____

3. Why do the people of the village not open their doors at night?

   _____

   _____

4. **Literary Analysis:** Which of the following is an example of fantasy from the story? Circle the letter of your choice.

   (a) India once had a king.

   (b) Temple doors are locked.

   (c) Two men are riding in a taxi in India.

   (d) A man in the story is 500 years old.

   Explain why this is fantasy.

   _____

   _____

5. **Reading Strategy:** Complete the chart by writing one real and one fantastic thing about each character.

| Character | Real | Fantastic |
|---|---|---|
| Talkative Man (narrator) | | |
| Doss | | |
| Old Man | | |

# Writing

## Travel Brochure

The story "Old Man of the Temple" is set in India. Many people visit India each year. Write a paragraph for a **travel brochure** that tells people about India. Your paragraph should tell visitors what they can see in India. It should also provide the kind of transportation travelers will need to get from the United States to India.

Here are places to find information about India. Make a checkmark next to the sources you use.

- books ____
- magazines ____
- encyclopedias ____
- travel brochures ____
- Internet information ____

Use these sentence starters to help you write your brochure. Include interesting details and descriptions so your reader will want to visit India.

1. India is located _____

2. When you are in India, you should visit _____

_____

3. An interesting thing to do in India is _____

_____

4. The most common way to get to India is _____

_____

Use the sentence starters above to write your paragraph for a travel brochure.

# Rules of the Game

## Amy Tan

## Summary

This story is set in San Francisco's Chinatown. Waverly Jong, the main character, is a nine-year-old girl with Chinese parents. When her brother Vincent gets a used chess set, Waverly becomes fascinated with the game. She challenges her brothers, the men at the park, and finally tournament players, eventually beating them all. At the end of the story, Waverly is frustrated with her mother's tendency to "show her off" to complete strangers. She feels her mother does not understand her, and runs away after an argument with her mother. When Waverly returns home two hours later, her mother refuses to talk with her. It is clear that Waverly and her mother have different perspectives because of their difference in age and where they were born.

## Visual Summary

| Main Characters: | Waverly Jong<br>Mrs. Jong (Waverly's mother) |
|---|---|
| Setting: | San Francisco's Chinatown |
| Conflict: | Waverly is embarrassed by her mother. Mrs. Jong thinks Waverly is ashamed of her. |

**Event 1:** Waverly pesters her mother for some plums and her mother gets angry. Waverly learns that if she wants something it is better to remain silent. → **Event 2:** Waverly's brother Vincent gets a used chess set for Christmas. → **Event 3:** Waverly learns chess and begins to win several tournaments. She becomes well known for her chess-playing ability.

**Climax:** Mrs. Jong's habit of introducing Waverly as a chess champion embarrasses her. Waverly tells her to stop, and she runs away when her mother gets angry.

**Resolution:** Waverly returns home—only to find her mother is giving her the "silent treatment." She goes to her room to ponder her next move in this mother-daughter conflict.

## LITERARY ANALYSIS

### Generational Conflict

Ideas about the way we live change from one generation to another. A **generational conflict** is a struggle that exists between characters when beliefs and values change from one generation to the next. This causes people from different generations to disagree. It also causes people of different ages to not understand each other.

In the story "Rules of the Game," a daughter from a younger generation and a mother from an older generation struggle to understand each other. The chart below explains the conflict that occurs during one event in the story.

| Event |
|---|
| Waverly's mother tells everyone she meets that Waverly is her daughter because she is very proud of her. |

| Younger Generation | Older Generation |
|---|---|
| Waverly is embarrassed by the attention. | Her mother does not understand why Waverly is embarrassed. |

Look for the generational conflict between characters as you read this story.

## READING STRATEGY

### Contrasting Characters

When you **contrast characters,** you notice the difference between characters. For example, in this story, the daughter is embarrassed by what her mother says. The mother is angry because the daughter is embarrassed by her.

As you read, notice the differences between the characters. Then, consider how each character must feel. Use a chart like this to contrast the characters.

| Character | Feeling |
|---|---|
| Waverly, the daughter | embarrassed |
| Mrs. Jong, the mother | angry |

# Rules of the Game

## Amy Tan

The narrator, Waverly, was six when she cried loudly for candy in a story. Her mother said, "Strongest wind cannot be seen," and she did not buy the candy. The next time they shopped, Waverly followed her mother's advice. She was quiet. This time her mother rewarded Waverly's good behavior. She bought a bag of candy for Waverly. Waverly had learned her first lesson in winning arguments.

◆ ◆ ◆

My mother imparted her daily truths so she could help my older brothers and me rise above our circumstances.[1] We lived in San Francisco's Chinatown.[2] Like most of the other Chinese children who played in the back alleys of restaurants and curio shops,[3] I didn't think we were poor. My bowl was always full, three five-course meals every day, beginning with a soup full of mysterious things I didn't want to know the names of.

◆ ◆ ◆

Waverly was named for the street she lived on, Waverly Place. She was the youngest and only daughter. She had two brothers, Vincent and Winston. One Christmas the family attended a holiday party. Each child received a present.

◆ ◆ ◆

Vincent got the chess set,[4] which would have been a very decent present to get at a church

---

1. **rise above our circumstances** to live a better life in the future.
2. **Chinatown** (CHĪ nuh town) *n.* a section of a city where Chinese people live.
3. **curio** (KYOOR ee oh) **shops** *n.* stores that sell strange or rare objects.
4. **chess set** *n.* thirty-two pieces and a checkerboard used to play the game of chess.

Christmas party except it was obviously used and, as we discovered later, it was missing a black pawn and a white knight. My mother graciously thanked the unknown <u>benefactor</u>, saying, "Too good. Cost too much." At which point, an old lady with fine white, wispy hair nodded toward our family and said with a whistling whisper, "Merry, merry Christmas."

When we got home, my mother told Vincent to throw the chess set away. "She not want it. We not want it," she said, tossing her head stiffly to the side with a tight, proud smile. My brothers had deaf ears. They were already lining up the chess pieces and reading from the dog-eared instruction book.

◆ ◆ ◆

At first, Waverly watched as her brothers played this new game. Then she begged them to let her play. Vincent would not let her play. But Waverly had Life Saver candies that could be used for the two missing chess pieces, so Vincent let her play. They decided that the winner would eat the Life Saver pieces.

Vincent explained the rules of the game, but Waverly didn't understand them. Her mother told Waverly that it is better to figure out the rules on her own.

◆ ◆ ◆

I read the rules and looked up all the big words in a dictionary. I borrowed books from the Chinatown library. I studied each chess piece, trying to absorb the power each contained.

◆ ◆ ◆

### Vocabulary Development

**benefactor** (BEN uh fak ter) *n.* a person who helps someone by giving a gift

---

◆ **Literary Analysis**

Reread the bracketed passage. There is a **generational conflict** over the gift of the used chess set. Explain how the different generations react to the gifts.

Younger generation (sons)

_____

_____

Older generation (mother)

_____

_____

◆ **Reading Check**

What did Waverly do to help her learn the game of chess?

On the lines, write the three things she did.

1. _____

2. _____

3. _____

Read the bracketed passage and **contrast the characters** of Waverly and her brothers. How did each one feel about the game of chess?

Waverly: _____

_____

_____

Brothers: _____

_____

_____

Why does Waverly pick up a roll of Life Savers before going back to the park?

_____

_____

_____

Waverly learned how to move the chess pieces on the checkerboard. She learned to plan her attacks. She learned to use her opponent's weaknesses to win. She also learned to not let her opponent know what she was going to do next.

◆　◆　◆

I loved the secrets I found within the sixty-four black and white squares. I carefully drew a handmade chessboard and pinned it to the wall next to my bed, where at night I would stare for hours at imaginary battles. Soon I no longer lost any games or Life Savers, but I lost my adversaries. Winston and Vincent decided they were more interested in roaming the streets after school in their Hopalong Cassidy[5] cowboy hats.

◆　◆　◆

One day Waverly saw old men playing chess at the playground. She ran home to get the box that held Vincent's chess set. She also picked up a roll of Life Savers. She returned to the park. She spoke to a man who was watching a chess game.

◆　◆　◆

"Want to play?" I asked him. His face widened with surprise and he grinned as he looked at the box under my arm.

"Little sister, been a long time since I play with dolls," he said, smiling benevolently. I quickly put the box down next to him on the bench and displayed my retort.

---

### Vocabulary Development

**adversary** (AD ver ser ee) *n.* person on the other side in a contest

**benevolently** (buh NEV uh lent lee) *adv.* in a kind and nice way

**retort** (ri TORT) *n.* a clever or sharp answer

---

5. **Hopalong Cassidy** *n.* popular cowboy story character from the 1950s.

Lau Po, as he allowed me to call him, turned out to be a much better player than my brothers. I lost many games and many Life Savers.

◆ ◆ ◆

Lau Po taught Waverly many secrets of how to win the game. He also taught her how to behave properly when playing. She learned to keep her pieces in neat rows. She learned to not lose her temper. By the end of the summer, Waverly was a better chess player.

People came to the park to watch Waverly play chess and win. Her mother watched too. She was proud of Waverly, but she told others that Waverly won because of luck. A man who saw Waverly play chess asked her to enter a chess <u>tournament</u>. Waverly wanted to go to the tournament, but she knew her mother would not agree. So Waverly told her mother that she did not want to play in the tournament. She said she did not want to lose. Her mother said she should not give up before she tried.

◆ ◆ ◆

During my first tournament, my mother sat with me in the front row as I waited for my turn. I frequently bounced my legs to unstick them from the cold metal seat of the folding chair. When my name was called, I leapt up. My mother unwrapped something in her lap. It was her chang, a small tablet of red jade which held the sun's fire. "Is luck," she whispered, and tucked it into my dress pocket.

◆ ◆ ◆

---

**Vocabulary Development**

**tournament** (TOR nuh ment) *n.* a contest played by many players

---

◆ **Stop to Reflect**

Waverly learned to play chess from Lau Po. She learned two other things from him. Write them here.

1. _____

_____

_____

2. _____

_____

_____

◆ **Read Fluently**

Read the bracketed passage aloud.

What did the mother give to Waverly?

_____

_____

Why did she give it to her?

_____

_____

There is a **generational conflict** over how to win at chess. Explain how Waverly and her mother each think a player should win.

Waverly:

_____

_____

_____

Mother:

_____

_____

_____

◆ **Reading Check**

How did Waverly's life at home change?

Underline the sentence that tells you the answer.

◆ **Stop to Reflect**

Do you think it is fair that Waverly no longer had to do house chores? _____

Why or why not?

_____

_____

_____

_____

Waverly remembered her chess lessons well. She beat her fifteen-year-old opponent. She won the tournament.

◆   ◆   ◆

My mother placed my first trophy next to a new plastic chess set that the neighborhood Tao society[6] had given to me. As she wiped each piece with a soft cloth, she said, "Next time win more, lose less."

"Ma, it's not how many pieces you lose," I said. "Sometimes you need to lose pieces to get ahead."

"Better to lose less, see if you really need."

◆   ◆   ◆

Waverly won her next tournament. Her mother was proud because Waverly had lost fewer pieces. This was not important in winning the game, but Waverly did not say this to her mother. Waverly won many more tournaments. The Chinatown community was very proud of her.

Waverly no longer needed to do household chores. She spent her free time practicing to be a better chess player. When she was nine-years-old, she became a national chess champion. Her picture appeared in a magazine. Waverly continued to play in tournaments, such as the one held at a large high school.

◆   ◆   ◆

Seated across from me was an American man, about the same age as Lau Po, maybe fifty. I remember that his sweaty brow seemed to weep at my every move. He wore a dark, <u>malodorous</u> suit. One of his pockets was

---

**Vocabulary Development**

**malodorous** (mal OH der uhs) *n.* having a bad smell

---

6. **Tao society** (DOW suh SI i tee) *n.* group of people who believe in the Chinese religion called Taoism (DOW izm).

stuffed with a great white kerchief on which he wiped his palm before sweeping his hand over the chosen chess piece with great flourish.

In my crisp pink-and-white dress with scratchy lace at the neck, one of two my mother had sewn for these special occasions, I would clasp my hands under my chin, the delicate points of my elbows poised lightly on the table in the manner my mother had shown me for posing for the press. I would swing my patent leather shoes back and forth like an impatient child riding on a school bus. Then I would pause, suck in my lips, twirl my chosen piece in midair as if undecided, and then firmly plant it in its new threatening place, with a triumphant smile thrown back at my opponent for good measure.

◆ ◆ ◆

Waverly spent her time going to school and practicing chess. She was given special attention at home. When she said her brothers were too noisy, she got her own bedroom. When she said she could not finish her dinner, she was permitted to leave the table. One thing did not change. She still had to go to the Saturday market with her mother.

◆ ◆ ◆

My mother would proudly walk with me, visiting many shops, buying very little. "This my daughter Wave-ly Jong," she said to who-ever looked her way.

One day, after we left a shop I said under my breath, "I wish you wouldn't do that, telling everybody I'm your daughter." My mother stopped walking. Crowds of people with heavy bags pushed past us on the sidewalk, bumping into first one shoulder, then another.

"Aiii-ya. So shame be with mother?" She grasped my hand even tighter as she glared at me.

◆ **Stop to Reflect**

How do you think this fifty year old man felt as he played against Waverly? Explain your answer.

_____

_____

_____

_____

◆ **Reading Check**

In what two ways did Waverly receive special attention? Circle the answers in the paragraph.

◆ **Literary Analysis**

There is a **generational conflict** between Waverly and her mother in the bracketed passage.

1. Why is Waverly embarrassed?

Underline the sentence that gives you the answer.

2. How do Waverly's words cause the mother to feel?

Draw a box around the sentence that gives you the answer.

I looked down. "It's not that, it's just so obvious. It's just so embarrassing."

"Embarrass you be my daughter?" Her voice was cracking with anger.

◆   ◆   ◆

Waverly lost her temper. She said she was embarrassed because her mother was showing off. This made her mother even angrier, and Waverly ran off. In her speed, Waverly ran into an old woman and knocked her groceries to the ground. When Waverly's mother stopped to help gather the cans and food, Waverly raced away. She ran and ran. She finally realized she had nowhere to go. She sat down to think. Two hours later, she went home.

When she returned home that evening, she was sent to bed with no supper. Waverly used the time in her room to plan the next move in her life. She remembered her mother's words of advice, "Strongest wind cannot be seen."

1. Circle two phrases that tell what Lau Po taught Waverly.

   how to shop at the market

   how to win

   how to behave when playing chess

   how to do housework

2. Which situation is an example of the saying "Strongest wind cannot be seen."?

   (a) attending a church party

   (b) quietly beating an opponent at chess

   (c) begging for candy in a store

   (d) losing one's temper at the market

   Explain why you chose this answer.

   _____

   _____

   _____

   _____

3. **Literary Analysis:** The chart shows two generational conflicts from the story. To complete the chart, explain Waverly's and the mother's ideas about each event in the first column.

| Event | Waverly's Ideas | Mother's Ideas |
|---|---|---|
| 1. Life in Chinatown | | |
| 2. Winning a chess game | | |

4. **Reading Strategy:** What are the differences between Waverly and her mother? Write each word or phrase in the correct side of the Venn Diagram to contrast these two characters. In the middle, write the words that describe how they are alike.

| | | |
|---|---|---|
| strong-willed | watches chess | proud |
| born in China | born in the U.S. | secretive |
| believes in luck | believes in skill | plays chess |

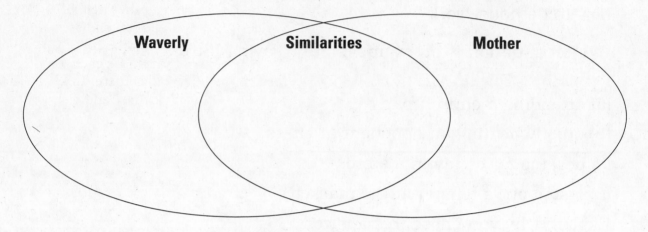

**Waverly**      **Similarities**      **Mother**

# Listening and Speaking

## Dialogue

Imagine that years have passed after the events in this story. Then, imagine that an adult Waverly and her mother are talking about what happened at the market at the end of the story.

- What details will each character remember?

Waverly remembers _____

Mrs. Jong remembers _____

- How does each character feel now?

Waverly was embarrassed then. Now she feels _____

_____

Mrs. Jong was angry then. Now she feels _____

_____

Use the information above to write a **dialogue** between the two characters. Decide whether you will play Waverly or her mother. Ask a partner to role play the other character. Then say your dialogue aloud with the partner. Switch characters and role-play the dialogue again.

# Checkouts

## Cynthia Rylant

## Summary

In this story, a teenage girl has just moved with her parents to Cincinnati. She is not happy with the move, and she spends a lot of time looking through photographs of her former home. The one activity she does enjoy in her new surroundings is grocery shopping. During one trip to the supermarket, she sees a bag boy whom she finds attractive. It is his first day on the job and he is nervous, but he notices her, too. Soon, the girl and boy are watching for each other at the supermarket. Though they do eventually see each other there, they never speak to each other or indicate their feelings. In the end, the boy and girl do find romance—but with other people.

## Visual Summary

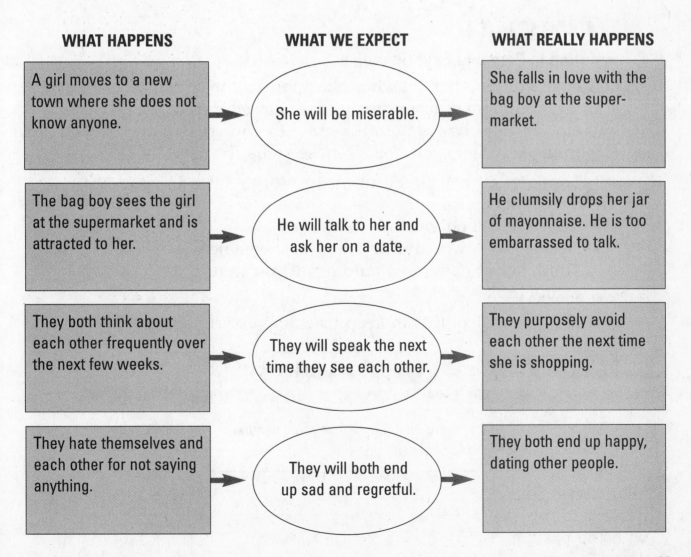

| WHAT HAPPENS | WHAT WE EXPECT | WHAT REALLY HAPPENS |
|---|---|---|
| A girl moves to a new town where she does not know anyone. | She will be miserable. | She falls in love with the bag boy at the supermarket. |
| The bag boy sees the girl at the supermarket and is attracted to her. | He will talk to her and ask her on a date. | He clumsily drops her jar of mayonnaise. He is too embarrassed to talk. |
| They both think about each other frequently over the next few weeks. | They will speak the next time they see each other. | They purposely avoid each other the next time she is shopping. |
| They hate themselves and each other for not saying anything. | They will both end up sad and regretful. | They both end up happy, dating other people. |

## LITERARY ANALYSIS

### Irony

**Irony** in a story is what happens when the outcome is not the usual or expected outcome.

- Irony in a story can be funny.
- Irony in a story can make you stop and think about events.

In the short story, "Checkouts," a grocery store bag boy tries to act cool in front of a girl. Instead, he drops a jar of mayonnaise. You might expect that the girl would think the boy is clumsy. Instead she falls in love with him. This unexpected outcome makes the reader stop to wonder why the girl falls in love. This is irony.

## READING STRATEGY

### Relating to Personal Experience

A character is a person who takes part in the action of a story. You can better understand a character in a story by **relating** what happens in the story **to your personal experience**. To help you, follow these steps.

- Think about how an event in the story relates to your own experiences.
- Notice how a character acts.
- Decide if you would have acted in the same way.
- Think about how you would feel if you were the character.

Make a chart like this to keep track of your thoughts.

| Event in the Story | Similar Event in My Life | How I Felt | How the Character Must Feel |
|---|---|---|---|
| The bag boy's first day on a new job. | The first time I had a job babysitting. | Nervous, unsure | Nervous, unsure |

# Checkouts
## Cynthia Rylant

As the story opens, we learn that a teenage girl and her family have moved to Cincinnati.

The girl is very sad after the move, but she finds that it is hard to be sad all the time. So she finally leaves her new room and goes to the supermarket.

◆  ◆  ◆

She liked to grocery shop. She loved it in the way some people love to drive long country roads, because doing it she could think and relax and wander. Her parents wrote up the list and handed it to her and off she went without <u>complaint</u> to perform what they regarded as a great sacrifice of her time and a sign that she was indeed a very nice girl.

◆  ◆  ◆

The girl does not tell her parents how much she enjoys grocery shopping. She keeps this fact about herself a secret. Pushing the cart around the store makes her calm. The supermarket makes her very happy.

◆  ◆  ◆

Then one day the bag boy dropped her jar of mayonnaise[1] and that is how she fell in love.

He was nervous—first day on the job—and along had come this fascinating girl, standing in the checkout line with the unfocused stare one often sees in young children, her face turned enough away that he might take several full looks at her as he packed sturdy bags full

---

### Vocabulary Development

**complaint** (kuhm PLAYNT) *n.*  an explanation of how much trouble something is

---

1. **mayonnaise** (MAY uh nayz) *n.* a creamy dressing made of eggs, oil, lemon juice, and seasonings that is used in salads and on sandwiches.

---

### ◆ Reading Fluently

Read aloud the bracketed passage. How does the girl feel when she shops? Circle the letter of the best answer below.

(a) happy      (c) nervous

(b) bored      (d) unhappy

### ◆ Literary Analysis

Write a sentence that describes what happens in a supermarket.

_____

_____

Why is it ironic that a super-market makes the girl calm?

_____

_____

_____

### ◆ Reading Strategy

How do you feel about shopping?

_____

_____

_____

Are the girl's feelings about shopping the same as or different from your feelings?

_____

_____

_____

of food and the goods of modern life.

◆ ◆ ◆

◆ Literary Analysis

Circle what the boy does that makes him feel foolish.

The **irony** is that the girl falls in love with the boy. Why are we surprised that she falls in love?

_____

_____

The bag boy likes the girl's red thick hair and the orange bow in her hair. He drops her jar of mayonnaise when she smiles at him. It breaks at his feet. He feels foolish. He wishes he had a second chance to know her. At that moment, she loves him.

The boy's and girl's thoughts about each other help each of them to get through their struggles and transitions.

After four weeks, they meet up again, but they both pretend not to see the other person. She does not bring her groceries to his checkout lane. The boy pretends not to notice her. She leaves the store. They both feel upset about not talking to each other.

◆ Reading Check

1. What happens the first time the boy and girl meet?

_____

_____

2. What happens the second time the boy and girl meet?

_____

_____

Soon after, things change. A boy who lives near the girl asks her to a movie. The bag boy switches jobs. He starts working at a bookstore. He sees many interesting girls at the bookstore.

◆ ◆ ◆

Some months later the bag boy and the girl with the orange bow again crossed paths, standing in line with their dates at a movie theater, and, glancing toward the other, each smiled slightly, then looked away, as strangers on public buses often do, when one is moving off the bus and the other is moving on.

◆ Stop to Reflect

Circle the words that tell what happens when the boy and girl meet for the third time.

Does their third meeting surprise you? Circle your answer.

yes    no

Why, or why not?

_____

_____

_____

1. Why is the girl sad in the beginning of the story? Circle the letter of the correct answer.

   (a) The bag boy does not speak to her.

   (b) Her parents moved the family to a new town.

   (c) She does not want to go grocery shopping.

   (d) The bag boy broke her jar of mayonnaise.

2. Circle two words that best describe the boy.

   busy       rude       nervous       lazy       talkative

3. Why do you think the girl liked the bag boy so much?

   _____

   _____

   _____

4. **Literary Analysis:** Find the **irony** in the third meeting between the boy and girl at the movies. Circle the letter of the correct answer.

   (a) What did the boy and girl do when they saw each other at the movie?

      (a) They said hello.

      (b) They said they loved each other.

      (c) They smiled and looked away.

      (d) They laughed.

   (b) What did you expect them to do when they saw each other again?

   _____

   _____

   _____

5. **Reading Strategy:** Relate the feelings of the girl to your own personal experience. Complete the chart for the following story event.

| Event in the Story | Similar Event in My Life | How I Felt | How the Character Must Feel |
|---|---|---|---|
| The girl sees the boy with another girl. She smiles and looks away. | | | |

## Writing Activity

### Character's Journal

A journal entry often records a person's feelings. The feelings might be about another person or about an event. Imagine that the boy and the girl in "Checkouts" each write their feelings in a journal.

Write a **journal entry** for each character that tells how they felt about their first meeting in the supermarket.

1. Decide how you think each character felt when they first met. Read the following list of words. Think about which words describe the girl and which words describe the boy.

   nervous       calm          foolish       happy

   in love       embarrassed   dreamy        interested

2. Sort the words by writing them in the chart. Some words may fit in both columns.

| Words that tell how the girl feels | Words that tell how the boy feels |
|---|---|
| | |

3. Use words and ideas from the chart to write a journal entry for the boy and a journal entry for the girl. Remember that you need to write the feelings of each characters.

# The Interlopers
## Saki (H. H. Munro)

### Summary

   Ulrich and Georg have always been enemies. Their families have been enemies for generations because of a dispute over land ownership. Each man thinks the other man is trespassing on his land. The two men meet in the forest, prepared to kill each other. Before they can act, however, a storm knocks down a tree, pinning both men to the ground. Badly hurt and unable to move, they continue to quarrel, vowing to fight until death. After threatening one another, they lie silently waiting to be rescued. Ulrich manages to open his flask, and he offers Georg a sip of wine. Georg refuses, but Ulrich makes an offer to end the feud. Georg agrees. They discuss what great friends they will be, and how surprised everyone will be to see them not fighting. Together they shout for help and soon hear the sound of movement in the woods. Ulrich can make out nine or ten figures approaching. They are excited and relieved at the thought of being rescued. Unfortunately, the figures are not men but wolves.

### Visual Summary

| **Ulrich:** | **Conflict** | **Georg:** |
|---|---|---|
| Ulrich wants to kill Georg because of a land dispute. | vs. | Georg wants to kill Ulrich because of a land dispute. |

| **Ulrich:** | | **Georg:** |
|---|---|---|
| Ulrich is trapped. He wants to be rescued so he can kill Georg. | vs. | Georg is trapped. He wants to be rescued so he can kill Ulrich. |

| **Ulrich and Georg:** | | **Nature:** |
|---|---|---|
| Ulrich and Georg try to put off death together by shouting out loudly for help. | vs. | The tree is crushing them. They could die from their injuries, the cold, or a new threat . . . wolves. |

## LITERARY ANALYSIS
## Conflict

**Conflict** in a story is when one side struggles against another side. Conflict can be internal conflict or external conflict.
- **Internal conflict** is the struggle inside the mind of a character.
- **External conflict** is the struggle between characters.
- External conflict can also be a struggle between characters and nature. For example, a character struggling to walk through a snow storm experiences a conflict with nature.

As you read "The Interlopers," use a chart like this to record conflicts in the story.

| Internal Conflict | External Conflict |
|---|---|
| Ulrich struggles against himself because he wants to kill the other man, but he knows killing is wrong. | The men struggle against each other when they try to kill each other. |

## READING STRATEGY
## Identifying Causes and Effects

**Identifying causes and effects** in a story helps you understand story events.
- The **effect** is the result of an action or event.
- The **cause** is the action or event that is the reason for the effect.

As you read the story, think about what causes events to happen. The chart below shows one cause and effect from the story.

| Cause | Effect |
|---|---|
| A tree falls. | The men are trapped. |

# The Interlopers
## Saki (H. H. Munro)

A man stands watching and listening in a forest in central Europe. He looks as if he is hunting an animal. But he is not. He is hunting a human enemy. The man's name is Ulrich von Gradwitz (OOL rik von Grad vitz). He is hunting on his own forest lands. But another family also claims this land. Who really owns this land? The two families have quarreled over this question for three generations.

◆　◆　◆

The neighbor <u>feud</u> had grown into a personal one since Ulrich had come to be head of his family; if there was a man in the world whom he detested and wished ill to it was Georg Znaeym (GAY org ZNAY im), the inheritor of the quarrel and the tireless game-snatcher and raider of the disputed border-forest.[1]

◆　◆　◆

Ulrich and Georg hated each other when they were children. Now, as men, they still hate each other. On this stormy winter night, Ulrich wanders away from his huntsmen. The huntsmen continue to hunt for animals. But Ulrich hopes that he will find his enemy, Georg.

◆　◆　◆

And as he stepped round the trunk of a huge <u>beech</u> he came face to face with the man he sought.

◆ **Reading Strategy**

What has caused the feud between the families? Underline two sentences that help you answer this question. Then write your answer here.

**Cause**

_____

_____

_____

↓

**Effect**
feud between families _____

◆ **Reading Check**

Who does Ulrich face when he steps around the tree?

_____

---

### Vocabulary Development

**feud** (FEWD) *n.*　a long quarrel and hatred between families

**beech** (BEECH) *n.*　tree with smooth gray bark and shiny leaves

---

1. **border-forest** *n.* trees along the edge of an area of land.

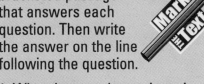

Circle the word in the bracketed passage that answers each question. Then write the answer on the line following the question.

1. What does each man have in his hand?

_____

2. What does each man have in his heart?

_____

3. What does each man have in his mind?

_____

◆ **Literary Analysis**

Read the bracketed passage. Which of the following sentences best explains the **conflict** in the passage? Circle the letter of your answer.

(a) Ulrich struggles against Georg.

(b) Georg struggles against nature.

(c) Ulrich struggles against the storm.

Is this conflict an example of internal or external conflict?

_____

The two enemies stood glaring at one another for a long silent moment. Each had a rifle in his hand, each had hate in his heart and murder uppermost in his mind.

◆ ◆ ◆

Ulrich wants to shoot Georg, but he waits just a moment. In that moment there is a crash over their heads. A large tree falls on the two men before they can move. Ulrich is knocked to the ground. He is trapped beneath the heavy branches of the tree.

◆ ◆ ◆

His heavy shooting-boots had saved his feet from being crushed to pieces, but if his <u>fractures</u> were not as serious as they might have been, at least it was evident that he could not move from his present position till someone came to release him. The descending twigs had slashed the skin of his face, and he had to wink away some drops of blood from his eyelashes before he could take in a general view of the disaster. At his side, so near that under ordinary circumstances he could almost have touched him, lay Georg Znaeym, alive and struggling, but obviously as helplessly <u>pinioned</u> down as himself.

◆ ◆ ◆

Ulrich is thankful for being alive. Yet he is angry at being trapped beneath the tree. Georg's face is covered in blood. When Georg hears Ulrich shouting at the tree, he speaks to his enemy.

◆ ◆ ◆

---

### Vocabulary Development

**fracture** (FRAK chur) *n.* broken bone
**pinioned** (PIN yuhnd) *v.* bound, held

"So you're not killed, as you ought to be, but you're caught, anyway," he cried; "caught fast. Ho, what a jest, Ulrich von Gradwitz snared in his stolen forest. There's real justice for you!"

◆ ◆ ◆

Ulrich says he is sure that his men will be along soon to release him. He tells Georg that he has caught him poaching on Gradwitz land.[2]

Georg says that maybe his men will arrive first and release him first. Then he says he will tell his men to roll the tree on top of Ulrich.

Ulrich says that is a good idea, but that it would be his men who will arrive first. He says he would be the one released first, and Georg would die under the tree.

◆ ◆ ◆

"Good," snarled Georg, "good. We fight this quarrel out to the death, you and I and our foresters, with no cursed interlopers to come between us. Death and damnation to you, Ulrich von Gradwitz."

"The same to you, Georg Znaeym, forest-thief, game-snatcher."

◆ ◆ ◆

The men stop struggling to free themselves. Ulrich reaches for a flask of wine he has in his pocket. He takes out the flask and he drinks. The wine warms him on the cold

### Vocabulary Development

**justice** (JUHS tis) *n.* fairness

**interloper** (IN ter loh pers) *n.* unwanted person or thing that gets in the way

**flask** (FLASK) *n.* a small bottle with flat sides that is carried in a pocket

---

2. **poaching on Gradwitz land:** wrongly hunting for animals on land owned by Gradwitz.

Read the underlined sentence. Georg says Ulrich is caught fast. Who or what has caught Ulrich?

_____

_____

◆ Literary Analysis

Reread the bracketed passage. Who is the conflict between?

_____

Is the conflict internal or external?

_____

_____

◆ Stop to Reflect

Do you think the conflict with the men will continue?

_____

Why, or why not?

_____

_____

_____

◆ Literary Analysis

Ulrich used to hate Georg. Then,
he felt sorry for Georg. Is this
internal or external conflict?

_____

Explain your answer.

_____

_____

_____

◆ ◆ ◆

"Could you reach this flask if I threw it over
to you?" asked Ulrich suddenly; "there is good
wine in it, and one may as well be as comfortable as one can. Let us drink, even if tonight
one of us dies."

"No, I can scarcely see anything; there is so
much blood caked round my eyes," said Georg,
"and in any case I don't drink wine with an
enemy."

◆ ◆ ◆

◆ Reading Check

Georg said he does not drink
with an enemy. Who is his
enemy?

_____

Ulrich is quiet. He grows weaker. His
hate for Georg grows weaker, too. Then
Ulrich gets an idea. He tells Georg that he
has changed his mind. He says that he will
tell his men to help Georg. He says he wants
their feud to end. He tells Georg he wants to
be his friend.

Slowly, Georg replies. He says the
people in the town will be surprised if he
and Ulrich become friends. He says their
friendship will bring peace among the
people. He says that no one could stop
them from being friends.

◆ ◆ ◆

◆ Reading Strategy

Georg says he will be
Ulrich's friend.
Underline what
causes Georg to
change his mind
about the friendship.

"I never thought to have wanted to do other
than hate you all my life, but I think I have
changed my mind about things too, this last
half-hour. And you offered me your wine
flask . . . Ulrich von Gradwitz, I will be your
friend."

◆ ◆ ◆

◆ Reading Check

Reread the bracketed passage.
What do the men do as they lie
in silence?

_____

_____

_____

Both men lie in silence thinking of the
wonderful things their friendship will bring.
They were happy about the changes
friendship would make. Still, they were cold
in the dark forest. They waited for help to
arrive and save them. Each man hoped his

own men would arrive to save them. Each man wanted to be able to be respectful toward his new friend by saving him. When the howling wind stops, both men shout for help. They shout as loud as they can, but they hear no response. Finally, they hear noise. Ulrich is the first to see someone coming toward them.

◆ ◆ ◆

"They hear us! They've stopped. Now they see us. They're running down the hill toward us," cried Ulrich.

"How many of them are there?" asked Georg.

"I can't see distinctly," said Ulrich; "nine or ten."

"Then they are yours," said Georg; "I had only seven out with me."

"They are making all the speed they can, brave lads," said Ulrich gladly.

"Are they your men?" asked Georg. "Are they your men?" he repeated impatiently as Ulrich did not answer.

"No," said Ulrich with a laugh, the idiotic chattering laugh of a man unstrung with hideous fear.

"Who are they?" asked Georg quickly, straining his eyes to see what the other would gladly not have seen.

"*Wolves.*"

---

◆ **Reading Check**

How do the men want to show their respect for each other?

_____

_____

◆ **Read Fluently**

Read the bracketed passage aloud. Say the word *wolves* as Ulrich said it.

Circle the word below that tells how Ulrich felt when he said *wolves*.

glad      afraid      sad

◆ **Stop to Reflect**

Who were the interlopers?

_____

What do you think happened after the men saw the interlopers at the end of the story?

_____

_____

_____

1. Why did the families feud in this story?

   _____

2. Were the two men friends at the beginning of the story? _____
   Support your answer with an event from the story.

   Beginning: _____

3. Were the two men friends at the end of the story? _____
   Support your answer with an action from the story.

   End: _____

4. **Literary Analysis:** Circle the letter of the best answer for each
   question.

   1. Which of the following is an example of internal conflict?

   (a) Ulrich hates Georg. Ulrich also feels sorry for Georg.

   (b) Ulrich tries to loosen himself from under the tree.

   2. Which of the following is an example of external conflict?

   (a) The two men are hunting for each other.

   (b) Georg says Ulrich is his enemy, and then changes his mind.

5. **Reading Strategy:** Fill in the chart to identify causes and effects from
   the story.

| Cause | → | Effect |
|---|---|---|
| _____ | → | The two men were enemies. |
| _____ | → | The two men were trapped. |
| Ulrich asks Georg to be his friend. | → | _____ |
| The men shout. | → | _____ |

# Listening and Speaking

**Debate**

A **debate** is a well-planned argument between two sides.

Imagine that the two families in the story are going to debate the question: Who owns the land? Imagine that you are a member of one family. You are going to speak in the debate. Plan what you will say in the debate. Make your notes here.

First, choose a family side. Make a checkmark next to the family you choose.

____ Ulrich's family

____ Georg's family

Write a sentence that tells the topic of the debate.

_____

List three reasons why your family should have the land.

1. _____

_____

2. _____

_____

3. _____

_____

List three reasons why the other family should not have the land.

1. _____

_____

2. _____

_____

3. _____

_____

Use your notes to debate a partner who chose to be a member of the opposing family.

# The Secret Life of Walter Mitty

## James Thurber

### Summary

Walter Mitty is an ordinary man who escapes from his boring life and nagging wife by daydreaming. The story begins in the middle of one of his dreams. He is a naval officer leading his airplane through a powerful storm. Mitty is jolted from his dreams of heroism by his wife. She is scolding him for driving too fast. All of the dreams that follow are triggered by ordinary events on a shopping trip with his wife. He dreams of being a world-famous surgeon, a sharpshooting criminal, a fearless soldier, and a proud man facing a firing squad. Each time Mitty drifts off, reality intrudes somehow—he almost gets in a car accident, he remembers some errand, or his wife pesters him about something he is doing wrong.

### Visual Summary

| Daydream | Jolt Back to Reality | Reality | Dream Trigger |
|---|---|---|---|
| Mitty is a commander guiding a seaplane through a storm. | His wife scolds him for driving too fast. | Mitty and his wife are driving into town to go shopping. | Mitty passes a hospital and takes off his gloves. |
| Mitty is a surgeon operating on a dying patient. | A parking attendant yells at Mitty. | Mitty parks the car to buy rain shoes. | A newsboy is shouting news about a trial. |
| Mitty is a criminal standing trial in a courtroom. | Mitty remembers he is supposed to buy puppy biscuits. | He buys the biscuits and waits for his wife in a chair. | Mitty sees a newspaper with war photographs. |
| Mitty is a soldier on a dangerous mission. | His wife returns and scolds him. | His wife goes on another errand. | Mitty smokes a cigarette while he waits. |
| Mitty is a man facing a firing squad. | | | |

## LITERARY ANALYSIS

### Point of View

Point of view is one way to describe how a narrator tells a story.

- In **first-person point of view,** the narrator is a character in the story. The narrator takes part in the action.
- In **third-person point of view,** the narrator is not a story character. The narrator takes no part in the action.

The third-person point of view can be *omniscient,* in which the narrator focuses on the thoughts and feelings of all the characters. The third-person point of view can also be *limited,* in which the narrator focuses on the thoughts and feelings of only one character.

"The Secret Life of Walter Mitty" is told from a limited third-person point of view. As you read, see how the narrator takes you inside the mind of the main character, Walter Mitty.

## READING STRATEGY

### Reading Back and Reading Ahead

In this story, Walter Mitty's thoughts move back and forth between daydreams and reality. Sometimes he imagines an event. Then, his mind switches back to the real world. You may better understand the story changes by **reading back and reading ahead**.

Suppose a part of the story is not clear to you. Look back to see if you missed any important details. You can also look ahead to find helpful information. As you read, find exactly where each of Walter Mitty's daydreams begins and ends. A chart like this can help you.

| Unclear Situation | What I Learned by Reading Back | What I Learned by Reading Ahead |
| --- | --- | --- |
| A scene in which a commander leads his Navy crew switches to a man and woman driving a car. | The man was day-dreaming about being in the war. | He daydreams often. |

# The Secret Life of Walter Mitty
## James Thurber

◆ **Reading Strategy**

The story begins with Walter Mitty's daydream. **Read ahead** to find where the daydream ends. Underline the last sentence of the daydream.

"We're going through!" The Commander's voice was like thin ice breaking. He wore his full-dress uniform, with the heavily braided white cap pulled down <u>rakishly</u> over one cold gray eye. "We can't make it, sir. It's spoiling for a hurricane, if you ask me." "I'm not asking you, Lieutenant Berg," said the Commander. "Throw on the power lights! Rev her up to 8,500! We're going through!"

◆ ◆ ◆

The Commander flies the plane into the storm. The crew has faith in their brave Commander.

◆ ◆ ◆

◆ **Literary Analysis**

The narrator takes you inside the mind of Walter Mitty. Circle the words in the bracketed passage that tell you Mitty's inner thoughts and feelings.

"Not so fast! You're driving too fast!" said Mrs. Mitty. "What are you driving so fast for?"

"Hmm?" said Walter Mitty. He looked at his wife, in the seat beside him, with shocked astonishment. She seemed grossly unfamiliar, like a strange woman who had yelled at him in a crowd. "You were up to fifty-five," she said. "You know I don't like to go more than forty. You were up to fifty-five."

◆ ◆ ◆

Walter Mitty continues driving with his wife to Waterbury. He drops her off to have her hair done. He drives past the hospital on his way to the parking lot.

Mitty begins another fantasy. He imagines that he is a world-famous doctor. He takes over an operation in an emergency. The other doctors are relieved that Mitty can save the patient.

◆ ◆ ◆

◆ **Reading Check**

What causes Walter Mitty to suddenly imagine that he is a world-famous doctor? Write your answer on the lines below.

_____

_____

_____

---

### Vocabulary Development

**rakishly** (RAYK ish lee) *adv.* in a happy, careless way

---

"Back it up, Mac! Look out for that Buick!" Walter Mitty jammed on the brakes. "Wrong lane, Mac," said the parking-lot attendant, looking at Mitty closely. "Gee. Yeh," muttered Mitty. He began cautiously to back out of the lane marked "Exit Only." "Leave her sit there," said the attendant. "I'll put her away."

◆ ◆ ◆

Mitty leaves his car. He starts to walk along Main Street. He buys overshoes that his wife told him to get. He tries to remember what else he is supposed to buy. A newsboy walks by, shouting about a trial in Waterbury.

◆ ◆ ◆

. . . "Perhaps this will refresh your memory." The District Attorney suddenly thrust a heavy automatic at the quiet figure on the witness stand. "Have you ever seen this before?" Walter Mitty took the gun and examined it expertly. "This is my Webley-Vickers 50.80," he said calmly. An excited buzz ran around the courtroom.

◆ ◆ ◆

Mitty continues his courtroom fantasy. He is an expert shot with any gun. He brags that he could have killed Gregory Fitzhurst from three hundred feet away. The courtroom goes wild with excitement.

◆ ◆ ◆

"Puppy biscuit," said Walter Mitty. He stopped walking and the buildings of Waterbury rose up out of the misty courtroom and surrounded him again. A woman who was passing laughed. "He said, 'Puppy biscuit,'" she said to her companion. "That man said 'Puppy biscuit' to himself." Walter Mitty hurried on.

◆ ◆ ◆

---

◆ **Stop to Reflect**

Walter Mitty is in the wrong lane at the parking lot. Why do you think he is driving so poorly?

_____

_____

_____

◆ **Reading Strategy**

What causes Mitty to suddenly imagine that he is in a courtroom? **Read back** to find the reason. Write the words that tell you.

_____

_____

_____

◆ **Stop to Reflect**

This story is meant to be humorous at times. Why is the phrase "Puppy biscuit" funny? _____

_____

_____

◆ **Literary Analysis**

The narrator describes what Walter Mitty sees when he stops walking. Circle the sentence that tells you what he sees.

Mitty buys a box of puppy biscuits at a supermarket. Then he goes to a hotel lobby to wait for his wife while she gets her hair done. He sits in the lobby with a magazine. An article is titled "Can Germany Conquer the World Through the Air?"

Suddenly, Mitty fantasizes about being a hero pilot in the war. He must blow up a key enemy target. He will have to fly through heavy gunfire.

◆ ◆ ◆

Something struck his shoulder. "I've been looking all over this hotel for you," said Mrs. Mitty. "Why did you have to hide in this old chair? How did you expect me to find you?" "Things close in," said Walter Mitty <u>vaguely</u>. "What?" Mrs. Mitty said. "Did you get the what's-its-name? The puppy biscuit? What's in that box?" "Overshoes," said Mitty. "Couldn't you have put them on in the store?" "I was thinking," said Walter Mitty. "Does it ever occur to you that I am sometimes thinking?" She looked at him. "I'm going to take your temperature when I get home," she said.

◆ ◆ ◆

Mitty and his wife walk toward the parking lot. She goes into a drugstore to buy something. Mitty lights a cigarette. He leans against the drugstore wall and smokes.

Suddenly, Mitty imagines he is standing in front of a firing squad. He smokes from his cigarette one last time. He is about to be shot. Bravely, he stands ready to face his death.

---

**Vocabulary Development**

**vaguely** (VAYG lee) *adv.* in an unclear way

1. Why is Mrs. Mitty unhappy with her husband's driving?

_____

2. Why is Mrs. Mitty unhappy with her husband after getting her hair done?

_____

3. How is Walter Mitty different in his daydreams than in his real life?

_____

_____

4. **Literary Analysis:** Suppose the narrator had presented the inner thoughts of Mrs. Mitty instead of her husband. How would your view of Walter Mitty be different than it is now?

_____

_____

5. **Reading Strategy:** Complete this chart that describes each of Walter Mitty's daydreams. **Read back or read ahead** from the real-life situation in the story to find the details you need.

| His Real Life | His Daydream |
|---|---|
| He drives fast in the car with his wife. | He is a Commander flying a plane in a storm. |
| He drives past the Waterbury hospital. | |
| He hears a newsboy shout about a trial. | |
| He reads a magazine article about German air power. | |
| He leans against a wall and smokes a cigarette. | |

# Writing

## Character Profile

Walter Mitty often imagines himself as a brave person. Choose one of Mitty's imaginary characters. Write a **character profile** that describes Mitty as that person. Follow these steps.

First, check the person you wish to describe from the choices below.

____ Mitty the airplane pilot

____ Mitty the doctor

____ Mitty the shooting expert

Next, write different words to describe Mitty as the person you chose. Write one word in each circle.

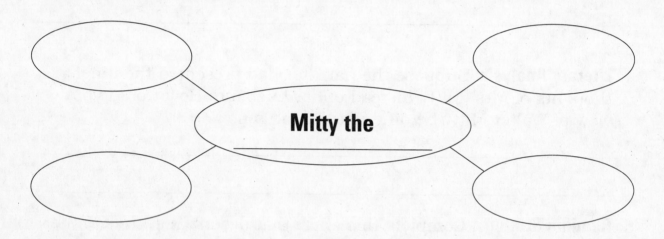

**Mitty the**
_____

Now, write a paragraph that describes Mitty's imaginary character in detail. Use the words you wrote in the circles. Also, tell what Mitty says and does that makes him brave.

_____

_____

_____

_____

_____

_____

# Go Deep to the Sewer
## Bill Cosby

**Summary**

In this essay, Bill Cosby remembers what it was like to play as a child on the city streets of Philadelphia. Instead of a grassy playing field with goals and bases, Cosby and his friends used city streets, garbage cans, and parked cars. They had to improvise, or "make do," with the materials they had at hand. Sometimes, Cosby's friends had to invent new rules to deal with unexpected situations—like the time the car serving as third base drove away while the ball was in play. Through it all, Cosby finds the humor in the situation as he describes their creative games of football and stickball.

**Visual Summary**

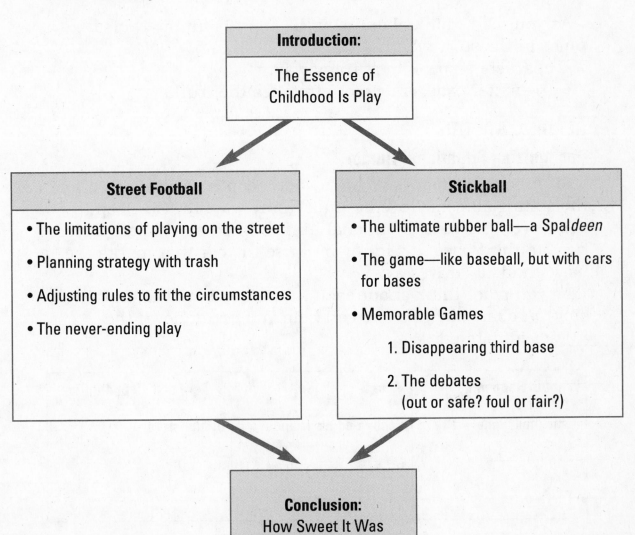

**Introduction:**

The Essence of Childhood Is Play

**Street Football**

- The limitations of playing on the street
- Planning strategy with trash
- Adjusting rules to fit the circumstances
- The never-ending play

**Stickball**

- The ultimate rubber ball—a Spal*deen*
- The game—like baseball, but with cars for bases
- Memorable Games
    1. Disappearing third base
    2. The debates (out or safe? foul or fair?)

**Conclusion:**
How Sweet It Was

## LITERARY ANALYSIS

### Humorous Remembrance

A **humorous remembrance** is a funny story that a writer recalls from his or her past. "Go Deep to the Sewer" is a humorous remembrance. Bill Cosby recalls playing football with his friends as a child. The boys didn't have a ball field to play on. So they played in the street instead.

In this passage, the quarterback plans the next play with his teammates.

> . . . Arnie, you go down to the corner of Locust an' fake takin' the bus. An' Cos, you do a zigzag out to the bakery. See if you can shake your man before you hit the rolls.

As you read, think about why the story is funny. Notice times in the story when

- characters speak in a funny way.
- the writer exaggerates, or stretches the truth.

## READING STRATEGY

### Recognizing Situational Humor

**Situational humor** is created when people, their actions, and the setting all come together in a funny way. In "Go Deep to the Sewer," there is situational humor when a stickball player runs to third base. It's funny because the car that marks the base suddenly drives away.

As you read, think about each humorous situation in the story. A chart like this one can help you break down the humor into its parts.

| What Is Happening? | Who Is Involved? | Where Is It Happening? |
|---|---|---|
| a stickball game | Cosby and his friends | on the street |
| | | |
| | | |

# Go Deep to the Sewer

## Bill Cosby

Bill Cosby recalls how he and his friends played football in the streets as a child. The players had to watch out for traffic as they ran. The quarterback would plan plays with pieces of garbage.

◆ ◆ ◆

"Okay, Shorty," Junior Barnes would say, "this is you: the orange peel."

"I don' wanna be the orange peel," Shorty replied. "The orange peel is Albert. I'm the gum."

"But let's make 'em *think* he's the orange peel," I said, "an' let 'em think Albert's the manhole."

◆ ◆ ◆

Cosby recalls the awkward way he caught a football as a kid. It looked like he was catching a load of wet laundry. He also recalls how the games went on till dark. It became hard to see the ball. Yet most players were not willing to quit.

◆ ◆ ◆

"Hey, you guys, dontcha think we should call the game?" said Harold one summer evening.

"Why do a stupid thing like that?" Junior replied.

"'Cause I can't see the ball."

"Harold, that don't make you special. Nobody can see the ball. But y'*know* it's up there."

And we continued to <u>stagger</u> around as night fell on Philadelphia and we kept looking for a football that could have been seen only on radar screens.

◆ ◆ ◆

### Literary Analysis

What part of his life does Cosby recall in his **humorous remembrance**? Circle the words that tell you.

### Reading Strategy

**Situational humor** is created when the players use objects to represent themselves. Circle three items that they use.

### Stop to Reflect

The boys want to continue to play in the dark. What does that tell you about them?

_____

_____

_____

### Literary Analysis

Cosby is funny when he exaggerates, or stretches the truth. In the bracketed passage, underline the words that show Cosby using exaggeration.

---

### Vocabulary Development

**stagger** (STAG er) *v.* walk in an unsure way, as if about to fall

Why is it funny when Cosby calls a Spaldeen "a pink rocket in orbit"?

_____

_____

_____

**Situational humor** is created when Junior runs to third base. What happens that makes the event funny? Circle the words that tell you.

*Mark the Text!*

Read the bracketed passage aloud. Who sounds more frustrated, Junior or Eddie?

_____

Explain your answer.

_____

_____

_____

Cosby now recalls how he and his friends played stickball[1] in the street. They used a pink rubber ball called a Spaldeen. The boys always pronounced it Spal*deen*.

◆ ◆ ◆

Baseball fans talk about the lively ball, but a lively baseball is a sinking stone compared to a Spal*deen*, which could be dropped from your eye level and bounce back there again, if you wanted to do something boring with it. And when you connected with a Spal*deen* in stick-ball, you put a pink rocket in orbit, perhaps even over the house at the corner and into another neighborhood, where it might gently bop somebody's mother sitting on a stoop.[2]

◆ ◆ ◆

In Cosby's stickball games, home plate and second base were manhole covers.[3] First base and third base were the fenders of parked cars. In one game, Junior was running to third base. Suddenly, the car that marked the base drove away. Eddie tagged him out.

◆ ◆ ◆

"I'm not out!" cried Junior in outrage. "I'm right here on third!"

And he did have a point, but so did Eddie, who replied, not without a certain logic of his own, "But third ain't there anymore."

◆ ◆ ◆

Parts of the field might have disappeared, but the stickball games were still fun for Cosby and his friends. Cosby says it was a complete thrill to have your stick connect with a Spaldeen.

---

1. **stickball** a game similar to baseball.
2. **stoop** (stoop) *n.* a porch with steps in front of a house.
3. **manhole covers** round sewer covers.

1. Where do Cosby and his friends play their games?

_____

2. Why is the football game funny when it is played at night?

_____

_____

_____

3. How is a Spaldeen different from a baseball?

_____

_____

4. **Literary Analysis:** What time in his life does Cosby recall in his **humorous remembrance?**

_____

_____

5. **Reading Strategy:** How do the players use an orange peel and gum in a funny way?

_____

_____

6. **Reading Strategy:** Cosby describes a humorous situation during a stickball game. Fill in the missing details.

   a. Manhole covers serve as home plate and _____.

   b. _____ serve as first base and third base.

   c. Junior runs to third base.

   d. The car that marked the base _____.

   e. Eddie tags out Junior.

# Listening and Speaking

## Monologue

A **monologue** is a speech or story told by one person. Imagine you are a comedian. Create a monologue based on a funny event. It may be an event that really happened to you. It may be an event you saw in a movie, television show, or book. Make your story as funny as possible. Follow these steps:

When did the event happen?

_____

_____

_____

Where did the event take place?

_____

Who took part in the event?

_____

_____

What happened that made the event so funny?

_____

_____

_____

Later, ask a partner to listen to your monologue. Talk about ways you can make your story even funnier. Then present it to a small group of friends or classmates.

# Talk

## African (Ashanti) Folk Tale

## retold by Harold Courlander and George Herzog

### Summary

"Talk" is a strange and humorous folk tale set in West Africa. In this story, various objects talk to a farmer, startling and frightening him. The tale begins with the farmer digging yams. One yam tells the farmer to go away and leave him alone. Next, the dog speaks up, the palm tree responds, and a stone talks. Frightened, the farmer runs toward the village. As he meets others along the way, they too hear objects talking: a fish trap, a bundle of cloth, the river, and finally the chief's stool. The chief's stool speaks the final line of the story when it says, "Imagine, a talking yam."

### Visual Summary

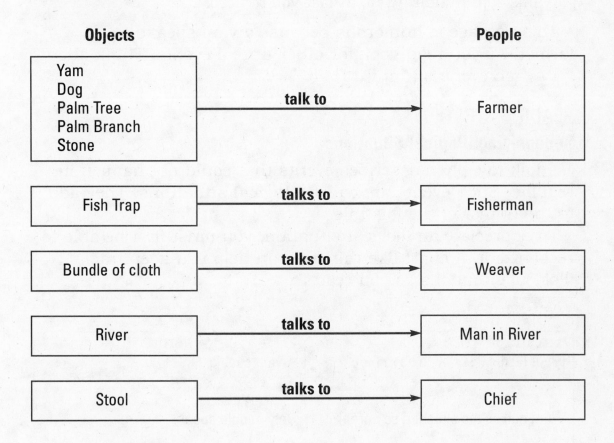

| Objects | | People |
|---|---|---|
| Yam<br>Dog<br>Palm Tree<br>Palm Branch<br>Stone | **talk to** → | Farmer |
| Fish Trap | **talks to** → | Fisherman |
| Bundle of cloth | **talks to** → | Weaver |
| River | **talks to** → | Man in River |
| Stool | **talks to** → | Chief |

## LITERARY ANALYSIS
### Humorous Folk Tale

A folk tale is a popular story that has been passed on from one generation to the next. A **humorous folk tale** tells a funny story.

A folk tale has these qualities:
- It has simple characters and language.
- It often describes unreal events.
- It teaches about life and how people behave.

Read this passage from "Talk." It is an example of part of a humorous folk tale.

> . . . a country man went out into his garden to dig up some yams to take to market. While he was digging, one of the yams said to him, "Well, at last you're here. . . ."

This passage is humorous because a yam speaks to a farmer. As you read, look for other unreal events. Think about why each event is funny.

## READING STRATEGY
### Recognizing Illogical Situations

A folk tale often describes events that could not happen in real life. Such events are called **illogical situations**. They add to the humor of the folk tale.

To appreciate an illogical situation, you must first be able to recognize it. A chart like this one can help you keep track of illogical situations as you read.

| | |
|---|---|
| What illogical situation have I found? | A yam speaks. |
| What makes the situation so unreal? | Only people speak. |
| Why is the illogical situation funny? | The speaking yam confuses the countryman. |

# Talk
## African (Ashanti) Folk Tale
### Retold by Harold Courlander
### and George Herzog

A farmer is digging up yams to sell at the market.

◆ ◆ ◆

While he was digging, one of the yams said to him, "Well, at last you're here. You never weeded me, but now you come around with your digging stick. Go away and leave me alone!"

◆ ◆ ◆

The farmer does not realize who spoke to him. His dog tells him it was the yam. The angry farmer takes a tree branch to whip the dog. The tree orders the farmer to put the branch down. The branch asks to be set down gently. The farmer places it on a stone. The stone tells him to remove the branch.

The farmer is frightened by all the talking items. He runs to the village. He meets a fisherman on the way. He tells him what has happened.

◆ ◆ ◆

"Is that all?" the man with the fish trap asked. "Is that so frightening?"

"Well," the man's fish trap said, "did he take it off the stone?"

"Wah!" the fisherman shouted. He threw the fish trap on the ground and began to run with the farmer, and on the trail they met a weaver with a bundle of cloth on his head.

◆ ◆ ◆

© Pearson Education, Inc.

---

◆ **Literary Analysis**

Circle the words in the bracketed passage that describe an unreal event.

◆ **Reading Strategy**

Why are the events with the dog, tree, branch, and stone **illogical situations**?

_____

_____

_____

◆ **Reading Check**

When does the fisherman become frightened?

_____

_____

_____

The stool thinks it's odd for a yam to talk. Why is that funny?

_____

_____

_____

How do you think the chief reacted in the end? Explain your answer.

_____

_____

_____

Both men tell their story to the weaver. The story does not scare him, but he grows scared when his cloth speaks.

◆　◆　◆

"Wah!" the weaver shouted. He threw his bundle on the trail and started running with the other men. They came panting to the <u>ford</u> in the river and found a man bathing. "Are you chasing a gazelle?" he asked them.

◆　◆　◆

They tell the bather their stories. The bather is scared when the river speaks. The four men tell their story to the village chief. The chief sits on his stool and listens. He says their story is too wild to be true. He orders the men to leave.

◆　◆　◆

"Fantastic, isn't it?" his stool said. "Imagine, a talking yam!"

---

### Vocabulary Development

**ford** (FORD) *n.* shallow place in a river that can be crossed

---

1. Why does the farmer become frightened?

_____

_____

2. How does each character feel after hearing what happened to the others? Check your answer.

|  | Scared | Not Scared |
|---|---|---|
| Fisherman | _____ | _____ |
| Weaver | _____ | _____ |
| Bather | _____ | _____ |

3. What does the village chief think of the men's story?

_____

_____

4. Why is the end of the story funny?

_____

_____

5. **Reading Strategy: Illogical situations** occur when things speak to characters. Complete this chart by listing the things that speak.

| Character | What Speaks to Him |
|---|---|
| farmer | yam, dog |
| fisherman | |
| weaver | |
| bather | |
| village chief | |

6. **Literary Analysis:** What does this **humorous folk tale** teach about the way people really behave? Check the correct sentence.

____ People rarely tell the truth.

____ People do not always believe something until it happens to them.

____ People often hear things that speak to them.

# Writing

## Humorous Folk Tale

Write a **humorous folk tale** that takes place in your school. Keep the characters and language very simple. Make your story funny by having a nonhuman item speak to people. Follow these steps:

List at least two people who will be characters.

a. _____    b. _____

Choose a nonhuman item that will speak to people.

book    desk    pencil    other: _____

Describe a problem that characters face. Base it on a problem that really took place in your school.

_____

_____

_____

_____

Tell how the problem is solved with the help of the talking item.

_____

_____

_____

_____

_____

## *from* The Road Ahead
### Bill Gates

### Summary

In this nonfiction excerpt, computer pioneer Bill Gates tells about the direction technology will take in our homes in the future. Gates remembers how frustrating it was when he was a child to miss a television show on the day and time it was broadcast. Today, videocassette recorders (VCRs) allow viewing whenever one wishes, although there is the inconvenience of timers and tapes. In the future, however, movies, television shows, and other kinds of digital information will be stored on servers. Computers will then access video-on-demand for home televisions connected to large home networks. Users will be able to call up selections from a large menu without the use of a VCR. Gates believes that in the near future video-on-demand will become a "killer app"—a use of technology that becomes a vital moneymaking venture.

### Visual Summary

**Television in the Future**

- Digitized data will be stored on servers.
- Data will be retrieved from servers and routed on demand to televisions, computers, and telephones.
- Individuals will be able to control when to view television shows, movies, and other kinds of video.

**Television Today**

- People can use VCRs to tape shows for later viewing.
- They can rent movies to watch on television via VCRs.
- Bandwidth is currently available in corporate networks for limited video-on-demand.

**Television Before the 1980s**

- People had to watch shows when they aired.
- If traveling, they would miss a show.
- Missing a show meant missing out on discussions of the show the next day.

## LITERARY ANALYSIS

### Expository Writing

**Expository writing** gives information on a subject. The writer presents one or more ideas about the subject. Each idea is supported with details, examples, and facts.

In *The Road Ahead,* author Bill Gates discusses an idea called "conventional television." He explains it with details.

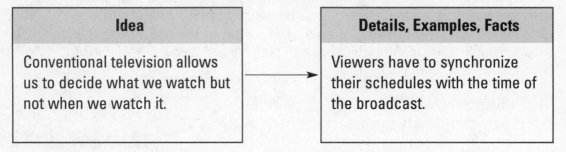

| Idea | | Details, Examples, Facts |
|------|---|--------------------------|
| Conventional television allows us to decide what we watch but not when we watch it. | → | Viewers have to synchronize their schedules with the time of the broadcast. |

As you read, look for ideas that the writer presents. Also look for details, facts, and examples that explain or support each idea.

## READING STRATEGY

### Recognizing a Writer's Bias

For expository writing, the writer should discuss both the good and bad points about the subject. Sometimes writers show **bias**—a strong feeling for or against their subject.

You can find a writer's bias by looking for these things:
- opinions that are not backed up with facts
- opinions that show only one side of an argument
- loaded words that stir up good or bad feelings in you

As you read, remember that Gates is the head of a giant computer company. Therefore, you might expect him to have strong feelings about the ideas he is discussing. As you read, consider what influences Gates to have such a strong feeling about his subject.

# *from* The Road Ahead
## Bill Gates

Gates recalls how Americans watched TV when he was a child. The Ed Sullivan Show came on at eight o'clock on Sunday night. Most people stayed home to watch it. People had to watch the program at the same time it was shown on TV. Otherwise they missed the show. Gates calls that kind of TV viewing "synchronous."[1]

◆ ◆ ◆

In the early 1980's, the videocassette recorder gave us more <u>flexibility</u>. If you cared enough about a program to fuss with timers and tapes in advance, you could watch it whenever you liked. You could claim from the broadcasters the freedom and luxury to serve as your own program scheduler—and millions of people do.

◆ ◆ ◆

Gates explains that taping a television show and using an answering machine on your telephone are forms of "asynchronous" communication.

Gates explains that books are also a form of asynchronous communication. That's because you can read a book whenever you like. It's only natural for people to want asynchronous communication. It gives them more control over their schedule. It also gives them more choices of movies to watch on TV. The choices will grow even greater once the Internet is able to carry high-quality videos.

◆ ◆ ◆

---

### Vocabulary Development

**flexibility** (fleks uh BIL uh tee) *n.* ability to make a change

---

1. **synchronous** (SING kru nus) *adj.* happening at the same time.

*from* The Road Ahead **99**

---

**◆ Literary Analysis**

Name two details in the bracketed section that help explain the idea of "synchronous" TV viewing.

_____

_____

**◆ Reading Strategy**

*Mark the Text*

Gates uses the loaded word *freedom* when discussing the VCR. The word probably stirs up a good feeling in you. Underline another word in the same sentence that stirs up a good feeling.

**◆ Reading Check**

*Asynchronous* has the opposite meaning of *synchronous*. Write the meaning of *asynchronous*.

asynchronous:

_____

_____

**◆ Literary Analysis**

Gates says it's only natural for people to want asynchronous communication. What are two reasons he gives to support his opinion?

Because consumers already understand the value of movies and are used to paying to watch them, video-on-demand is an obvious development. There won't be any <u>intermediary</u> VCR. You'll simply select what you want from countless available programs.

◆ ◆ ◆

Gates says that no one knows yet when video-on-demand will be available in the United States. It may not happen for another ten years or more. When it happens, a TV program will still be shown at its regular time. But you'll be able to watch it any time you choose after that. You'll just tell your TV when to start the show.

◆ ◆ ◆

Even if a show is being broadcast live, you'll be able to use your <u>infrared</u> remote control to start it, stop it, or go to any earlier part of the program, at any time. If somebody comes to the door, you'll be able to pause the program for as long as you like.

◆ ◆ ◆

The wonderful thing is that you will be able to view a show whenever you want except, of course, before it actually takes place.

Gates believes that most people will buy video-on-demand if the cost is low enough. He says video-on-demand might even become a "killer application." That's an invention so popular that people feel they must have it.

---

### Vocabulary Development

**intermediary** (in ter MEE dee air ee) *adj.* acting between two persons or things

**infrared** (in fruh RED) *adj.* of light waves that lie just beyond the red end of the color range

---

1. Complete each sentence with the word *synchronous* or *asynchronous*.

   a. You watch a TV program at the same time that it is broadcast. That is an example of _____ communication.

   b. You watch a TV program any time after it is broadcast. That is an example of _____ communication.

2. What does the term "video-on-demand" mean?

   _____

   _____

3. What does the term "killer application" mean?

   _____

   _____

4. **Literary Analysis:** Write one more detail that supports the idea shown below.

   Idea: <u>It's natural for people to want asynchronous communication.</u>

   Detail: <u>It gives you more control over your schedule.</u>

   Detail: _____

5. **Literary Analysis:** Why does Gates think video-on-demand will be very popular? Write one reason he gives.

   _____

6. **Reading Strategy:** Put a check in front of each statement that shows the **writer's bias** in *The Road Ahead.*

   ____ With video-on-demand, you'll be in absolute control.

   ____ You could claim the freedom and luxury to serve as your own program scheduler.

   ____ Video-on-demand is an obvious development.

   ____ *The Ed Sullivan Show* was broadcast on Sunday night.

# Writing

## Consumer Response

In his essay, Gates predicts how television will change in the future. As a consumer, you have experience using a television and a computer. Write your own essay about televisions and computers. Describe the changes you'd like to see in televisions or computers of the future. Follow these steps:

First, describe two things you like about televisions or computers right now.

_____

_____

_____

Next, describe two things that bother you about televisions or computers right now.

_____

_____

_____

Then, describe two changes you'd like to see in televisions or computers of the future.

_____

_____

_____

Finally, explain why you think most people will want the changes you've described.

_____

_____

_____

_____

Use the information above to write your consumer response essay.

# The Machine That Won the War
## Isaac Asimov

## Summary

In this futuristic story, a giant computer named Multivac is credited with winning a war between Earth and a rival planet named Deneb. As the three main characters discuss the victory, they reveal their own activities during the war. Henderson, Chief Programmer for Multivac, admits he was forced to "correct" computer data that had become meaningless. Jablonsky, whose job is to analyze Multivac's data, admits that he knew Multivac was unreliable but did nothing about it. To protect his job, he, too, adjusted data until it looked right. Finally, Swift, the Director, admits that he hadn't taken the data presented to him seriously anyway. In fact, when he had to make war decisions, he used the oldest computing device available: the flip of a coin.

## Visual Summary

**What Others Thought**

| About Henderson | About Jablonsky | About Swift |
|---|---|---|
| He programmed reliable data into Multivac to process statistical information about the armies of Earth and Deneb. | He analyzed the data processed by Multivac to obtain results to help form a plan for defeating the Denebians. | He used the statistical information from Henderson and technical reports from Jablonsky to make military decisions. |

**What Was Really True**

| | | |
|---|---|---|
| He created his own data based on intuition to develop more reliable statistical reports. | He adjusted his analyses of the computer data based on intuition to come up with more reliable results. | He relied on flipping a coin rather than reading Multivac's reports to help him make key decisions. |

## LITERARY ANALYSIS
### Science Fiction

**Science fiction** is a story with unreal settings, characters, or events. However, the unreal parts of the story are based on true science. For example, the characters might be robots who rule the earth. That situation does not exist in the real world. But science could be used to explain how the robots came to have such power.

Read this passage from Asimov's science fiction story, "The Machine That Won the War."

> What do you know of the data Multivac had to use . . . from a hundred . . . computers here on Earth, on the Moon, on Mars, even on Titan . . .

You can see the story is science fiction. Asimov's setting is unreal. There are computers on the Moon, Mars, and Titan. Yet science could explain how computers can get to outer space. As you read the story, think about what is real and what is not. Consider how science might be used to explain the unreal parts.

## READING STRATEGY
### Identifying Relevant Details

In a story, **relevant details** are the key descriptions or events. They are the details you need most to understand the story. Without them, you couldn't understand the setting, characters, or events.

Asimov's story mentions computers on the Moon, Mars, and Titan. That's a relevant detail. It helps you understand that the setting is in the future.

A chart like this one can help you. As you read, jot down relevant details about characters, setting, or events. Explain why each detail is so important.

| Detail | Why It's Important |
|---|---|
| There are computers on the Moon, Mars, and Titan. | The setting is in the future. |

# The Machine That Won the War
## Isaac Asimov

Earth has won a ten-year war against the planet of Deneb. Credit for the victory is given to a giant computer named Multivac. During the war, information was fed into the machine. Multivac then advised when and where battles should be fought.

Three men are discussing Multivac's role in the war. John Henderson is a programmer who supplied Multivac with data. Max Jablonsky is an engineer who interpreted the machine's advice. Lamar Swift is director of the Solar Federation.

◆ ◆ ◆

Henderson said, "Multivac had nothing to do with victory. It's just a machine."

"A big one," said Swift.

"Then just a big machine. No better than the data fed it." For a moment, he stopped, suddenly unnerved at what he was saying.

Jablonsky looked at him. "You should know. You supplied the data. Or is it just that you're taking the credit?"

"No," said Henderson angrily. "There is no credit. What do you know of the data Multivac had to use: <u>predigested</u> from a hundred <u>subsidiary</u> computers here on Earth, on the Moon, on Mars, even on Titan."

◆ ◆ ◆

---

**Vocabulary Development**

**predigested** (pree dī JEST ed) *v.* shortened and summarized in advance

**subsidiary** (sub SID ee air ee) *adj.* supporting

Henderson makes a surprising confession. During the war, he suspected that the data he was given to feed into Multivac was not reliable.

◆ ◆ ◆

"Well, then," said Henderson, "if I told you the data was unreliable, what could you have done but replace me and refuse to believe me? I couldn't allow that."

"What did you do?" said Jablonsky.

"Since the war is won, I'll tell you what I did. I corrected the data."

"How?" asked Swift.

"Intuition,[1] I presume. I juggled them till they looked right. At first I hardly dared. I changed a bit here and there to correct what were obvious impossibilities. When the sky didn't collapse about us, I got braver. Toward the end, I scarcely cared. I just wrote out the necessary data as it was needed."

◆ ◆ ◆

Jablonsky then makes a confession of his own. During the war, he doubted that Multivac was working correctly. In the war's last years, his best technicians weren't available to service the machine. He did not trust the work that other technicians did on it. As a result, he feared that Multivac's advice was not reliable.

◆ ◆ ◆

"What did you do?" asked Henderson.

"I did what you did, John. I introduced the bugger factor.[2] I adjusted matters in accordance with intuition—and that's how the machine won the war."

◆ ◆ ◆

---

1. **Intuition** (in too IH shun) *n.* a sense of knowing something without knowing why.
2. **bugger factor** (BUG er FAK ter) *n.* the possibility of errors.

Swift now makes a confession. He also didn't think Multivac was reliable.

♦ ♦ ♦

"I'm afraid I didn't. Multivac might seem to say, Strike here, not there; do this, not that; wait, don't act. But I could never be certain that what Multivac seemed to say, it really did say; or what it really said, it really meant. I could never be certain."

♦ ♦ ♦

Jablonsky wonders how Swift made war decisions without Multivac's advice. Swift explains that he used a very old kind of computer.

He shows old-fashioned coins from his pocket that were used before the current computer credit system went into effect. Swift puts all but one of the coins back into his pocket.

♦ ♦ ♦

He held the last coin between his fingers, staring absently at it. "Multivac is not the first computer, friends, nor the best-known, nor the one that can most efficiently lift the load of decision from the shoulders of the executive. A machine *did* win the war, John; at least a very simple computing device did; one that I used every time I had a particularly hard decision to make.

♦ ♦ ♦

Swift takes the coin and tosses it in the air. It lands in the palm of his hand. He covers the coin with his other hand to hide it.

♦ ♦ ♦

"Heads or tails, gentlemen?" said Swift.

---

**♦ Stop to Reflect**

Swift ignored Multivac's advice when making war decisions. What do his actions show about him? Write your ideas on these lines.

_____

_____

_____

**♦ Read Fluently**

Read the bracketed passage. Then underline the word that tells what kind of "machine" won the war.

# REVIEW AND ASSESS

1. **Reading Strategy:** Use **relevant details** to describe the job that each man had during the war.

| Character | Job |
| --- | --- |
| John Henderson | |
| Max Jablonsky | |
| Lamar Swift | |

2. What were the three men celebrating?

_____

_____

3. How are the confessions of the three men alike?

_____

_____

4. Asimov's story is titled "The Machine That Won the War." How does the meaning of the title change by the end of the story?

_____

_____

5. **Literary Analysis:** Put a check in front of the details that tell you the story is **science fiction**.

____ Henderson, Jablonsky, and Swift work with a computer.

____ There are computers on the Moon, on Mars, and on Titan.

____ There are no coins anymore because of a metal shortage.

____ Each of the men does something that is not honest.

6. **Reading Strategy:** Use **relevant details** to explain how Swift made decisions during the war.

_____

_____

# Listening and Speaking

## Discussion

In Asimov's story, the three men rely on their intuition to make important decisions. Intuition is a sense of knowing something without knowing why. Hold a small-group **discussion** with classmates. Talk about the following cases. Take notes on what group members say.

Your friend asks you to ride the elevator in a very old building. Your intuition tells you it is not safe. Should you ride the elevator? _____
Why, or why not?

_____

_____

_____

_____

Your teacher asks you to work with a new student on a class project. Your intuition tells you that you will not get along with the new student. Should you work together? _____
Why, or why not?

_____

_____

_____

_____

You are traveling somewhere for the first time. A map tells you to turn left at the lake. Your intuition tells you to turn right. Which way should you turn? _____
Explain.

_____

_____

_____

_____

_____

## *from* Silent Spring
### Rachel Carson

## Summary

   In this short fable, the author warns that environmental disasters might one day destroy many of the plants, animals, and natural settings that people in America enjoy today.  She begins by describing a time when there were prosperous fields of grain, fruitful orchards, continuous migrations of birds, and streams filled with fish. Then, a blight crept over the land, wiping out plant and animal life on farms and in orchards and streams. The blight seems to have been caused by a white powder.  At the end, the author notes that the town does not actually exist.  However, all of the disasters she describes have happened in different places and might happen everywhere unless Americans change the way they treat the environment.

## Visual Summary

| Before the Blight | After the Blight |
| --- | --- |
| • prosperous farms<br><br>• fields of grain<br><br>• hillsides of orchards<br><br>• beautiful roadsides<br><br>• countless birds<br><br>• streams filled with fish | • sick and dying chickens, cattle, and sheep<br><br>• sick and dying humans<br><br>• silence when birds become sick and die<br><br>• no pollination of fruit trees<br><br>• roadsides lined with brown and withered plants<br><br>• white powder remaining on houses and in fields and streams |

## LITERARY ANALYSIS
### Persuasive Appeal

A **persuasive appeal** is a writer's attempt to make you think or act in a certain way. The writer might warn you that something bad will occur if you fail to take action. In the book *Silent Spring*, Rachel Carson warns us that our careless use of chemicals will in time harm many plants, animals, and people. She starts by describing an American town where everything is beautiful. Then her warning begins:

> Then . . . everything began to change . . . the cattle and sheep sickened and died. Everywhere was a shadow of death. The farmers spoke of much illness among their families.

As you read, consider
• what Carson wants you to believe.
• what warnings Carson gives.
• what action Carson wants you to take.

## READING STRATEGY
### Distinguishing Between Fact and Opinion

In her persuasive appeal, Carson tries to convince her audience that chemicals are harmful to plants, animals, and people. She supports her belief, or opinion, with facts.
• A **fact** is a statement that can be proven true.
• An **opinion** states a personal belief. An opinion can never be proven.

This chart shows an opinion that Carson offers and a fact she uses to support it.

| Opinion | Fact |
|---|---|
| This imagined tragedy may easily become a stark reality we all shall know. | Every one of these disasters has actually happened somewhere. |

As you read, find more facts and opinions that Carson offers. Add them to a chart like the one above.

◆ Reading Strategy

Circle one **fact** in the bracketed passage. Draw a line under one **opinion**.

◆ Literary Analysis

Carson's **persuasive appeal** is a warning. How does the text on this page make you feel? _____

_____

Why? _____

_____

_____

# *from* Silent Spring
## Rachel Carson

Carson begins by describing an ideal American town that had beautiful trees, fields, and streams. It also had lots of birds, fish, and farm animals. After many years, however, a change occurred.

◆　◆　◆

Then a strange <u>blight</u> crept over the area and everything began to change. Some evil spell had settled on the community.

◆　◆　◆

Carson explains the terrible things that started to happen. People became sick and died unexplained deaths. Farm animals were born sick and died quickly. Plants dried up and turned brown. Apple trees failed to grow fruit. All the fish in the streams died. A strange white powder appeared on the roofs of houses.

◆　◆　◆

No witchcraft, no enemy action had silenced the rebirth of new life in this stricken world. The people had done it themselves.

This town does not actually exist, but it might easily have a thousand counterparts in America or elsewhere in the world. I know of no community that has experienced all the misfortunes I describe. Yet every one of these disasters has actually happened somewhere, and many real communities have already suffered a substantial number of them. A grim specter has crept upon us almost unnoticed, and this imagined tragedy may easily become a stark reality we all shall know.

---

**Vocabulary Development**

**blight** (BLĪT) *n.* something that destroys or prevents growth

---

1. What are three beautiful things in the town before it changes?

   a. _____

   b. _____

   c. _____

2. Complete this chart to tell what happens to people and things in the town after it changes.

| cattle and sheep | get sick and die |
|---|---|
| people | |
| plants | |
| apple trees | |
| fish | |

3. What appears on the roofs of houses after the town changes?

   _____

   _____

   _____

4. **Literary Analysis:** Put a check before each statement you feel is true about Carson's **persuasive appeal**.

   ____ a. She is warning us that chemicals can harm plants and animals.

   ____ b. She is warning us that the town she writes about is real.

   ____ c. She is warning us that chemicals can make people sick.

   ____ d. She is warning us to cut back our use of chemicals.

   ____ e. She is warning us to move away from farms.

5. **Literary Analysis:** Did Carson's **persuasive appeal** convince you to agree with her opinion? _____ Give two reasons why, or why not.

_____

_____

6. **Reading Strategy:** Write whether each statement from *Silent Spring* is a **fact** or an **opinion**.

_____ a. The cattle and sheep sickened and died.

_____ b. This town does not actually exist.

_____ c. Many real communities have already suffered.

_____ d. This imagined tragedy may easily become a stark reality we all shall know.

# Listening and Speaking

## Speech

Many people today are concerned about the problems of our earth or environment. Prepare a speech about one problem that you feel is most important. To help you write your speech, follow these steps.

First, choose a problem to write about. Check one of these, or name your own problem.

____ air pollution      ____ water pollution      ____ soil pollution

____ other _____

Next, list two facts about the problem. Your facts may come from *Silent Spring,* or your facts may come from newspapers or magazines.

Facts: 1. _____

2. _____

End your speech with your opinion on how to deal with the problem.

Opinion: _____

_____

Use your answers to write a two-paragraph speech. Practice your speech before reading it aloud to your class.

# The Gift of the Magi

## O. Henry

### Summary

   This story is about Jim and Della, a couple in love. Della is introduced to us first. She is thinking of a present for her husband Jim on Christmas Eve. Della is heartbroken that she does not have enough money to buy Jim the perfect present—a watch chain for his favorite watch. Suddenly, she has the idea to sell her most treasured possession—her hair—so that she can afford the watch chain. When Jim arrives home, he is shocked by Della's appearance. Jim had sold his watch so that he could afford a set of combs for Della's hair—hair that now no longer exists. Both presents are useless for the moment, but it does not matter. Such sacrifices are wise, the narrator concludes, since they are made in the true spirit of giving.

### Visual Summary

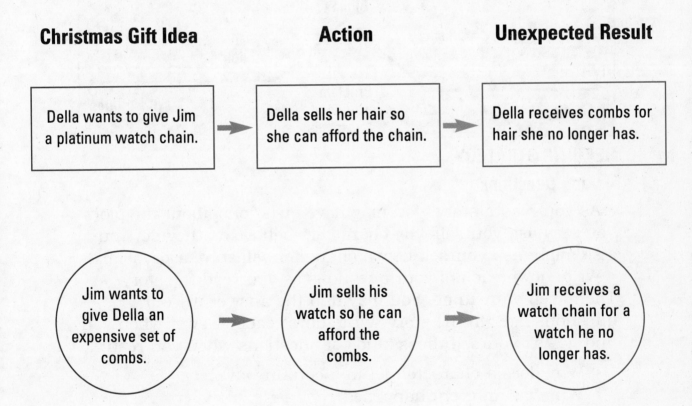

| Christmas Gift Idea | Action | Unexpected Result |
| --- | --- | --- |
| Della wants to give Jim a platinum watch chain. | Della sells her hair so she can afford the chain. | Della receives combs for hair she no longer has. |
| Jim wants to give Della an expensive set of combs. | Jim sells his watch so he can afford the combs. | Jim receives a watch chain for a watch he no longer has. |

## LITERARY ANALYSIS

### Plot

**Plot** is all the events that happen in a story. The plot has five parts:

- *Exposition*—The setting and characters in the story are introduced.
- *Rising action*—A problem arises for the main character or characters.
- *Climax*—The problem reaches its most dramatic point or moment.
- *Falling action*—The problem becomes easier to solve.
- *Resolution*—The problem is finally solved in some way.

A diagram like this can help you follow the plot of the story as you read.

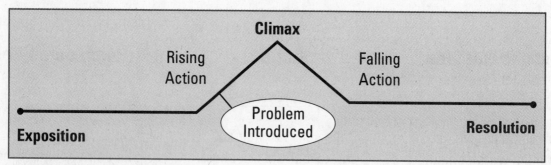

## READING STRATEGY

### Asking Questions

As you read a story, you may have questions about the plot. You may ask yourself why characters behave as they do. You also might ask yourself how a character will solve a problem.

Write down each of your questions as you read the story. Then keep on reading. You may find the answer to your questions later in the story. Write down each answer when you find it. Ask yourself these kinds of questions when you read:

- Why does a character act in a certain way?
- Why has an event happened?
- What information is left out of the story?

# The Gift of the Magi

## O. Henry

Della and Jim Young are a very poor couple. They live in a run-down apartment. Jim makes only twenty dollars a week. At home, Della counts the small amount of money she has managed to save. She is crying because it is so little.

◆  ◆  ◆

Della finished her cry and attended to her cheeks with the powder rag. She stood by the window and looked out dully at a gray cat walking a gray fence in a gray backyard. Tomorrow would be Christmas Day, and she had only $1.87 with which to buy Jim a present. She had been saving every penny she could for months, with this result. Twenty dollars a week doesn't go far. Expenses had been greater than she had <u>calculated</u>. They always are. Only $1.87 to buy a present for Jim. Her Jim. Many a happy hour she had spent planning for something nice for him.

◆  ◆  ◆

Della stands in front of the mirror. She lets down her long, beautiful hair. It reaches all the way below her knees. Della and Jim are both very proud of Della's hair. They are also very proud of Jim's gold watch. It was passed down from his grandfather to his father to him.

Della goes downstairs to the street. She enters the store of Madame Sofronie, a seller of hair goods. She speaks with Madame.

◆  ◆  ◆

◆ **Literary Analysis**

The first paragraph tells the **exposition** of the **plot**. Underline the sentences that give background information about Della and Jim.

◆ **Literary Analysis**

In the **rising action** of the **plot**, Della faces a problem. Circle the sentence or sentences that explain Della's problem.

◆ **Reading Strategy**

Read the bracketed passage. Then ask a question about Della's actions. Write it on the lines below.

_____

_____

_____

---

**Vocabulary Development**

**calculated** (KAL kyoo layt id) *v.*   figured out by counting

---

How do you think Jim will feel about Della's new haircut? Why?

_____

_____

_____

Jim behaves strangely when he first sees Della at home. Ask a question about his behavior. Write it on the lines below.

_____

_____

_____

"Will you buy my hair?" asked Della.

"I buy hair," said Madame. "Take yer hat off and let's have a sight at the looks of it."

Down rippled the brown cascade.

"Twenty dollars," said Madame, lifting the mass with a practiced hand.

"Give it to me quick," said Della.

◆　◆　◆

*Della goes shopping for Jim's Christmas present. She chooses a simple but handsome watch chain for twenty-one dollars. Della imagines how good Jim will look wearing his watch and new chain. Back home, she curls her short hair. Jim comes home from work later that night.*

◆　◆　◆

The door opened and Jim stepped in and closed it. He looked thin and very serious. Poor fellow, he was only twenty-two—and to be <u>burdened</u> with a family! He needed a new overcoat and he was without gloves.

Jim stepped inside the door, as <u>immovable</u> as a setter at the scent of quail. His eyes were fixed upon Della, and there was an expression in them that she could not read, and it terrified her. It was not anger, nor surprise, nor <u>disapproval</u>, nor horror, nor any of the <u>sentiments</u> that she had been prepared for. He simply stared at her fixedly with that particular expression on his face.

◆　◆　◆

---

### Vocabulary Development

**burdened** (BURd und) *v.* loaded down
**immovable** (im MOOV uh bul) *adj.* not able to be moved
**disapproval** (dis uh PROOV ul) *n.* being against an idea
**sentiments** (SEN tuh ments) *n.* feelings

Della begs Jim not to be upset with her. She explains that she sold her hair to buy him a Christmas present. She says that her hair will grow back. Jim finally stops staring at her. He tosses a package on the table.

◆ ◆ ◆

"Don't make any mistake, Dell," he said, "about me. I don't think there's anything in the way of a haircut or a shave or a shampoo that could make me like my girl any less. But if you'll unwrap that package you may see why you had me going a while at first."

◆ ◆ ◆

Della quickly opens Jim's package. She screams first in joy, then in tears. Jim has bought Della a set of expensive combs for her long hair. She reminds Jim that her hair will grow back quickly. She then gives Jim his gift. She wants to see how the watch and chain will look on him. She asks him for his watch.

◆ ◆ ◆

Instead of obeying, Jim tumbled down on the couch and put his hands under the back of his head and smiled.

"Dell," he said, "let's put our Christmas presents away and keep 'em a while. They're too nice to use just at present. I sold the watch to get the money to buy your combs. And now suppose you put the chops on."

◆ ◆ ◆

The narrator[1] explains that the Magi were wise men who brought gifts to the baby Jesus. Their gifts were very wise, says the narrator. Yet Jim and Della were the wisest gift givers of all. They gave up what they treasured most, out of love for each other. The narrator says Jim and Della are the magi.

---

1. **narrator** (NAR ray ter) *n.* a person who tells a story.

---

◆ **Reading Check**

Why does Della tell Jim that her hair will grow back? Write your answer on the lines below.

_____

_____

_____

◆ **Reading Strategy**

Della screams in joy and then in tears. You might ask, "What is in Jim's package that makes her act that way?" Underline the words that answer the question.

◆ **Literary Analysis**

The **plot** reaches its **climax** when Jim tells Della about his watch. What has happened to Jim's watch?

_____

_____

_____

◆ **Reading Check**

The narrator feels that Jim and Della are the wisest gift givers of all. Circle the sentence that explains why.

# REVIEW AND ASSESS

1. Why does Della visit Madame Sofronie's store?

_____

_____

_____

2. What gifts do Della and Jim buy for each other?

a. Della's gift for Jim: _____

b. Jim's gift for Della: _____

3. Put a check next to each reason that explains why Della and Jim are wise gift givers.

_____ They bring gifts to the baby Jesus.

_____ Their gifts show their love for each other.

_____ They each give up what they love to please the other.

_____ They spend very little money on their gifts.

4. **Literary Analysis:** Use information from the **exposition** of the **plot** on page 117 to complete these sentences.

a. Della and Jim are a very _____ couple.

b. They live in a _____.

5. **Literary Analysis:** What problem does Della face in the **rising action** of the **plot**?

_____

_____

_____

6. **Reading Strategy:**

a. Write two questions that came to your mind as you read this story.

_____

_____

_____

_____

b. Were the questions answered as you continued to read? _____

If so, write the answers here.

_____

_____

_____

_____

# Writing

## Story from Jim's Point of View

Imagine that Jim had narrated "The Gift of the Magi." You would have learned about the characters and events from his point of view. For example, Jim might have said, "I think Della is the most wonderful wife in the world." Write the answers to each of these questions in Jim's own words. Start with the word *I*.

What would Jim think about being poor?

I _____

_____

_____

What would Jim think after he sold his watch?

I _____

_____

_____

What would Jim think when he saw Della's short hair?

I _____

_____

_____

What would Jim say about their Christmas gifts?

I _____

_____

_____

## The Scarlet Ibis

### James Hurst

### Summary

The narrator of this story remembers his boyhood with his brother, Doodle. Doodle was a disappointment to his brother because he was weak and frail. When Doodle was born, the narrator had looked forward to having a new playmate. Instead, he often had to take care of Doodle and he resented this responsibility. Still, a bond developed between them, despite Doodle's physical disabilities. Pride drove the narrator to teach Doodle to walk. Encouraged by his success, the narrator decided he would teach Doodle how to run, swim, climb trees, and fight before Doodle started school. The deadline approached and the narrator knew that Doodle would not succeed. He was angry because of this failure and left Doodle behind in a lightning storm. When he returned to look for Doodle, the narrator was devastated to find Doodle lying dead under a bush.

### Visual Summary

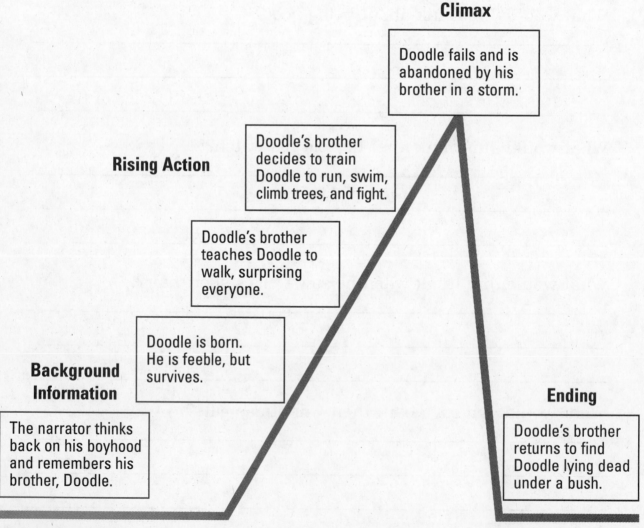

**Climax**

Doodle fails and is abandoned by his brother in a storm.

**Rising Action**

Doodle's brother decides to train Doodle to run, swim, climb trees, and fight.

Doodle's brother teaches Doodle to walk, surprising everyone.

Doodle is born. He is feeble, but survives.

**Background Information**

The narrator thinks back on his boyhood and remembers his brother, Doodle.

**Ending**

Doodle's brother returns to find Doodle lying dead under a bush.

## LITERARY ANALYSIS

### Point of View

**Point of view** is the position from which a narrator tells a story.

- In **first-person** point of view, the narrator is a character in the story. The narrator takes part in the action.
- In **third-person** point of view, the narrator is not a story character. The narrator takes no part in the action.

Look at this passage from "The Scarlet Ibis":

> . . . one afternoon as I watched him, my head poked between the iron posts of the foot of the bed, he looked straight at me and grinned.

This story is told from first-person point of view. The narrator takes part in the action. He refers to himself with the words *I*, *my*, and *me*. A story told in first person lets you learn the narrator's private thoughts and feelings.

## READING STRATEGY

### Identifying With a Character

The first-person point of view gives you an inside view of the person telling the story. It tells you the thoughts and feelings of the narrator. It lets you identify with the narrator, who is a character in the story.

**Identify with a character** in these ways:

- Put yourself in his or her place.
- Consider how you might act if the story were happening to you. Ask yourself if you would do and say the same things as the character.

In "The Scarlet Ibis," the narrator is an older brother. He tells about growing up with his younger brother, Doodle. As you read, consider what the narrator says and does. Think about whether you would act the same way if Doodle were your brother. A chart like this can help you.

| Event | Narrator's Feelings | Your Feelings |
|---|---|---|
| Narrator takes Doodle everywhere. | "He was a burden in many ways." | |

# The Scarlet Ibis
## James Hurst

The narrator tells about life with his younger brother when they were children. He tells the story many years after it happened.

◆ ◆ ◆

### ◆ Literary Analysis

Circle the word in the bracketed passage that shows the story is narrated from **first-person point of view.**

He was born when I was six and was, from the outset, a disappointment. He seemed all head, with a tiny body which was red and shriveled like an old man's. Everybody thought he was going to die—everybody except Aunt Nicey, who had delivered him. She said he would live because he was born in a <u>caul</u> and cauls were made from Jesus' nightgown. Daddy had Mr. Heath, the carpenter, build a little mahogany coffin for him. But he didn't die, and when he was three months old Mama and Daddy decided they might as well name him. They named him William Armstrong, which was like tying a big tail on a small kite. Such a name sounds good only on a tombstone.

◆ ◆ ◆

### ◆ Reading Check

Mama says that the baby may not be "all there." What does she mean by that? Write your answer on these lines.

_____

_____

_____

Mama warns the narrator that his baby brother may be limited physically. He may never be able to run and jump and climb. He may not even be "all there."

◆ ◆ ◆

### ◆ Reading Strategy

Circle the words that show how the narrator feels about having a sick brother. Then **identify with the character.** Explain how you would feel if you were in the narrator's place.

_____

_____

_____

It was bad enough having an <u>invalid</u> brother, but having one who possibly was not all there was unbearable, so I began to make plans to kill him by smothering him with a pillow. However, one afternoon as I watched him, my head poked between the

---

### Vocabulary Development

**caul** (KAWL) *n.*  thin layer of tissue that covers a baby at birth

**invalid** (IN vuh lid) *n.*  a weak, sick person

---

iron posts of the foot of the bed, he looked straight at me and grinned. I skipped through the rooms, down the echoing halls, shouting, "Mama, he smiled. He's all there! He's all there!" and he was.

◆   ◆   ◆

William Armstrong starts to grow. The narrator renames him Doodle because he crawls backwards like a doodle-bug. Doodle can't walk, so Daddy builds him a go-cart. The narrator pulls Doodle around in the cart.

◆   ◆   ◆

He was a burden in many ways. The doctor had said that he mustn't get too excited, too hot, too cold, or too tired and that he must always be treated gently. A long list of don'ts went with him, all of which I ignored once we got out of the house. To discourage his coming with me, I'd run with him across the ends of the cotton rows and <u>careen</u> him around corners on two wheels. Sometimes I accidentally turned him over, but he never told Mama.

◆   ◆   ◆

The narrator accepts that Doodle will always be with him. He often takes Doodle to his favorite field. When Doodle turns five, the narrator decides to teach him how to walk. Doodle says he can never walk. His brother disagrees, but the job of teaching is hard.

◆   ◆   ◆

It seemed so hopeless from the beginning that it's a miracle I didn't give up. But all of us must have something or someone to be proud of, and Doodle had become mine. I did not know then that pride is a wonderful, terrible thing, a seed that bears two vines, life and death.

◆   ◆   ◆

### Vocabulary Development

**careen** (kuh REEN) *v.* to tip or tilt

After many weeks, Doodle is finally able to take steps without falling. At age six, Doodle surprises his family by walking.

◆ ◆ ◆

Doodle told them it was I who had taught him to walk, so everyone wanted to hug me, and I began to cry.

"What are you crying for?" asked Daddy, but I couldn't answer. They did not know that I did it for myself; that pride, whose slave I was, spoke to me louder than all their voices, and that Doodle walked only because I was ashamed of having a crippled brother.

◆ ◆ ◆

The narrator now decides to teach Doodle to run, swim, climb, and fight. By summer's end, Doodle has made little progress. He has grown weaker. One day, the family hears a strange noise outside. A large red bird—a scarlet ibis—sits high in a tree. The bird looks tired and sick. It soon falls out of the tree

◆ ◆ ◆

Its long graceful neck jerked twice into an S, then straightened out, and the bird was still. A white veil came over the eyes and the long white beak <u>unhinged</u>. Its legs were crossed and its clawlike feet were delicately curved at rest. Even death did not mar its grace, for it lay on the earth like a broken vase of red flowers, and we stood around it, awed by its <u>exotic</u> beauty.

◆ ◆ ◆

Doodle buries the dead ibis. He and his brother then go out in a boat. Doodle grows tired while rowing. Back on land, the boys start to race home as a storm approaches.

◆ ◆ ◆

---

### Vocabulary Development

**unhinged** (un HINJD) *adj.* opened

**exotic** (ig ZAWT ik) *adj.* strangely beautiful

---

The faster I walked, the faster he walked, so I began to run. The rain was coming, roaring through the pines, and then, like a bursting Roman candle, a gum tree ahead of us was shattered by a bolt of lightning. When the <u>deafening</u> peal of thunder had died, and in the moment before the rain arrived, I heard Doodle, who had fallen behind, cry out, "Brother, Brother, don't leave me!"

The knowledge that Doodle's and my plans had come to <u>naught</u> was bitter, and that streak of cruelty within me awakened. I ran as fast as I could, leaving him far behind with a wall of rain dividing us.

◆   ◆   ◆

Later the narrator waits for Doodle to catch up. When Doodle doesn't come, the narrator goes back for him. Doodle is on the ground, dead. He has been bleeding from the mouth. His neck and shirt are bright red.

◆   ◆   ◆

I began to weep, and the tear-blurred vision in red before me looked very familiar. "Doodle!" I screamed above the pounding storm and threw my body to the earth above his. For a long long time, it seemed forever, I lay there crying, sheltering my fallen scarlet ibis from the <u>heresy</u> of rain.

◆ Reading Strategy

The narrator is angry, so he leaves Doodle behind in the rain. Would you do the same thing? Circle your answer.

yes          no

Explain your answer.

_____

_____

_____

◆ Stop to Reflect

The narrator sees Doodle on the ground. In what ways is Doodle now like the ibis?

_____

_____

_____

◆ Literary Analysis

The narrator is very upset over Doodle's death. Circle the words in the bracketed passage that show how he feels.

Mark the Text!

### Vocabulary Development

**deafening** (DEF uh ning) *adj.* extremely loud
**naught** (NAWT) *n.* nothing
**heresy** (HEHR uh see) *n.* idea that goes against a religion or set of beliefs

1. Write three words or phrases to describe Doodle as a baby.

   a. _____   b. _____   c. _____

2. What is the real reason the narrator wants Doodle to walk?

   _____

   _____

   _____

3. Why does Doodle's death make the narrator think of the scarlet ibis?

   _____

   _____

4. **Literary Analysis:** Put a check in front of each sentence that shows the story is told from first-person **point of view.**

   ____ He was born when I was six.

   ____ Everybody thought he was going to die except Aunt Nicey.

   ____ The baby was named William Armstrong.

   ____ I began to make plans to kill him.

   ____ The doctor said that he mustn't get too excited.

   ____ I did not know then that pride is a wonderful, terrible thing.

5. **Reading Strategy:** Doodle is weak, yet the narrator pushes him hard to walk, run, and swim. Imagine that you were the narrator. Read each sentence below. Then, complete the sentence which best states your feelings.

   ____ I would work Doodle hard because _____

   _____

   _____

   ____ I would not work Doodle hard because _____

   _____

# Writing

## Journal Entry

Put yourself in the place of the narrator in "The Scarlet Ibis." Write a journal entry that explains your feelings about Doodle. For each item below, write the answer you think Doodle's brother would write.

Describe the qualities of Doodle that made you feel happy.

_____

_____

_____

Describe one thing about Doodle that made you feel ashamed or embarrassed.

_____

_____

_____

Describe one thing Doodle did that got you angry or upset.

_____

_____

_____

Describe one strong feeling you had when Doodle died.

_____

_____

_____

Describe one thing you will miss most about Doodle.

_____

_____

_____

Use these notes to write a journal entry on a separate sheet of paper.

# The Necklace

## Guy de Maupassant

### Summary

This story takes place in nineteenth-century Paris. Madame Loisel is the unhappy wife of a middle class government official. She constantly dreams of being rich. Her husband is content, but he knows his wife is miserable. To please her, he obtains an invitation to an exclusive dinner party. Madame Loisel borrows a diamond necklace from a friend so she can look respectable at the party. After a wonderful evening, they are horrified to discover that the necklace is missing. Quietly, the Loisels buy a replacement for the diamond necklace. They can only afford this expensive purchase by taking out an enormous loan. It takes them ten years of saving to repay the loan. At that time, Madame Loisel finally tells the owner of the necklace what really happened. She is shocked when the owner tells her that the necklace she borrowed was inexpensive jewelry that contained only fake diamonds.

### Visual Summary

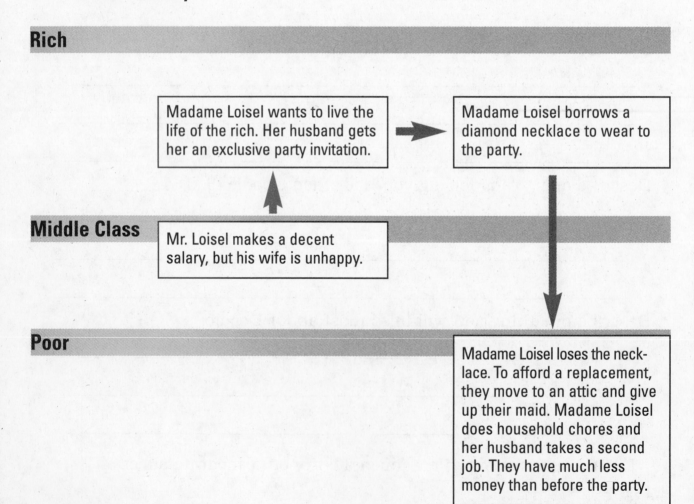

**Rich**

Madame Loisel wants to live the life of the rich. Her husband gets her an exclusive party invitation. → Madame Loisel borrows a diamond necklace to wear to the party.

**Middle Class**

Mr. Loisel makes a decent salary, but his wife is unhappy.

**Poor**

Madame Loisel loses the necklace. To afford a replacement, they move to an attic and give up their maid. Madame Loisel does household chores and her husband takes a second job. They have much less money than before the party.

## LITERARY ANALYSIS
### Theme

The **theme** of a story is its general message or lesson about life. In some stories, the theme is stated directly.

For example, the story might actually say, "If you're too greedy, you'll end up with nothing." In most stories, the theme is not stated directly. You need to figure it out for yourself. To figure out the theme, you must think about

- the characters' words.
- the characters' actions.
- the lesson you can learn from the story.

As you read "The Necklace," consider the woman's behavior. Consider why she marries her husband. Those details will help you find an important theme in the story.

## READING STRATEGY
### Drawing Conclusions

To find a theme, you must **draw conclusions** about characters and events. When you draw conclusions, you look at details and make decisions about what those details tell you about a character or an event. Follow these steps:

- Pay close attention to the characters. Notice what they are like. Notice what they do. Notice what happens to them as a result.
- Decide why characters behave as they do.
- Think what might have happened had a character acted differently.

A chart like this can help you draw conclusions in a story.

| Characters | What They're Like | What They Do | Conclusions |
|---|---|---|---|
| | | | |

# The Necklace

## Guy de Maupassant

She was one of those pretty, charming young women who are born, as if by an error of Fate, into a petty official's family. She had no <u>dowry</u>, no hopes, not the slightest chance of being appreciated, understood, loved, and married by a rich and distinguished man; so she slipped into marriage with a minor civil servant at the Ministry of Education.

◆　◆　◆

The woman is Madame Mathilde Loisel. She is bitter and unhappy about not being rich. She feels that she deserves a gracious, luxurious life and hates her old, plain home and life of poverty. She dreams of living in a fancy house with servants, beautiful furniture, and fine food. Her husband is content, but she constantly wishes for fancy clothes and jewels that others would envy.

◆　◆　◆

She had a rich friend, a schoolmate from the convent she had attended, but she didn't like to visit her because it always made her so miserable when she got home again. She would weep for whole days at a time from sorrow, regret, despair, and <u>distress</u>.

◆　◆　◆

---

### Vocabulary Development

**dowry** (DOW ree) *n.* property that a woman brings to her husband at marriage

**distress** (dis TRES) *n.* pain, suffering

Madame Loisel and her husband are invited to a fancy party at the Ministry of Education. Madame Loisel says she can't go. She has no nice dress to wear. Her husband gives her money to buy one. She gets a dress but is still unhappy. She complains that she has no jewelry to wear.

◆ ◆ ◆

"No . . . there's nothing more humiliating than to look poverty-stricken among a lot of rich women."

Then her husband exclaimed:

"Wait—you silly thing! Why don't you go and see Madame Forestier and ask her to lend you some jewelry. You certainly know her well enough for that, don't you think?"

She let out an awful cry.

"You're right. It never occurred to me."

◆ ◆ ◆

She visits her friend the next day and explains her problem. Madame Forestier is very understanding and gets her jewel case. She tells Madame Loisel to choose any piece.

Madame Loisel eagerly tries on several pieces of jewelry. Finally, she borrows a beautiful diamond necklace.

At the party, the pretty Madame Loisel is the center of attention. All the men want to dance with her.

◆ ◆ ◆

She danced enraptured—carried away, intoxicated with pleasure, forgetting everything in this triumph of her beauty and the glory of

---

### Vocabulary Development

**intoxicated** (in TOK suh kayt id) *adj.* wild with excitement or happiness

---

◆ **Reading Strategy**

Madame Loisel says she can't go to the party without a nice dress and jewelry. What does that tell you about her? **Draw a conclusion** and write it here:

_____

_____

_____

◆ **Read Fluently**

Read the bracketed passage aloud. Then circle the words that tell why Madame Loisel plans to visit Madame Forestier.

◆ **Stop to Reflect**

Madame Loisel is the center of attention at the party. What do you think is the reason?

_____

_____

_____

◆ **Reading Check**

Why is Madame Loisel so happy at the party? Write your answer on these lines.

_____

_____

her success, floating in a cloud of happiness formed by this <u>homage</u>, all this admiration, all the desires she had stirred up—by this victory so complete and so sweet to the heart of a woman.

◆ ◆ ◆

Back home, Madame Loisel discovers to her horror that the necklace is gone. The couple search their clothes but do not find it. Loisel retraces his steps outdoors. He still does not find the necklace.

◆ ◆ ◆

By the end of the week, they had lost all hope.

Loisel, who had aged five years, declared: "We'll have to replace the necklace."

The next day they took the case in which it had been kept and went to the jeweler whose name appeared inside it. He looked through his <u>ledgers</u>:

"I didn't sell this necklace, madame. I only supplied the case."

Then they went from one jeweler to the next, trying to find a necklace like the other, racking their memories, both of them sick with worry and distress.

◆ ◆ ◆

The couple finally find a necklace that looks like the lost one. It costs 36,000 francs. Loisel must borrow 18,000 francs to pay for it. Madame Loisel gives the necklace to Madame Forestier. She doesn't tell her where it really came from.

◆ **Reading Check**

Why does Madame Loisel become very upset upon returning home?

◆ **Reading Strategy**

You can assume that Madame Forestier didn't keep her necklace in its original case. Circle the words that help you **draw that conclusion**.

◆ **Stop to Reflect**

Why do you think Madame Loisel chooses not to tell the truth about the necklace?

_____

_____

_____

---

### Vocabulary Development

**homage** (HOM ij) *n.*  anything done to show respect or honor

**ledgers** (LEJ erz) *n.*  record books

---

Madame Loisel begins her life of poverty, since she knows the debt has to be paid. She does all the hated household chores. She lives like a working-class woman.

Her husband works a second job at night. After ten long, hard years, their debt is finally paid.

◆ ◆ ◆

Madame Loisel looked old now. She had become the sort of strong woman, hard and coarse, that one finds in poor families. <u>Disheveled</u>, her skirts askew, with reddened hands, she spoke in a loud voice, slopping water over the floors as she washed them. But sometimes, when her husband was at the office, she would sit down by the window and <u>muse</u> over that party long ago when she had been so beautiful, the <u>belle</u> of the ball.

[ How would things have turned out if she hadn't lost that necklace? Who could tell? How strange and <u>fickle</u> life is! How little it takes to make or break you!

◆ ◆ ◆

One day, Madame Loisel meets Madame Forestier in the street. Madame Forestier is shocked by how old she looks. Madame Loisel explains that it's all because of the diamond necklace she borrowed.

◆ ◆ ◆

◆ Literary Analysis

Madame Loisel gives up many things to pay back her debt. What lesson does this teach you about spending money?

_____

_____

_____

◆ Reading Check

How long does it take the Loisels to pay off their debt?

◆ Literary Analysis

Read the bracketed passage. What theme is stated directly in the passage?

_____

_____

_____

_____

---

### Vocabulary Development

**disheveled** (di SHEV uld) *adj.*  messy
**muse** (MYOOZ) *v.*  to think
**belle** (BEL) *n.*  a pretty woman
**fickle** (FIK ul) *adj.*  easily changing

◆ **Reading Strategy**

Madame Loisel now tells the truth about the necklace. What does that show about her?

_____

_____

_____

◆ **Literary Analysis**

The lost necklace had really been worth very little. What **theme**, or lesson, can be learned from this story?

_____

_____

_____

"You remember the diamond necklace you lent me to wear to the party at the Ministry?"

"Yes. What about it?"

"Well, I lost it."

"What are you talking about? You returned it to me."

"What I gave back to you was another one just like it. And it took us ten years to pay for it. You can imagine it wasn't easy for us, since we were quite poor . . . Anyway, I'm glad it's over and done with."

Madame Forestier stopped short.

"You say you bought a diamond necklace to replace that other one?"

"Yes. You didn't even notice then? They really were exactly alike."

And she smiled, full of a proud, simple joy.

Madame Forestier, profoundly moved, took Mathilde's hands in her own.

"Oh, my poor, poor Mathilde! Mine was false. It was worth five hundred francs at the most!"

---

**Vocabulary Development**

**profoundly** (proh FOWND lee) *adj.* deeply

---

1. Why is Madame Loisel unhappy in her marriage?

_____

_____

2. Name two things Madame Loisel needs in order to go to the party.

   a. _____ b. _____

3. Complete each sentence to tell how the Loisels save money to pay their debt.

   a. The Loisels get rid of their _____.

   b. The couple move into _____.

   c. Madame Loisel does all the _____.

   d. Her husband works at _____.

4. What surprise does Madame Forestier reveal at the end of the story?

   _____

5. **Literary Analysis:** Put a check mark in front of each sentence that you think is a **theme** of this story.

   ____ Money should not be the most important thing in your life.

   ____ Being jealous of others can lead to unhappiness.

   ____ Never borrow anything that you can not afford to repay.

   ____ People in the Ministry of Education are not to be trusted.

   ____ Something that looks costly may not be that valuable.

6. **Reading Strategy:** Why is Madame Loisel so happy at the party? **Draw a conclusion** based on what happens there.

   _____

   _____

# Listening and Speaking

## Improvisation

An **improvisation** is a scene that you make up as you go along. With a classmate, make up a conversation between Madame Loisel and her husband. Madame Loisel has just returned after meeting Madame Forestier ten years later. Now she's telling her husband about it. Make up something each character might say about each topic below.

**Topic:** Meeting Madame Forestier after ten years:

Madame Loisel: _____

_____.

Her Husband: _____

_____.

**Topic:** Madame Loisel's confession that she lost and replaced the necklace:

Madame Loisel: _____

_____.

Her Husband: _____

_____.

**Topic:** Madame Forestier's confession that the necklace was false:

Madame Loisel: _____

_____.

Her Husband: _____

_____.

You and your classmate should each take the role of one of the characters. Use the information above as a guide, but improvise, or make up more as you go along.

## Single Room, Earth View

### Sally Ride

### Summary

In this nonfiction account, Sally Ride tells about her space shuttle voyage. Ride is amazed by the way the Earth looks from space. Although she is 200 miles away, she is able to see many details on Earth. For example, she can see the different colors of the oceans, environmental problems such as air pollution, natural events like typhoons forming, and man-made structures like skyscrapers in New York City.

### Visual Summary

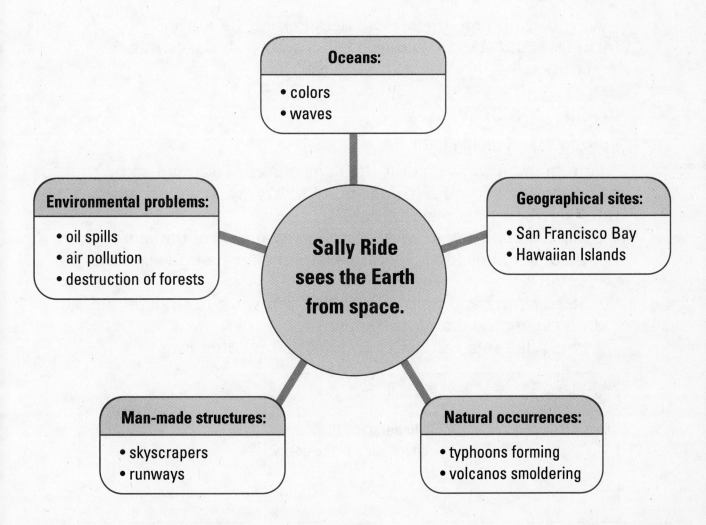

**Oceans:**
- colors
- waves

**Geographical sites:**
- San Francisco Bay
- Hawaiian Islands

**Environmental problems:**
- oil spills
- air pollution
- destruction of forests

**Sally Ride sees the Earth from space.**

**Natural occurrences:**
- typhoons forming
- volcanos smoldering

**Man-made structures:**
- skyscrapers
- runways

## LITERARY ANALYSIS

### Observation

An **observation** describes an event that the writer witnessed in person. It includes many details. It also uses exact and colorful words. The writer wants readers to feel as if they, too, are there watching.

Read this passage from "Single Room, Earth View."

> We could see smoke rising from fires that dotted the entire coast of Africa, and in the same orbit only moments later, ice floes jostling for position in the Antarctic. We could see the Ganges River dumping its murky, sediment-laden water into the Indian Ocean . . .

As you read, note the special details that the author includes. Find the colorful and exact words she uses in her description.

## READING STRATEGY

### Varying Your Reading Rate

You do not always read at the same speed. You read some things slowly and other things quickly. You **vary your reading rate** based on your reading goal.

- Read quickly if you want just a general idea of the material. Also, read quickly if you are searching for just one specific detail.
- Read slowly and more carefully if you want to understand all the material and its details.

A chart like this can help you choose a reading rate.

| Passage | Reading Goal | Rate |
| --- | --- | --- |
| First paragraph | To understand the general idea of the essay | fast |

# Single Room, Earth View
## Sally Ride

Sally Ride says that people often ask her what it is like to travel in space. It is not easy for her to answer. Earth looks much different from far away than from close up.

◆ ◆ ◆

And the difference is enormous: Spaceflight moves the traveler another giant step farther away. Eight and one-half thunderous minutes after launch, an astronaut is orbiting high above the Earth, suddenly able to watch typhoons form, volcanoes smolder, and meteors streak through the atmosphere below.

◆ ◆ ◆

During her space trip, Ride circled the Earth every 90 minutes. She had to look out the window all the time to know where she was. If she looked away for too long, she could have missed an entire continent.

◆ ◆ ◆

We could see smoke rising from fires that dotted the entire coast of Africa, and in the same orbit only moments later, ice floes[1] jostling for position in the Antarctic. We could see the Ganges River dumping its murky, sediment-laden[2] water into the Indian Ocean and watch ominous hurricane clouds expanding and rising like biscuits in the oven of the Caribbean.

◆ ◆ ◆

### Vocabulary Development

**jostling** (JOS ling) *v.* pushing
**murky** (MUHR kee) *adj.* dark
**ominous** (OM uh nus) *adj.* threatening

1. **ice floes** (ĪS flohz) *n.* pieces of floating ice.
2. **sediment-laden** (SED uh ment LAY duhn) *adj.* filled with sand that settles to the bottom of the water.

---

### ◆ Reading Strategy

At what **rate** would you read to learn the general topic of the article? Circle your answer.

slow      fast

Why? _____

_____

### ◆ Literary Analysis

Circle three things that Ride sees after 8 1/2 minutes in space.

### ◆ Reading Check

Why must Ride keep looking out the window at all times? Write your answer on these lines.

_____

_____

_____

### ◆ Literary Analysis

In the bracketed passage, underline five places that Ride observes.

From space, Ride saw mountains and rivers. The view helped her to imagine how those features were formed. It also helped her to appreciate the wonders of nature.

♦   ♦   ♦

One day, as I scanned the sandy expanse of Northern Africa, I couldn't find any of the familiar landmarks—colorful outcroppings of rock in Chad, irrigated patches of the Sahara. Then I realized they were <u>obscured</u> by a huge dust storm, a cloud of sand that enveloped the continent from Morocco to the Sudan.

♦   ♦   ♦

Ride describes many places on Earth that she recognized from space. She also describes signs of pollution that she saw.

♦   ♦   ♦

Oil slicks <u>glisten</u> on the surface of the Persian Gulf, patches of pollution-damaged trees dot the forests of central Europe. Some cities look out of focus, and their colors <u>muted</u>, when viewed through a pollutant haze. Not surprisingly, the effects are more noticeable now than they were a decade ago.

♦   ♦   ♦

An astronaut who flew in 1973 and in 1983 did say there was a visible difference after ten years.

Ride explains that cameras on the space shuttle take pictures of the pollution. Other equipment measures the pollution. The information helps scientists understand how pollution affects the Earth.

♦   ♦   ♦

### Vocabulary Development

**obscured** (ub SKYOORD) *adj.* blocked from view
**glisten** (GLIS un) *v.* shine
**muted** (MYOOT id) *adj.* weaker

Most of Earth's surface is covered with water, and at first glance it all looks the same: blue. But with the right lighting conditions and a couple of orbits of practice, it's possible to make out the intricate patterns in the oceans—<u>eddies</u> and spirals become visible because of the <u>subtle</u> differences in water color or <u>reflectivity</u>.

◆ ◆ ◆

Cameras in space take pictures of the oceans. The photos help scientists study the sea. When the lighting was right, Ride could see ships and their travel paths.

Ride says she could also view the Earth in darkness during part of each orbit.

◆ ◆ ◆

The lights of cities sparkle; on nights when there was no moon, it was difficult for me to tell the Earth from the sky—the twinkling lights could be stars or they could be small cities. On one nighttime pass from Cuba to Nova Scotia, the entire East Coast of the United States appeared in twinkling outline.

When the moon is full, it casts an <u>eerie</u> light on the Earth. In its light, we see ghostly clouds and bright reflections on the water.

◆ ◆ ◆

To Ride, the most amazing sight from space may have been lightning. It looked like bursting balls of light, like a fireworks show. Another amazing sight was sunrise. Blue and orange bands would streak along the horizon. The drama is too great to describe. Ride says that a trip into space is like nothing you can experience on Earth.

---

### Vocabulary Development

**eddies** (ED eez) *n.* round water movements
**subtle** (SUT el) *adj.* not obvious
**reflectivity** (ri flek TIV uh tee) *n.* shining light
**eerie** (IHR ee) *adj.* mysterious

◆ **Reading Check**

What are two things Ride can see in the ocean with the right lighting? Circle the words that tell you.

◆ **Read Fluently**

Read the bracketed passage aloud. Then tell what was difficult for Ride on nights with no moon.

_____

_____

_____

◆ **Literary Analysis**

Circle the words that Ride uses to describe lightning. Draw a line under the words she uses to describe sunrise.

Do you think Ride enjoyed the view? _____

Why, or why not?

_____

_____

1. Why does Ride think it's hard to describe a space trip?

_____

_____

_____

2. Why do some cities look fuzzy and weakly colored to Ride?

_____

_____

_____

3. What does Ride feel are the two most amazing sights from space?

a. _____  b. _____

4. **Literary Analysis:** What event does Sally Ride describe in her observation?

_____

5. **Literary Analysis:** Ride describes many sights and tells where they are. Complete the list in this chart.

| What Ride Sees | Where She Sees It |
| --- | --- |
| smoke rising from fires | Africa |
| ice floes | |
| hurricane clouds | |
| dust storm | |
| oil slicks | |

6. **Reading Strategy:** At what rate would you read to learn about all the sights that Ride describes?

_____

# Writing

## Observation from Space

Imagine that you are an astronaut in space. Write an observation that describes the event. Follow these steps:

First, decide exactly where you are in space. Check one of these sentences or make up your own.

____ I am riding in a spaceship around the Earth.

____ I am walking on the moon.

____ I am _____

Next, name two amazing things that you see. Tell what each one looks like:

1. First thing I see: _____

_____

What it looks like: _____

_____

2. Second thing I see: _____

_____

What it looks like: _____

_____

Now, describe one activity that you do in space. Use colorful and exact words.

_____

_____

_____

Last, describe your feelings about the whole event.

_____

_____

_____

# On Summer

## Lorraine Hansberry

## Summary

The author of "On Summer" explains that as a young person, summer was not her favorite season. She thought the season was too intense; with bright, long days, loud noises, and other unpleasant aspects. She preferred the sadness of autumn, and the bleakness of winter, to summer's heat and glare. Over time, her opinion of summer changed. She came to associate summer with strong-willed people—her grandmother and a woman she met one summer in Maine who was fighting cancer.

## Visual Summary

**Feelings about the seasons when young**

**Realizations about the seasons when older**

| | |
|---|---|
| **Spring**<br>She is connected to spring because she was born in May. | **Spring**<br>It can provide false promises. |
| **Winter**<br>She admires its cold distance as an older child. | **Winter**<br>It shuts dying people up inside. |
| **Autumn**<br>As a teenager, she loves its sadness. | **Autumn**<br>Its sadness can seem artificial. |
| **Summer**<br>Summer is too hot and loud, and the days are too long. Summer seems like a mistake. | **Summer**<br>It offers life at its fullest. |

**What happens to her in the summer**

- She enjoys sleeping outside.
- She meets her grandmother.
- She visits many places.
- She meets a woman in Maine whom she admires. This woman loves summer. Seeing summer through this woman's eyes helps the author appreciate summer.

## LITERARY ANALYSIS

### Persuasive Essay

A **persuasive essay** is a short piece of nonfiction. The writer expresses a personal opinion about a topic. The writer wants you to agree with the opinion. Therefore, many reasons and examples are offered to support the opinion.

In "On Summer," Lorraine Hansberry wants the reader to understand why she once disliked summer.

> . . . my earliest memory of anything at all is of waking up in a darkened room where I had been put to bed for a nap on a summer's afternoon, and feeling very, very hot. I acutely disliked the feeling then and retained the bias for years.

As you read the essay, follow these steps:
- Look for the writer's opinion about the topic.
- Find reasons and examples that explain the writer's opinion.
- Decide if you agree with the writer's opinion.

## READING STRATEGY

### Identifying the Author's Attitude

In a persuasive essay, the author shows a personal feeling, or **attitude,** toward the subject. For example, the author's attitude might be positive and supportive; or, the attitude might be negative and suspicious.

You can **identify the author's attitude** by paying attention to details.
- Note how the author describes the subject.
- Notice the arguments that the author uses to persuade you to agree.
- Consider whether the arguments support the subject or argue against it.

Use a chart like this to help you identify the author's attitude.

| Words That Describe Subject | Attitude |
| --- | --- |
|  |  |
|  |  |

# On Summer
## Lorraine Hansberry

Hansberry explains that it took her many years to learn to like summer. As a child, she liked the other seasons, but not summer.

♦ ♦ ♦

In fact, my earliest memory of anything at all is of waking up in a darkened room where I had been put to bed for a nap on a summer's afternoon, and feeling very, very hot. I <u>acutely</u> disliked the feeling then and <u>retained</u> the <u>bias</u> for years. It had originally been a matter of heat but, over the years, I came actively to associate displeasure with most of the usually celebrated natural features and social by-products of the season: the too-grainy texture of sand; the <u>too-cold coldness</u> of the various waters we constantly try to escape into, and the icky-perspiry feeling of bathing caps.

♦ ♦ ♦

Hansberry says summer days in Chicago were too long and too sunny for her. During the day she played street games. At night she sat on the back porch. On very hot nights her family slept in the park.

One summer, Hansberry visited her grandmother in Tennessee. During the trip, she learned how her grandfather had been a slave. When she met her grandmother, she was shocked by how old she looked. But her grandmother liked to talk, and she made delicious cupcakes.

As an adult, Hansberry spent her summers in beautiful places. One summer she stayed at a

---

♦ **Literary Analysis**

What is Hansberry's opinion of summer as a child?

_____

_____

_____

♦ **Reading Strategy**

Circle three words or phrases in the bracketed passage that show the **author's attitude** toward summer.

♦ **Literary Analysis**

List two reasons why Hansberry dislikes summer.

(a) _____

_____

(b) _____

_____

♦ **Reading Check**

What does Hansberry like about her grandmother? Draw a box around the words that tell you.

---

### Vocabulary Development

**acutely** (uh KYOOT lee) *adv.* in an extreme way
**retained** (ri TAYND) *v.* kept
**bias** (BĪ us) *n.* a feeling for or against something

lodge on the coast of Maine. There, she met a brave woman who was dying of cancer.

◆ ◆ ◆

She had, characteristically, just written a book and taken up painting. She had also been of radical viewpoint all her life; one of those people who energetically believe that the world can be changed for the better and spend their lives trying to do just that.

◆ ◆ ◆

Hansberry was amazed by the dying woman's courage. She spoke with her a lot. She also watched as the woman sat quietly and looked out at the bay.

◆ ◆ ◆

Her face softened with love of all that beauty and, watching her, I wished with all my power what I knew that she was wishing: that she might live to see at least one more *summer*. Through her eyes I finally gained the sense of what it might mean; more than the coming autumn with its <u>pretentious</u> <u>melancholy</u>; more than an <u>austere</u> and silent winter which must shut dying people in for precious months; more even than the <u>frivolous</u> spring, too full of too many false promises, would be the gift of another summer with its stark and intimate assertion of neither birth nor death but life at the <u>apex</u>; with the gentlest nights and, above all, the longest days.

I heard later that she did live to see another summer. And I have retained my respect for the noblest of the seasons.

---

### Vocabulary Development

**pretentious** (pri TEN shus) *adj.* pretending to be more important than it really is

**melancholy** (MEL un kol ee) *n.* sadness

**austere** (aw STEER) *adj.* very plain

**frivolous** (FRIV uh lus) *adj.* not important

**apex** (AY peks) *n.* the highest point

---

◆ **Stop to Reflect**

How is summer different for Hansberry when she is an adult than when she is a child?

_____

_____

_____

_____

_____

◆ **Reading Strategy**

Circle the sentence in the bracketed passage that shows the **author's attitude** toward the dying woman.

◆ **Read Fluently**

Read aloud the sentence that begins "Her face softened." Then underline the words that tell what Hansberry wishes for the woman.

◆ **Literary Analysis**

How does Hansberry's opinion of summer change by the end of her **persuasive essay?**

_____

_____

1. What does Hansberry wish for the dying woman?

_____

_____

_____

2. Why does Hansberry's opinion of summer change as she gets older?

_____

_____

_____

3. **Literary Analysis:** List three reasons why Hansberry doesn't like summer when she is a child.

a. _____

b. _____

c. _____

4. **Reading Strategy:** What is the **author's attitude** toward her grandmother?

_____

_____

_____

5. **Reading Strategy:** What is the **author's attitude** toward the woman dying of cancer? _____

_____

_____

6. **Reading Strategy:** Complete the second column of the chart with words that Hansberry uses, as an adult, to describe each season. In the third column use your own words to explain Hansberry's ideas. Then, in the fourth column, circle a + or − to show whether these words show a positive or negative attitude.

| Season | Descriptive Words | My Explanation | +/− |
|---|---|---|---|
| autumn | pretentious melancholy | a fake sadness | + ⊖ |
| winter | | | + − |
| spring | | | + − |
| summer | | | + − |

# Writing

## Essay on Summer

Write an essay on summer. Explain why you agree or disagree with Hansberry's opinions of summer. Give reasons to support your views. Use your own summer experiences as reasons. Discuss these points:

1. As a child, Hansberry thought summer days were too hot.

   Do you agree or disagree? _____ Explain. _____

   _____

2. As a child, Hansberry thought summer water felt too cold.

   Do you agree or disagree? _____ Explain. _____

   _____

3. As an adult, Hansberry thought summer was a good time to visit new places.

   Do you agree or disagree? _____ Explain. _____

   _____

4. As an adult, Hansberry thought summer nights were gentle.

   Do you agree or disagree? _____ Explain. _____

   _____

# A Celebration of Grandfathers

## Rudolfo A. Anaya

## Summary

In "A Celebration of Grandfathers," the author remembers the quiet ways of the "old ones" of his grandfather's generation. They understood the seasons, worked hard, appreciated the land in which they lived, and had a deep inner strength. The author believes today's world puts too much emphasis on youth and ignores the reality of aging. He urges us to understand and respect our grandparents.

## Visual Summary

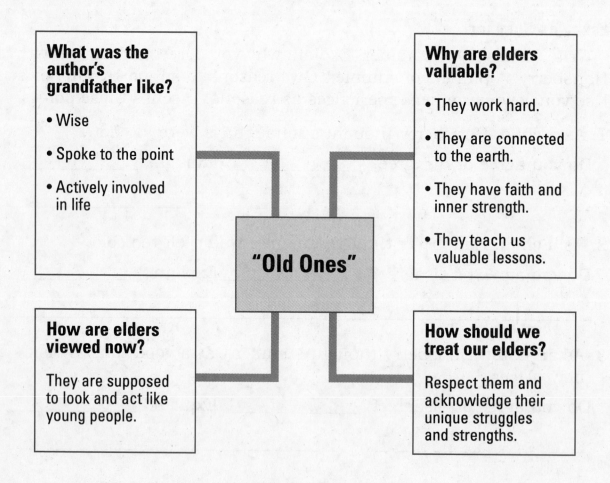

**What was the author's grandfather like?**

- Wise

- Spoke to the point

- Actively involved in life

**Why are elders valuable?**

- They work hard.

- They are connected to the earth.

- They have faith and inner strength.

- They teach us valuable lessons.

**"Old Ones"**

**How are elders viewed now?**

They are supposed to look and act like young people.

**How should we treat our elders?**

Respect them and acknowledge their unique struggles and strengths.

## LITERARY ANALYSIS

### Reflective Essay

A **reflective essay** is a short piece of nonfiction. The writer shares personal feelings about a topic that is special for him or her.

In "A Celebration of Grandfathers," Rudolfo Anaya describes his feelings about his grandfather and others like him. He does more than just offer facts about his grandfather. He shares his personal views and opinions as well. Read this passage:

> My grandfather touched me, looked up into the sky and whispered, "Pray for rain." . . . He felt connected to the cycles that brought the rain or kept it from us.

As you read the essay, follow these steps:

- Look for facts that the writer presents.
- Look for the author's personal views and opinions.
- Find details that explain the author's views and opinions.

## READING STRATEGY

### Identifying the Author's Attitude

In a reflective essay, the author shows a personal feeling, or **attitude**, toward the subject. For example, the author's attitude might be loving and respectful. Or, the attitude might be angry and resentful.

You can **identify the author's attitude** by paying attention to details.

- Notice how the author describes the subject.
- Notice the words he uses.
- Think about whether the author makes the subject look good or bad. Look at this example from the text:

| Details About His Grandfather | Anaya's Attitude |
|---|---|
| He felt connected to the cycles that brought the rain or kept it from us. → | Respect for his grandfather's connection to nature |

# A Celebration of Grandfathers
## Rudolfo A. Anaya

**♦ Literary Analysis**

Circle the words in the bracketed passage that express the author's personal feelings about old people.

"Buenos dias le de Dios, abuelo."[1] God give you a good day, grandfather. This is how I was taught as a child to greet my grandfather, or any grown person. It was a greeting of respect, a cultural value to be passed on from generation to generation, this respect for the old ones.

The old people I remember from my childhood were strong in their beliefs, and as we lived daily with them we learned a wise path of life to follow. They had something important to share with the young, and when they spoke the young listened.

♦     ♦     ♦

**♦ Stop to Reflect**

The old people help each other in their work and lives. What do their actions tell you about them? Write your ideas on these lines.

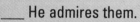
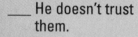
_____

_____

_____

Anaya says that the old people had been farmers all their lives. Therefore, they understood the value of growth. They worked together and helped each other.

♦     ♦     ♦

They shared good times and hard times. They helped each other through the epidemics and the personal tragedies, and they shared what little they had when the hot winds burned the land and no rain came. They learned that to survive one had to share in the process of life.

♦     ♦     ♦

**♦ Reading Strategy**

What is the **author's attitude** toward old people? Check one.

____ He admires them.

____ He doesn't trust them.

Underline one sentence from the essay to support your answer.

The old people had great faith, says Anaya. They prayed sincerely. They celebrated good times together. They taught their traditions to the next generation, so their ways of life would not be lost.

---

### Vocabulary Development

**epidemics** (ep uh DEM iks) *n.* wide-spread diseases

---

1. **Buenos dias le de Dios, abuelo** (BWAY nuhs DEE ahs lay day DEE ohs ah BWAY loh).

For Anaya, time seems to stand still when he meets the old people. He feels their strength. He then recalls his own grandfather. As a child, Anaya spent summers on his farm. The experience affected him deeply.

◆ ◆ ◆

I remember once, while out hoeing the fields, I came upon an anthill, and before I knew it I was badly bitten. After he had covered my <u>welts</u> with the cool mud from the irrigation ditch, my grandfather calmly said: "Know where you stand." That is the way he spoke, in short phrases, to the point.

One very dry summer, the river dried to a trickle, there was no water for the fields. The young plants <u>withered</u> and died. In my sadness and with the impulses of youth I said, "I wish it would rain!" My grandfather touched me, looked up into the sky and whispered, "Pray for rain." In his language there was a difference. He felt connected to the cycles that brought the rain or kept it from us. His prayer was a meaningful action, because he was a participant with the forces that filled our world, he was not a bystander.

◆ ◆ ◆

Anaya recalls how his grandfather drove his farm crops to market. Anaya sat next to him in the wagon. He felt honored to share in his grandfather's way of life. But today's children don't want to take part in that past, says Anaya. They ignore the old values. Our link to the past is threatened.

◆ ◆ ◆

## Literary Analysis

Circle the words in the bracketed passage that reveal Anaya's personal feelings.

## Stop to Reflect

What does the grandfather mean when he says "Know where you stand"?

_____

_____

_____

## Reading Strategy

Anaya admires his grandfather for the way he prays. Circle the words that show the **author's attitude.**

## Reading Check

What does Anaya say is different about children today than in the past?

_____

_____

_____

## Vocabulary Development

**welts** (WELTZ) *n.* marks on the skin from a blow or a bite

**withered** (with urd) *v.* dried up

We need to know where we stand. We need to speak softly and respect others, and to share what we have. We need to pray not for material gain, but for rain for the fields, for the sun to nurture growth, for nights in which we can sleep in peace, and for a harvest in which everyone can share. Simple lessons from a simple man. These lessons he learned from his past which was as deep and strong as the currents of the river of life, a life which could be stronger than death.

◆ ◆ ◆

Anaya recalls his grandfather just before his death at age 94. He had grown very weak. He needed much care. Anaya says that youth need patience to deal with the elderly. American society celebrates youth but not old age. TV ads show old people as healthy and lively, but that's not the way it really is with many of the elderly.

◆ ◆ ◆

Real life takes into account the natural cycle of growth and change. My grandfather pointed to the leaves falling from the tree. So time brings with its transformation the often painful, wearing-down process. Vision blurs, health wanes; even the act of walking carries with it the painful reminder of the autumn of life. But this process is something to be faced, not something to be hidden away by false images.

◆ ◆ ◆

As an adult, Anaya returns to visit his grandfather's land. He fondly remembers his grandfather. He says everyone today should show respect and kindness to the elderly.

---

**Vocabulary Development**

**transformation** (tranz for MAY shun) *n.* change

1. Write three words that Rudolfo Anaya might use to describe old people?

   a. _____   b. _____   c. _____

2. What does Anaya say is the difference between youth today and youth of the past?

   _____

   _____

3. **Literary Analysis:** Why does Anaya call his **reflective essay** "A Celebration of Grandfathers"?

   _____

4. **Reading Strategy:** Complete the chart to show how the **author's attitudes** are supported with examples.

| Author's Attitude Toward His Grandfather | Supporting Example |
|---|---|
| He is sincere. | He says, "Pray for rain." |
| He is hard-working. | |
| He is wise. | |
| He is caring. | |

5. **Reading Strategy:** Check the **attitudes** that Anaya expresses in his essay.

   ____ Young people deserve more respect today.

   ____ Young people should listen more to old people.

   ____ Young people can teach old people valuable lessons.

   ____ Young people need patience to deal with old people.

# Listening and Speaking

**Interview**

Conduct an interview with an elderly person. You might choose your grandparent or someone else you know. Prepare a list of questions in advance. Jot down the answers you receive during the interview. Follow these steps:

1. Ask about the person's schooling.
Your question:

_____

The person's reply:

_____

_____

2. Ask about the person's work or career.
Your question:

_____

The person's reply:

_____

_____

3. Ask about the person's attitude toward today's youth.
Your question:

_____

The person's reply:

_____

_____

4. Ask about the person's attitude toward getting older.
Your question:

_____

The person's reply:

_____

_____

Later, present some of the information you learned from the interview to a small group of classmates.

# The Tragedy of Romeo and Juliet, *Act II, Scene ii*

## William Shakespeare

## Summary

In this scene, Romeo visits Juliet under cover of darkness. He calls to Juliet from below her window and speaks of his love for her. Juliet says it is dangerous for Romeo to visit her, since their families are bitter enemies. If any member of her family spots him, he will be killed. They both agree that their love is stronger than their families' hatred. Juliet wants proof that Romeo's love will last. Romeo leaves her with the promise that he will send word the next day about his plans to marry her. The nurse calls Juliet, but she and Romeo find it hard to say good night. Finally, they separate. Juliet goes inside, and Romeo goes to find the friar to ask for his help in arranging the marriage.

## Visual Summary

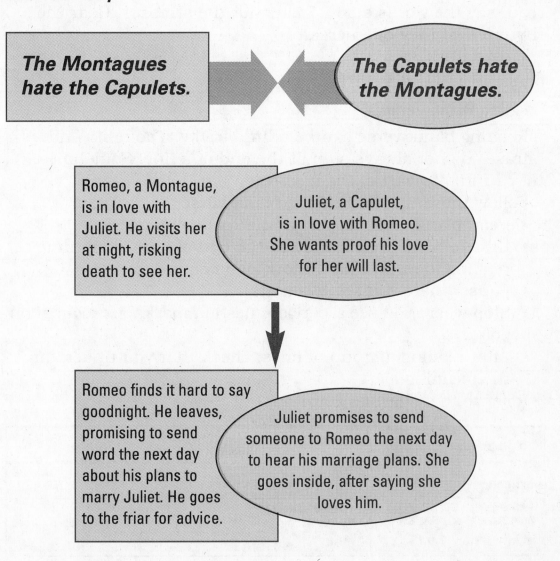

The Montagues hate the Capulets.

The Capulets hate the Montagues.

Romeo, a Montague, is in love with Juliet. He visits her at night, risking death to see her.

Juliet, a Capulet, is in love with Romeo. She wants proof his love for her will last.

Romeo finds it hard to say goodnight. He leaves, promising to send word the next day about his plans to marry Juliet. He goes to the friar for advice.

Juliet promises to send someone to Romeo the next day to hear his marriage plans. She goes inside, after saying she loves him.

## LITERARY ANALYSIS

### Blank Verse

**Blank verse** is poetry with these features:
- Each line has ten syllables.
- Every second syllable is stressed in each line.
- The words at the ends of the lines don't rhyme.

Read aloud these lines from Act II Scene ii of *The Tragedy of Romeo and Juliet.* Listen for the stressed syllables. They are underlined in the text.

> But <u>soft</u>! What <u>light</u> through <u>yonder window breaks</u>?
> It <u>is</u> the <u>East</u>, and <u>Juliet is</u> the <u>sun</u>!

Much of *Romeo and Juliet* is written in blank verse. As you read, say the words aloud. Listen for the stresses. Hear the rhythm that they often create.

## READING STRATEGY

### Reading Blank Verse

Reading blank verse can be a little tricky. Thoughts and phrases do not always stop at the end of a line. Sometimes, they run on to part of the next line.

Follow these tips for **reading blank verse:**
- Read blank verse as you would read sentences.
- If there is no punctuation at the end of a line, continue reading the next line without pausing.
- Pause where you see a comma.
- Stop where you see a period, question mark, or exclamation point.
- After reading a group of lines, check that you understand the meaning.

Refer to this chart as you read.

| no punctuation | keep reading |
|---|---|
| comma | pause |
| period, question mark, exclamation point | stop |

# The Tragedy of Romeo and Juliet
## *Act II Scene ii*
### William Shakespeare

In Act I, Romeo and Juliet meet. They fall in love immediately. But their families, the Montagues and Capulets, hate each other.

In Act II Scene ii, Romeo stands in the orchard outside Juliet's home. She appears at her balcony window above him.

◆ ◆ ◆

ROMEO. But soft![1] What light through yonder
    window breaks?
It is the East, and Juliet is the sun!
Arise, fair sun, and kill the envious moon,
Who is already sick and pale with grief
That thou her maid art far more fair
    than she.

◆ ◆ ◆

Juliet steps out onto her balcony. She does not see Romeo in the dark. He is tempted to speak to her, but he is too shy. Instead he praises her eyes and cheek. He says they shine like the brightest stars. Juliet then declares her love for Romeo. She does not know that Romeo is listening below.

◆ ◆ ◆

JULIET. O Romeo, Romeo! Wherefore art thou
    Romeo?[2]
Deny thy father and refuse thy name;
Or, if thou wilt not, be but sworn my love,
And I'll no longer be a Capulet.

◆ ◆ ◆

◆ **Reading Check**

How do Romeo's and Juliet's families feel about each other?

_____

_____

◆ **Literary Analysis**

Romeo's first speech is in **blank verse.** Circle each stressed syllable in the bracketed passage.

◆ **Reading Check**

Why is Juliet unaware that Romeo is listening to her?

_____

_____

_____

◆ **Reading Strategy**

Read aloud Juliet's first speech. Circle the commas that show where to pause. Draw a line under each punctuation mark that shows where to stop.

---

1. **soft** quiet.
2. **Wherefore...Romeo?** Why must you be Romeo, of the enemy family of Montague?

**Stop to Reflect**

Romeo and Juliet are willing to give up their own names for the sake of love. What does that show about their feelings for each other?

_____

_____

_____

**Reading Strategy**

Read aloud Romeo's speech that begins "By a name." Draw a circle around the word that ends the first sentence.

**Reading Check**

Why is it dangerous for Romeo to be near Juliet's family?

_____

_____

_____

Romeo remains silent. Juliet says she'll be his if he gives up his name. He now decides to speak out to her.

◆ ◆ ◆

**ROMEO.**          I take thee at thy word.
  Call me but love, and I'll be new baptized;
  <u>Henceforth</u> I never will be Romeo.
**JULIET.** What man art thou, thus <u>bescreened</u> in night,
  So stumblest on my counsel?³
**ROMEO.**               By a name
  I know not how to tell thee who I am.
  My name, dear saint, is hateful to myself
  Because it is an enemy to thee.
  Had I it written, I would tear the word.

◆ ◆ ◆

Juliet realizes that she is speaking to Romeo. She says it's dangerous for him to be near her family. Romeo says that no walls or danger could stop his love. Juliet asks Romeo to declare his love for her.

◆ ◆ ◆

**ROMEO.** Lady, by yonder blessed moon I vow,
  That tips with silver all these fruit-tree
    tops—
**JULIET.** O, swear not by the moon, th'
                    <u>inconstant</u> moon,
  That monthly changes in her circle orb,
  Lest that thy love prove likewise <u>variable</u>.

---

### Vocabulary Development

**henceforth** (HENS forth) _adv._ from now on
**bescreened** (bee SKREEND) _adj._ hidden
**inconstant** (in KON stunt) _adj._ changing
**variable** (VAR ee uh bul) _adj._ changing

---

3. **So...counsel** who has overheard my secret thoughts.

**ROMEO.** What shall I swear by?

**JULIET.**                    Do not swear at all;
  Or if thou wilt, swear by thy gracious self,
  Which is the god of my idolatry,
  And I'll believe thee.

◆   ◆   ◆

    Juliet worries that their love may be moving too fast. She fears it will end as quickly as it began. Juliet wants to say good-night, but she has a hard time leaving Romeo. Her Nurse calls to her. Juliet tells Romeo to wait so she can talk to him some more. She goes inside but soon returns.

◆   ◆   ◆

**JULIET.** Three words, dear Romeo, and good
    night indeed.
  If that thy bent[4] of love be honorable,
  Thy purpose marriage, send me word
    tomorrow,
  By one that I'll <u>procure</u> to come to thee,
  Where and what time thou wilt perform
    the rite;
  And all my fortunes at thy foot I'll lay
  And follow thee my lord throughout the
    world.

◆   ◆   ◆

    The Nurse calls to Juliet again. Juliet goes inside. She soon returns to speak to Romeo one last time. She asks what time she should send her messenger tomorrow. He says to do it by nine o'clock. The lovers hate to part, but they must now do so.

◆   ◆   ◆

---

◆ **Literary Analysis**

A ten-syllable line of **blank verse** may be shared by two speakers. Circle Romeo's question and Juliet's answer that total ten syllables. Draw a line under the five stressed syllables.

◆ **Reading Check**

Why is it hard for Juliet to say goodnight to Romeo?

_____

_____

_____

◆ **Read Fluently**

Read Juliet's speech that begins "Three words." Circle the words that tell what news the messenger is supposed to bring.

_____

_____

_____

◆ **Reading Check**

Romeo and Juliet speak for one last time. Circle the words in the bracketed passage that tell what they discuss.

---

**Vocabulary Development**

**procure** (proh KYOOR) *v.* get

---

4. **thy bent** your purpose.

Read Juliet's speech that starts "'Tis almost morning." Circle each stressed syllable.

◆ Reading Strategy

Read Juliet's final speech in the bracketed passage. Should you pause after the words "Parting is such sweet sorrow"? Circle one.

yes            no

Explain your answer.

_____

_____

_____

JULIET. 'Tis almost morning. I would have thee
        gone—
And yet no farther than a wanton's[5] bird,
That lets it hop a little from his hand,
Like a poor prisoner in his twisted gyves,[6]
And with a silken thread plucks it back
        again,
So loving-jealous of his liberty.
ROMEO. I would[7] I were thy bird.
JULIET.                         Sweet, so would I.
Yet I should kill thee with much cherishing.
Good night, good night! Parting is such
        sweet sorrow
That I shall say good night till it be morrow.
        [*Exit.*]
        ◆   ◆   ◆

Romeo stands alone in the dark for a moment. He wishes Juliet a good night's sleep. Then he leaves to tell his priest about Juliet. He plans to ask the priest for help.

---

5. **wanton's** spoiled, playful child's.
6. **gyves** (JIVEZ) chains.
7. **would** wish.

1. Why does Romeo hide when he goes to see Juliet?

_____

_____

2. What are Romeo and Juliet willing to give up in order to be together?

_____

_____

3. What plan does Juliet make with Romeo?

_____

_____

4. To whom does Romeo go for help?

_____

_____

5. **Literary Analysis:** Read the following lines of **blank verse.** Circle each stressed syllable.

> JULIET. Three words, dear Romeo, and good night indeed.
> If that thy bent of love be honorable,
> Thy purpose marriage, send me word tomorrow,
> By one that I'll procure to come to thee,
> Where and what time thou wilt perform the rite;
> And all my fortunes at thy foot I'll lay
> And follow thee my lord throughout the world.

6. **Reading Strategy:** Read aloud the following lines. Circle the punctuation marks that tell you to pause. Draw a line under the punctuation marks that tell you to stop.

> ROMEO. But soft! What light through yonder window breaks?
> It is the East, and Juliet is the sun!
> Arise, fair sun, and kill the envious moon,
> Who is already sick and pale with grief
> That thou her maid art far more fair than she.

# Writing

## Adaptation

An **adaptation** is a retelling of a story, with changes made to reflect a different time or place. Write an adaptation of the balcony scene between Romeo and Juliet. Imagine the scene took place today in your city or town. Have the characters speak in modern English. Follow these steps:

Write something that Romeo says while hiding in the dark.

Romeo: _____

_____

_____

Write something that Juliet says, not knowing Romeo is there.

Juliet: _____

_____

_____

Write what Romeo and Juliet say to each other about their love.

Romeo: _____

_____

Juliet: _____

_____

Write what Romeo and Juliet say when planning what to do next.

Romeo: _____

_____

_____

Juliet: _____

_____

_____

# Memory
## Margaret Walker

### Summary

In this poem, Margaret Walker describes a certain type of rainy day in the city. She presents images of cold, windy, rainy days that depress people's spirits. The weather brings out the worst in people, who appear hurt, confused, and angry because of the rain. These are the same miserable people the poet sees alone at work or in their apartment buildings.

### Visual Summary

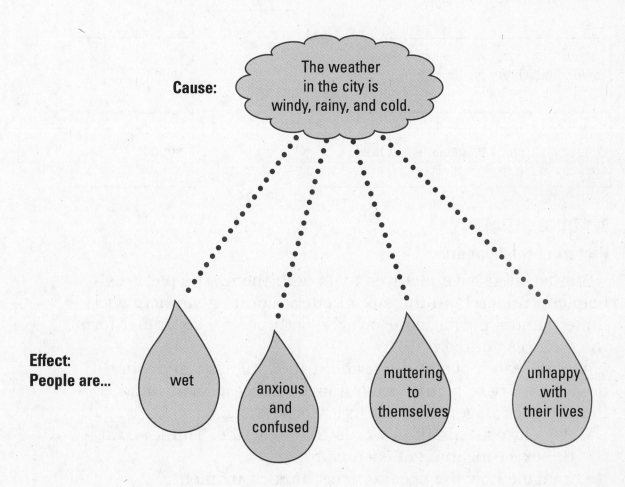

**Cause:** The weather in the city is windy, rainy, and cold.

**Effect:
People are...** wet | anxious and confused | muttering to themselves | unhappy with their lives

## LITERARY ANALYSIS

### Imagery

**Imagery** is language that forms a picture in the reader's mind. The picture, or **image**, may appeal to any of the five senses. These senses are sight, sound, taste, smell, and touch.

As you read, use a chart like this to track language that appeals to the five senses.

| Language | Sense |
|---|---|
| wind-swept streets of cities | sight |
| cold and blustery nights | touch |
| ghostly marching on pavement stones | sound |

## READING STRATEGY

### Picturing the Imagery

Stories often have pictures to go with them. The pictures help you understand the story better. Pictures can help you understand a poem, too. However, with poetry, you must form the pictures yourself.

As you read a poem, think about the language and what it describes. Try to picture each image clearly in your mind. **Picture the imagery** in a poem in these ways:

- Pay close attention to words that describe. Think about the exact meaning of each word.
- Imagine how the speaker feels at each moment.
- Remember not just to *see* an image. Also *hear, feel, taste,* and *smell* it.
- Try to connect the image in the poem to something you have experienced in real life.

# Memory
## Margaret Walker

In this poem, the speaker remembers
the unhappy people she has seen in cities.

◆  ◆  ◆

I can remember wind-swept streets of cities
on cold and <u>blustery</u> nights, on rainy days;
heads under shabby felts[1] and <u>parasols</u>
and shoulders hunched against a sharp
   concern;
seeing hurt <u>bewilderment</u> on poor faces,
smelling a deep and <u>sinister</u> unrest
these <u>brooding</u> people cautiously <u>caress</u>;
hearing ghostly marching on pavement
   stones
and closing fast around their squares of hate.
I can remember seeing them alone,
at work, and in their <u>tenements</u> at home.
I can remember hearing all they said:
their <u>muttering</u> protests, their whispered
   oaths,
and all that spells their living in <u>distress</u>.

◆ **Stop to Reflect**

*Shabby* means "old and worn
out." What do the shabby hats
and parasols suggest about the
people who own them?

_____

_____

_____

◆ **Reading Strategy**

Circle the words in the
bracketed passage that
create an image of
unhappy people.

◆ **Literary Analysis**

Underline the words in the
poem's last three lines
that appeal to the sense
of sound.

---

### Vocabulary Development

**blustery** (BLUS tuh ree) *adj.*  having strong winds

**parasols** (PAHR uh solz) *n.*  umbrellas

**bewilderment** (bee WIL der munt) *n.*  confusion

**sinister** (SIN is tuhr) *adj.*  threatening harm

**brooding** (BROOD ing) *adj.*  worrying

**caress** (kuh RES) *v.*  touch in a gentle way

**tenements** (TEN uh munts) *n.*  apartments

**muttering** (MUT er ing) *adj.*  spoken in a low, angry way

**distress** (dis TRES) *n.*  pain or suffering

---

1. **felts** hats made of felt.

1. What is the weather like in the cities?

_____

_____

2. Which word describing the felt hats and parasols gives a clue that the people are poor?

_____

3. What kind of look does the speaker see on the people's faces?

_____

_____

4. Would you want to live like the people in the poem? Circle one.

yes                    no

Explain why or why not.

_____

_____

_____

5. **Literary Analysis:** Complete the chart with the sense that each group of words appeals to. Choose either *sight, sound, taste, smell,* or *touch.*

| Language | Sense |
|---|---|
| a. cold and blustery nights | |
| b. smelling a deep and sinister unrest | |
| c. hearing ghostly marching on pavement stones | |
| d. seeing them alone, at work | |

6. **Reading Analysis:** Circle the word that best describes the way you picture the people in the poem.

smiling          angry          sleepy

Which words in the poem make you picture the people that way?

_____

# Writing

### Letter About a Memorable Moment

In Walker's poem, she describes the city people that she remembers. Write a letter to describe a special event that you remember. It might be something that really happened to you. If not, it might be an event from a book or movie. Follow these steps:

Explain when and where the event took place.

_____

_____

Explain who took part in the event.

_____

List three details about the way things looked.

1. _____

2. _____

3. _____

List two details about the way things sounded or smelled.

1. _____

2. _____

List two details about the way things felt or tasted.

1. _____

2. _____

Use your answers to write your letter.

# Woman's Work
## Julia Alvarez

## Summary

The speaker of this poem recalls helping her mother with the housework as a child. She resented having to do the housework while her friends played. In the end, though, she realizes she is similar to her mother, with one small difference. Instead of putting her heart into her housework, she puts it into her writing.

## Visual Summary

| | |
|---|---|
| **INTRODUCTION** | **Lines 1–3**<br>The speaker introduces her mother, who treated housework as if it were art. |

| | | | |
|---|---|---|---|
| **DETAILS** | **Lines 4–6**<br>The speaker recalls working hard instead of playing with her friends. | **Lines 7–9**<br>The speaker was not allowed to stop working until her mother was satisfied. | **Lines 10–12**<br>Her mother cleaned everything. She viewed cleaning as a way to express herself. | **Lines 13–15**<br>Her mother encouraged her daughter to be a good house-keeper. |

| | |
|---|---|
| **CONCLUSION** | **Lines 16–18**<br>The speaker rebels against her mother's wishes. She does not wish to be a good housekeeper like her mother. Then she realizes she *is* like her mother—only her art form is writing, instead of housekeeping. |

## LITERARY ANALYSIS

### Imagery

**Imagery** is language that forms a picture in the reader's mind. The picture, or image, may appeal to any of the five senses. They are sight, sound, taste, smell, and touch.

Read this passage from "Woman's Work." See how it appeals to the senses of sight and sound.

> We'd clean the whole upstairs before we'd start
> downstairs. I'd sigh, hearing my friends outside.

A chart like this can help you understand how language in the poem appeals to the senses.

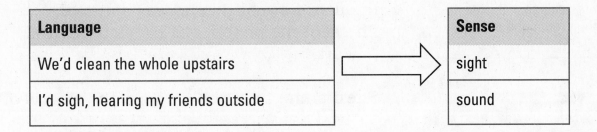

| Language | | Sense |
|----------|---|-------|
| We'd clean the whole upstairs | | sight |
| I'd sigh, hearing my friends outside | | sound |

## READING STRATEGY

### Picturing the Imagery

As you read a poem, think about the language. Try to **picture each image** in your mind. Doing this will help you appreciate the poem more.

Picture the imagery in a poem in these ways:

- Pay close attention to words that describe. Think about the exact meaning of each word.
- Imagine how the speaker feels at each moment. Try to experience that same feeling.
- Remember not just to see an image. Also *hear, feel, taste,* and *smell* it.
- Try to connect the image in the poem to something you've experienced in real life.

In Woman's Work, a daughter remembers how she and her mother used to clean the house together. Try to picture the details of the daughter's memories as you read.

# Woman's Work
## Julia Alvarez

◆ **Literary Analysis**

Circle the words in the poem's first three lines that appeal to the sense of touch.

Who says a woman's work isn't high art?
She'd challenge as she scrubbed the
   bathroom tiles.
Keep house as if the address were your
   heart.

We'd clean the whole upstairs before we'd
   start
downstairs. I'd sigh, hearing my friends
   outside.
Doing her woman's work was a hard art

◆ **Reading Strategy**

Underline the words in the bracketed passage that create the image of a prisoner in a prison. Does this image make the daughter feel good or bad?

_____

to practice when the summer sun would bar
the floor I swept till she was satisfied.
She kept me prisoner in her housebound
   heart.

She'd shine the tines of forks, the wheels of
   carts,
cut lacy <u>lattices</u> for all her pies.
Her woman's work was nothing less than art.

◆ **Stop to Reflect**

The mother both praised and scolded her daughter. How do you think the daughter felt toward her mother?

_____

_____

_____

And, I, her masterpiece since I was smart,
was <u>primed</u>, praised, polished, <u>scolded</u>, and
   advised
to keep a house much better than my heart.

I did not want to be her <u>counterpart</u>!
I struck out . . . but became my mother's
   child:
a woman working at home on her art,
housekeeping paper as if it were her heart

◆ **Read Fluently**

Read the last four lines of the poem. Circle the words that tell what kind of person the speaker became.

---

### Vocabulary Development

**lattices** (LAT is uhz) *n.*  strips in a crisscross pattern
**primed** (PRIMED) *v.*  prepared
**scolded** (SKOHL did) *v.*  criticized strongly
**counterpart** (KOUN ter pahrt) *n.*  a person who is very
   much like another

1. List three jobs the mother does as part of her woman's work.

   a. _____

   b. _____

   c. _____

2. What does the mother teach her daughter about cleaning?

   _____

   _____

3. Why does the girl dislike cleaning as a child?

   _____

   _____

4. The speaker says that she became her "mother's child"? What does she mean by that?

   _____

   _____

   _____

5. **Literary Analysis:** Complete the chart with the sense that each group of words appeals to. Choose either *sight, sound, taste, smell,* or *touch.*

| Language | Sense |
|---|---|
| a. she scrubbed the bathroom tiles | touch |
| b. I'd sigh, hearing my friends outside | |
| c. the summer sun would bar the floor | |
| d. She'd shine the tines of forks | |

6. **Reading Analysis:** Do you picture the daughter as smiling or frowning as a girl? Circle one.

smiling          frowning

Explain your answer.

_____

_____

## Listening and Speaking

**Presentation of Artwork**

Alvarez's poem creates strong images of women doing "woman's work." You can easily picture the mother and daughter in your mind. Now, find and present actual pictures on the same subject. Look in newspapers and magazines. Find photographs of women at work. Some may show women working at home. Others may show women working in offices or other places.

Prepare to show each picture to your class. Use the chart here to gather information. In the first column, identify each picture. In the second column, explain where you found each picture. In the third column, describe exactly what each picture shows. Use colorful and exact words. In the fourth column, tell why you chose the picture to go with "Woman's Work."

| Picture | Where I Found It | Description | Connection to Poem |
|---|---|---|---|
|  |  |  |  |
|  |  |  |  |
|  |  |  |  |

Use the information in your chart to help you present the pictures to your class.

# The Raven
## Edgar Allan Poe

## Summary

"The Raven" opens with the speaker describing a night alone with his books. He is reading to forget his lost love, Lenore. Suddenly, the speaker hears someone tapping at the door. When he opens the door, no one is there. The tapping continues. Then he opens the window, and a raven flies into the room. The bird perches on a sculpture of a Greek goddess. Asked its name, the raven replies, "Nevermore." This is all the bird can say. At first, the speaker is amused. But by the end of the poem, the speaker believes the raven is mocking him and his loneliness. The speaker does not succeed in driving the raven from the room, however, and this only intensifies his gloom.

## Visual Summary

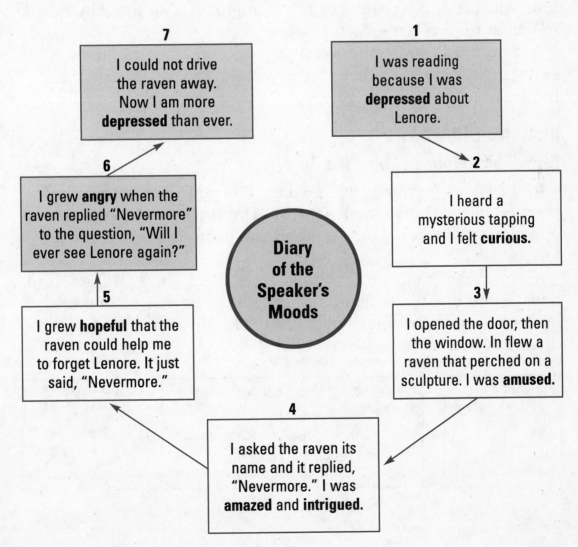

**7** I could not drive the raven away. Now I am more **depressed** than ever.

**1** I was reading because I was **depressed** about Lenore.

**6** I grew **angry** when the raven replied "Nevermore" to the question, "Will I ever see Lenore again?"

**Diary of the Speaker's Moods**

**2** I heard a mysterious tapping and I felt **curious.**

**5** I grew **hopeful** that the raven could help me to forget Lenore. It just said, "Nevermore."

**3** I opened the door, then the window. In flew a raven that perched on a sculpture. I was **amused.**

**4** I asked the raven its name and it replied, "Nevermore." I was **amazed** and **intrigued.**

## LITERARY ANALYSIS

### Narrative Poem

A **narrative poem** is a poem that tells a story. It has characters, a setting, and a plot.

- The *characters* are the people or animals who take part in the action.
- The *setting* is the time and place of the action.
- The *plot* is the action and events of the story.

"The Raven" is a narrative poem. It begins the way a short story might begin:

> Once upon a midnight dreary, while I
>    pondered, weak and weary,

The poem's opening line gives some helpful information. It tells you the time of the story—midnight. It also introduces an important character—the speaker.

As you read the poem, see what else you learn about the setting. Notice what other characters you meet. Learn what happens to them in the plot.

## READING STRATEGY

### Drawing Inferences About the Speaker

In a narrative poem, the speaker tells you the story. Many people believe that the speaker in "The Raven" is really based on Edgar Allan Poe. You can read the poem and then decide for yourself.

As you read, notice everything the speaker says, thinks, and does. Then use those details to **draw inferences**, or make guesses, about the speaker. A chart like this one can help you draw inferences.

| Speaker's Words | | Speaker's Thoughts | | Speaker's Actions | | Inferences |
|---|---|---|---|---|---|---|
| weak weary | + | thinks sadly about lost Lenore | + | nodding, nearly napping | = | Speaker is very sad and tired |

# The Raven

### Edgar Allan Poe

Once upon a midnight dreary, while I
   pondered, weak and weary,
Over many a <u>quaint</u> and curious volume of
   forgotten lore,[1]
While I nodded, nearly napping, suddenly there
   came a tapping,
As of someone gently rapping, rapping at my
   <u>chamber</u> door.
"'Tis some visitor," I muttered, "tapping at my
   chamber door—
      Only this, and nothing more."

◆　◆　◆

> The speaker thinks sadly and fondly
> about a lost woman named Lenore. He has
> tried to find in old books a magical way to
> bring her back to him. However, he has
> failed. He opens his door because of the
> tapping he hears. He sees nothing but
> darkness.

◆　◆　◆

Deep into that darkness peering, long I stood
   there wondering, fearing,
Doubting, dreaming dreams no mortal ever
   dared to dream before;
But the silence was unbroken, and the
   darkness gave no token,[2]
And the only word there spoken was the
   whispered word, "Lenore!"
This *I* whispered, and an echo murmured back
   the word, "Lenore!"
      Merely this, and nothing more.

◆　◆　◆

---

### Vocabulary Development

**quaint** (KWAYNT) *adj.* strange; unusual

**chamber** (CHAYM ber) *n.* a room in a house

---

1. **quaint . . . lore** strange book of ancient learning.
2. **token** (TOH kun) *n.* sign.

---

◆ **Literary Analysis**

This **narrative poem** tells a story. Circle the words in the bracketed passage that identify the story's *setting*—its time and place.

◆ **Reading Check**

What has the speaker tried to find in old books?

_____

_____

_____

◆ **Reading Strategy**

Circle a word that the speaker whispers. Then **draw inferences** from his remark. What do you think the remark tells you about the speaker?

_____

_____

_____

_____

◆ **Reading Check**

Who or what has been making the tapping sound that the speaker hears? Write your answer here.

_____

_____

◆ **Stop to Reflect**

The speaker believes the raven will leave tomorrow. Why does he think that?

_____

_____

_____

_____

◆ **Reading Check**

The speaker says that _she_ will never again press her head against his velvet cushion. Reread the bracketed passage. Who is _she_?

_____

Explain how you know.

_____

_____

_____

The speaker now hears an even louder tapping. He lets in light through the window. He sees a raven sitting above his door. The speaker asks the bird its name. The raven replies, "Nevermore." The speaker is amazed by this strange bird.

◆ ◆ ◆

But the raven, sitting lonely on the placid bust, spoke only
That one word, as if his soul in that one word he did outpour.
Nothing farther then he uttered—not a feather then he fluttered—
Till I scarcely more than muttered, "Other friends have flown before—
On the morrow _he_ will leave me, as my hopes have flown before."
    Quoth[3] the raven, "Nevermore."

◆ ◆ ◆

The speaker wonders why the raven says only the word "nevermore." He guesses that the raven's owner must have lived a life without hope. "Nevermore" is probably the only word the bird ever heard from its master. The speaker tries to find other reasons why the raven says only this word.

◆ ◆ ◆

This I sat engaged in guessing, but no syllable expressing
To the fowl whose fiery eyes now burned into my bosom's core;
This and more I sat divining,[4] with my head at ease reclining
On the cushion's velvet lining that the lamplight gloated o'er,
But whose velvet violet lining with the lamplight gloating o'er,
    _She_ shall press, ah, nevermore!

◆ ◆ ◆

---

3. **quoth** (KWOHTH) _v._ said.
4. **divining** (di VĪN ing) _v._ guessing.

The speaker smells perfume in the air. He says angels must have sent the raven to ease his pain of losing Lenore. The raven replies only, "Nevermore." The upset speaker now thinks perhaps the devil has sent the bird. He asks the raven if his suffering will ever end. He asks if he will ever hold his lost Lenore again. The speaker grows angry because the bird's only answer is "Nevermore."

♦   ♦   ♦

"Be that word our sign of parting, bird or
     fiend!" I shrieked,
     upstarting—
"Get thee back into the tempest and the Night's
     Plutonian[5] shore!
Leave no black plume as a token of that lie thy
     soul hath spoken!
Leave my loneliness unbroken!—quit the bust
     above my door!
Take thy beak from out my heart, and take thy
     form from off my door!"
          Quoth the raven, "Nevermore."

♦   ♦   ♦

The raven refuses to leave. It remains sitting above the speaker's door. The speaker thinks the bird's eyes look like those of a devil. The speaker fears that his suffering will never end.

5. **Plutonian** (ploo TOH nee un) *adj.* like the underworld, ruled over by the ancient Roman god Pluto.

The Raven **181**

---

◆ **Reading Strategy**

Circle two things the speaker asks the raven. Then explain what his questions show about him.

_____

_____

_____

_____

◆ **Read Fluently**

Read aloud the bracketed passage. How do you think the speaker feels as he says these words?

_____

_____

◆ **Literary Analysis**

What happens to the characters at the end of the **narrative poem**? Write your answers on the lines.

The speaker: _____

_____

_____

The raven: _____

_____

_____

1. Why is the speaker reading old books at the start of the poem?

   _____

2. What is strange about the raven that sits above the door?

   _____

   _____

3. Why does the speaker grow very upset with the raven?

   _____

   _____

4. **Literary Analysis:** What is the setting of this **narrative poem?**

   time: _____     place: _____

5. **Literary Analysis:** Below are some events that happen in the narrative poem. Fill in other events from the plot.

   a. The speaker hears a tapping at his door.

   b. _____

   c. The speaker asks the raven questions about Lenore.

   d. _____

   e. The speaker orders the raven to leave.

   f. _____

6. **Reading Strategy:** Use the chart to list things that the speaker thinks, says, and does. Then **draw inferences** about the speaker.

What he thinks: _____

_____

What he says: _____

_____

What he does: _____

_____

Inferences: _____

_____

# Writing

## Scene for a Movie

Imagine that you plan to make a movie based on "The Raven." You want to grab the audience's attention in the very first scene. Close your eyes and picture the scene in your mind. Then write a paragraph about everything the audience will see and hear. First fill in the information below.

1. Write four words to describe the room where "The Raven" is set.

_____   _____

_____   _____

2. Write a sentence to describe each character.

The Speaker: _____

The Raven: _____

3. Do you think the room would have dim lighting or bright lighting?

_____

4. What kind of music would be playing in the background?

_____

Use all of your answers from above to help you write a paragraph describing the first scene.

# The Seven Ages of Man
## William Shakespeare

## Summary

The speaker in this poem notes that we all have our time in the world and then we die. Then he traces the journey of all people from the cradle to the grave. The stages he mentions are the infant, the schoolboy, the lover, the soldier, the judge, the old man, and finally, the dying man. In each stage, a person grows older, but not necessarily any wiser. In the end, according to the speaker, the entire journey proves meaningless.

## Visual Summary

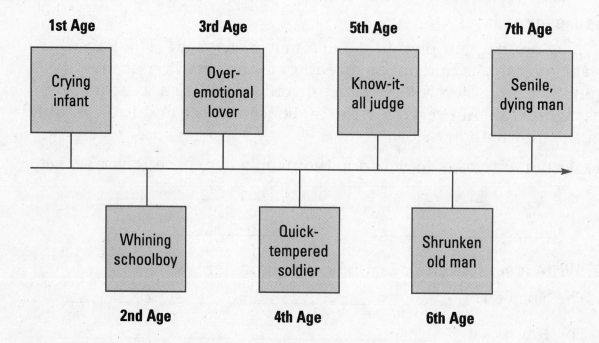

1st Age — Crying infant

2nd Age — Whining schoolboy

3rd Age — Over-emotional lover

4th Age — Quick-tempered soldier

5th Age — Know-it-all judge

6th Age — Shrunken old man

7th Age — Senile, dying man

## LITERARY ANALYSIS

### Dramatic Poem

A **dramatic poem** is a poem in which the speaker expresses his or her thoughts and feelings. "The Seven Ages of Man" is a dramatic poem. It is spoken by a character named Jacques in Shakespeare's play *As You Like It*. Jacques is a servant with bitter feelings about life. He opens the poem with these famous words:

> All the world's a stage,
> And all the men and women merely players:

As you read the poem, notice how the speaker describes people and things. Try to find words that reflect his cold and bitter feelings about life.

## READING STRATEGY

### Drawing Inferences About the Speaker

In a dramatic poem, the speaker shares his thoughts and feelings. Sometimes those feelings are stated directly. Other times you must guess, or **draw inferences**, about the speaker's feelings.

**Draw inferences about the speaker** in these ways:

- Notice words that the speaker uses to describe people and things.
- Think about the meanings of the words. Are they kind words or unkind words?
- Guess how the speaker feels, based on his language.

A chart like this one can help you draw inferences.

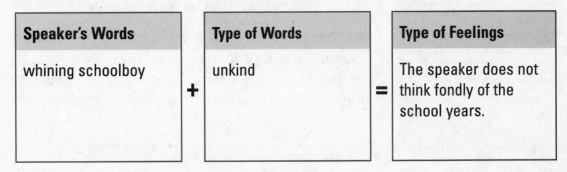

| Speaker's Words | | Type of Words | | Type of Feelings |
|---|---|---|---|---|
| whining schoolboy | **+** | unkind | **=** | The speaker does not think fondly of the school years. |

# The Seven Ages of Man
## William Shakespeare

All the world's a stage,
And all the men and women merely players:[1]
They have their exits and their entrances;
And one man in his time plays many parts,
His acts being seven ages.[2] At first the infant,
Mewling[3] and puking in the nurse's arms.
And then the whining schoolboy, with his
   satchel,
And shining morning face, creeping like snail
Unwillingy to school. And then the lover,
Sighing like furnace, with a woeful ballad
Made to his mistress' eyebrow.

◆ ◆ ◆

    The fourth age is the soldier. He desires honor and argues a lot. The fifth age is the justice, or judge. He is a fat man with mean eyes who quotes wise sayings. The sixth age is the pantaloon, or old foolish man. His high-pitched voice sounds like a child's.

◆ ◆ ◆

    Last scene of all,
That ends this strange eventful history,
Is second childishness, and mere oblivion,
Sans[4] teeth, sans eyes, sans taste, sans
   everything.

---

### Vocabulary Development

**satchel** (SATCH ul) *n.* a small bag for carrying books
**woeful** (WOH ful) *adj.* sad
**ballad** (BAL ud) *n.* a slow, sad song, often about love
**oblivion** (uh BLIV ee un) *n.* a state of forgetting

---

1. **players** actors.
2. **ages** periods of life.
3. **mewling** (MYOOL ing) *adj.* crying weakly.
4. **sans** (sanz) *prep.* without.

1. Why is the soldier an unpleasant person?

   _____

   _____

2. Name three things the speaker says are gone in the final age of man.

   a. _____  b. _____  c. _____

3. **Literary Analysis:** A speaker in a dramatic poem expresses his thoughts or feelings. Put a check in front of the sentence that best expresses the speaker's feelings.

   ____ Life is an exciting adventure to be lived with joy.

   ____ Life is a sad experience from birth to death.

   ____ Life is wonderful most of the time but hard at some times.

4. **Reading Strategy:** Complete this chart to show each age of man and the speaker's unkind words that describe the age.

   | Age of Man | Unkind Words |
   | --- | --- |
   | infant | mewling and puking |
   | schoolboy | |
   | lover | |
   | soldier | |
   | justice | |
   | pantaloon | |
   | second childishness | |

5. **Reading Strategy:** Based on the chart, what can you infer about the speaker's point of view?

   _____

   _____

# Listening and Speaking

## Debate

Hold a **debate** based on "The Seven Ages of Man." Form two teams, each with two to four members. The teams will debate this idea: *Life is an unhappy experience.* One team will argue in favor of the idea. The other team will argue against the idea. Members of each team should back up their arguments with examples from real life. Team speakers should do the following:

Check off the position you will defend.

Life is a happy experience. _____

Life is an unhappy experience. _____

Explain how the life of a student could support this position.

_____

_____

Explain how being in love could support this position.

_____

_____

Explain how having a job could support this position.

_____

_____

Explain how living to one hundred could prove this position.

_____

_____

## *from the* Odyssey

### Homer (Translated by Robert Fitzgerald)

### Summary

This epic tells the story of the Greek hero Odysseus, who is trying to return home to Ithaca after the Trojan War. Odysseus and his men arrive at the land of the Cyclopes, a race of one-eyed giants. Odysseus decides to wait for one of them. The Cyclops finds them in his cave and eats two men. Odysseus finds a large club and uses part of it to make a spike. He gives the giant some brandy, and the Cyclops—Polyphemus—gets drunk. Odysseus and his men blind the giant by ramming the spike into his eye. Polyphemus calls for help from the other Cyclopes but is foiled by the fact that Odysseus gave him a false name: Nohbdy. Odysseus ties the Cyclops' sheep together and hides his men under them. When Polyphemus lets the sheep out, Odysseus and his men escape. Odysseus taunts the giant from his ship, and Polyphemus realizes that he was warned about Odysseus long ago. He asks the god Poseidon to curse Odysseus.

### Visual Summary

| Setting | Land of the Cyclopes | | |
|---|---|---|---|
| Characters | Odysseus | Odysseus' men | Polyphemus, a Cyclops |
| Problem | Odysseus and his men must escape from the Cyclops before he kills them all. | | |
| Events | 1. Odysseus and his men arrive at the land of the Cyclopes. 2. Odysseus decides to wait for one of the Cyclopes. 3. Polyphemus, a Cyclops, finds them and eats two men. 4. Odysseus finds an enormous club and turns it into a spike. 5. Odysseus gives the Cyclops wine to get him drunk. 6. Odysseus tells Polyphemus his name is *Nohbdy*. 7. Odysseus and his men blind Polyphemus with a spiked club. 8. Polyphemus calls for help but is foiled by Odysseus' false name. 9. Odysseus ties the sheep together and hides his men under them. | | |
| Outcome | When the Cyclops lets the sheep out, Odysseus and his men escape. Odysseus taunts the giant from his ship, and Polyphemus realizes that he was warned about Odysseus long ago. He asks Poseidon to curse Odysseus. | | |

## LITERARY ANALYSIS

### The Epic Hero

An epic is a long poem about the adventures of gods or heroes. The main character is the **epic hero.** He bravely faces all kinds of danger. He shows courage, loyalty, and honor.

As you read, consider the actions and qualities that make Odysseus an epic hero.

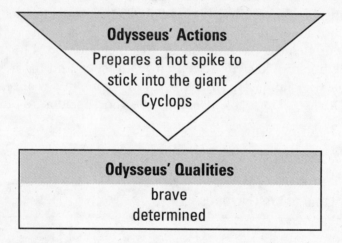

**Odysseus' Actions**

Prepares a hot spike to stick into the giant Cyclops

**Odysseus' Qualities**

brave
determined

## READING STRATEGY

### Reading in Sentences

An epic tells a story in poetry form. The lines appear in verses. However, thoughts and phrases do not always stop at the end of a line. Sometimes they run on to part of the next line.

For the story to make sense, you must **read in sentences.** Follow these steps:

- Read the poem the same way you might read a book or magazine article.
- Pause where you see a comma, colon, or semicolon.
- Stop where you see a period, question mark, or exclamation point.
- If necessary, restate the sentence in your own words to make the meaning clearer.

# *from* the Odyssey, Part 1
# The Cyclops

## Homer
## Translated by Robert Fitzgerald

Odysseus is traveling home to Ithaca
after fighting in the Trojan War. He is asked
to tell about his adventures. In one story, he
tells about his visit to the island of the
Cyclopes. They are wild, one-eyed giants
who live in large caves.

◆　◆　◆

　　　　　A <u>prodigious</u> man
slept in this cave alone, and took his flocks
to graze afield—remote from all companions,
knowing none but savage ways, a brute
so huge, he seemed no man at all of those
who eat good wheaten bread; but he seemed
　rather
a shaggy mountain reared in <u>solitude</u>.
We beached there, and I told the crew
to stand by and keep watch over the ship:
as for myself I took my twelve best fighters
and went ahead.

◆　◆　◆

Odysseus and his men walk into the
cave of a Cyclops. They find lambs and goats
and lots of cheese there. Odysseus' men
want to steal the items and leave quickly.

◆　◆　◆

---

### Vocabulary Development

**prodigious** (proh DIJ us) *adj.*　huge
**solitude** (SOL uh tood) *n.*　being alone

---

◆ **Reading Strategy**

**Read** the first bracketed passage **in sentences**. Circle the punctuation marks that show where to pause. Draw a box around the punctuation marks that show where to stop.

◆ **Literary Analysis**

Underline the words in the second bracketed passage that show that Odysseus is a leader.

◆ **Reading Check**

Read the passage that starts "Neither reply nor pity." Then describe in your own words what the Cyclops does.

_____

_____

_____

Ah, how sound that was! Yet I refused. I wished
to see the cave man, what he had to offer—
no pretty sight, it turned out, for my friends.
We lit a fire, burnt an offering,
and took some cheese to eat; then sat in
   silence
around the embers, waiting. When he came
he had a load of dry <u>boughs</u> on his shoulder
to stoke his fire at suppertime. He dumped it
with a great crash into that hollow cave,
and we all scattered fast to the far wall.

◆  ◆  ◆

The Cyclops blocks the entrance to his cave with a huge rock. Then he milks his animals. He sees Odysseus and his men hiding in the corner. He asks them who they are. Odysseus says they are Trojans returning from the war. Odysseus asks for help or gifts that the Cyclops might wish to offer them.

◆  ◆  ◆

Neither reply nor pity came from him,
but in one stride he clutched at my
   companions
and caught two in his hands like squirming
   puppies
to beat their brains out, spattering the floor.
Then he <u>dismembered</u> them and made his
   meal,
gaping and crunching like a mountain lion—
everything: <u>innards</u>, flesh, and marrow
   bones.

◆  ◆  ◆

---

### Vocabulary Development

**boughs** (BOUZ) *n.*  tree branches
**dismembered** (dis MEM burd) *v.*  tore apart
**innards** (IN urds) *n.*  insides

Odysseus is shocked by the Cyclops' violence. He can't kill the giant right away, or he and his men will be trapped inside the cave. The next morning, the Cyclops eats two more men for breakfast. Then he leaves the cave with his sheep. Odysseus makes a plan. He and his men sharpen a long wooden pole.

That evening, the Cyclops returns. Odysseus gives him wine. He tells the giant that his name is Nohbdy. Soon the Cyclops falls asleep. Odysseus heats up the pole in the fire. He and his men jam the sharp end into the Cyclops' eye.

◆ ◆ ◆

So with our brand we <u>bored</u> that great eye socket
while blood ran out around the red-hot bar.
Eyelid and lash were <u>seared</u>; the pierced ball hissed broiling, and the roots popped.

◆ ◆ ◆

The blind Cyclops screams for help. Other Cyclopes come to his cave. They ask him what is wrong.

◆ ◆ ◆

'Nohbdy, Nohbdy's tricked me, Nohbdy's ruined me!'

To this rough shot they made a <u>sage</u> reply:

'Ah, well, if nobody has played you foul, there in your lonely bed, we are no use in pain

---

**Vocabulary Development**

**bored** (BORD) *v.* made a hole in
**seared** (SEERD) *adj.* burned on the surface
**sage** (SAYJ) *adj.* wise

given by great Zeus.[1] Let it be your father,
Poseidon Lord,[2] to whom you pray.'
                    So saying,
they trailed away. And I was filled with
  laughter
to see how like a charm the name <u>deceived</u>
  them.

◆ ◆ ◆

Odysseus makes a plan to escape from
the cave. He ties the Cyclops' sheep together
in groups of three. Then he ties his men to
the bellies of the sheep. Odysseus clings to
the belly of the ram with the most wool. In
the morning, the Cyclops lets the animals
out of the cave.

◆ ◆ ◆

He sent us into the open, then. Close by,
I dropped and rolled clear of the ram's belly,
going this way and that to untie the men.
With many glances back, we rounded up
his fat, stiff-legged sheep to take aboard,
and drove them down to where the good
  ship lay.

◆ ◆ ◆

Odysseus and his men row their ship
away from the island. The angry Odysseus
yells at the Cyclops on shore. His men beg
him to be quiet. They fear that the blind
giant will figure out their sea position from
his voice. The Cyclops may throw a huge
rock at them.

◆ ◆ ◆

### Vocabulary Development

**deceived** (di SEEVD) *v.* tricked

---

1. **Zeus** (ZOOS) king of the gods.
2. **Poseidon** (poh SĪ dun) god of the sea.

---

---

**◆ Stop to Reflect**

Odysseus ties his men to the
sheep's bellies. Why don't they
ride on the sheep's backs
instead?

_____

_____

_____

**◆ Reading Strategy**

Read the bracketed
passage. Circle the
lines that you would
stop after reading.

**◆ Reading Check**

Draw a box around the
words that explain
why Odysseus' men
want him to stop
yelling.

I would not heed them in my glorying spirit,
but let my anger flare and yelled:
              'Cyclops,
if ever mortal man inquire
how you were put to shame and blinded, tell
    him
Odysseus, raider of cities, took your eye:
Laertes' son, whose home's on Ithaca!'
                    ◆  ◆  ◆

The Cyclops now knows Odysseus' real
name. He prays to his father, Poseidon. He
asks that Odysseus never be allowed to
reach home. The Cyclops then picks up a
huge rock. He throws it at Odysseus' ship,
but it misses. The ship meets other ships
with Trojan soldiers. They soon reach an
island.
                    ◆  ◆  ◆

Then we unloaded all the Cyclops' flock
to make division, share and share alike,
only my fighters voted that my ram,
the prize of all, should go to me. I slew him
by the seaside and burnt his long thighbones
to Zeus beyond the stormcloud, Cronus'[3]
    son,
who rules the world. But Zeus <u>disdained</u> my
    offering:
destruction for my ships he had in store
and death for those who sailed them, my
    companions.
                    ◆  ◆  ◆

That night Odysseus and his men feast.
The next morning they set sail again.

---

**Vocabulary Development**

**disdained** (dis DAYND) *v.* rejected angrily

---

3. **Cronus** (KROH nus) father of Zeus, ruler of the world before Zeus.

# REVIEW AND ASSESS

1. Write three words that describe the Cyclops.

   a. _____  b. _____  c. _____

2. What violent act does the Cyclops do in his cave?

   _____

   _____

3. What do Odysseus and his men steal from the Cyclops?

   _____

   _____

4. **Literary Analysis:** Complete the chart to show actions and qualities that make Odysseus an **epic hero.**

| Odysseus' Actions | Odysseus' Qualities |
| --- | --- |
| He speaks for the men when the Cyclops asks questions. | leadership |
| He gives the Cyclops wine to make him fall asleep. | |
| He jams a sharp pole into the giant's eye. | |
| He helps his men escape by tying them to sheep. | |

5. **Reading Strategy: Read** the following passage **in sentences.** Circle the punctuation marks that tell you to pause. Draw a line under the punctuation marks that tell you to stop.

   Ah,
   how sound that was! Yet I refused. I wished
   to see the cave man, what he had to offer—
   no pretty sight, it turned out, for my friends.

# Writing

## Comparison-and-Contrast Paragraph

When you **compare,** you show how things are alike. When you **contrast,** you show how things are different. Write a **paragraph** that compares and contrasts Odysseus to another hero. It might be a real person or a character from a book or movie. Follow these steps:

Name the hero you are comparing and contrasting to Odysseus.

_____

Name a quality your hero has (such as bravery) that Odysseus also has.

_____

Describe something your hero did to show that quality.

_____

_____

_____

_____

Name a quality your hero has that Odysseus does not have.

_____

Describe something your hero did to show that quality.

_____

_____

_____

_____

Use your answers to write your comparison-and-contrast paragraph.

# Part 2

## Selection Summaries with Alternative Reading Strategies

Part 2 contains summaries of all selections in *Prentice Hall Literature: Timeless Voices, Timeless Themes*. An alternative reading strategy follows each summary.

• Use the summaries in Part 2 to preview or review the selections.

• Use the alternative reading strategies in Part 2 to guide your reading or to check your understanding of the selection.

## "The Cask of Amontillado" by Edgar Allan Poe

**Summary** This spine-tingling tale of vengeance is set in Italy during carnival season. Montresor, a man from an old aristocratic family, seeks revenge against his one-time friend Fortunato. Knowing that Fortunato prides himself on his ability to judge fine wine, Montresor lures his victim to the family palace to judge a cask of Amontillado sherry. The men descend twisted stairways to an underground tunnel, past burial caves, to a room in which the wine is supposedly stored. Once inside, Montresor chains Fortunato to the wall and then walls up the entrance from the outside. As the entrance wall rises, Fortunato moans, protests, and finally suggests that the whole incident is a joke. Montresor ignores the pleas. When he places the last stone in the wall, he hears only the bells jingling on Fortunato's holiday costume.

**Resumen** Este escalofriante relato ocurre en Italia, durante el Carnaval. Montresor, un aristócrata, busca vengarse de Fortunato, quien había sido su amigo. Montresor sabe que Fortunato se enorgullece de poder reconocer buenos vinos y lo invita a su palacio para que pruebe un jerez Amontillado. Los hombres descienden por una escalera en espiral hasta un túnel, pasan frente a tumbas, y llegan a un cuarto, donde supuestamente está el vino. Una vez adentro, Montresor encadena a Fortunato a la pared y comienza a tapiar la entrada del cuarto. Fortunato se queja, protesta y finalmente cree que todo es una broma. Montresor no le hace caso y continúa tapiando la entrada. Cuando finalmente coloca la última piedra, sólo escucha los cascabeles del disfraz de Fortunato.

**Form a Mental Picture** Good readers picture in their mind's eye what an author describes. Listen to the audiocassette recording of the story as you read. Picture each scene as you listen. Use this page to jot down notes to describe what you picture in your mind. Then work with a partner to draw sketches of what Poe describes in each of the following five scenes.

1. Fortunato's costume in the street
2. The passage through the vaults
3. The prison chamber
4. Fortunato chained to the wall
5. Montresor building the wall

_____

_____

_____

_____

_____

_____

_____

_____

_____

_____

_____

# "The Most Dangerous Game" by Richard Connell

**Summary** This spine-tingler is set on an island in the Caribbean Sea. Rainsford, an expert hunter, is traveling by boat in search of big game. He accidentally falls overboard and is forced to swim to a nearby mysterious island. There, he comes upon a palace owned by a General Zaroff. Over dinner, Zaroff explains that since hunting animals is no longer a challenge, he now stocks the island with more interesting game—shipwrecked sailors. Shocked, Rainsford refuses to join the hunt. He quickly learns, however, that *he* will be the hunted and can leave only if he stays alive for three days. Cornered on the third evening, Rainsford jumps into the sea. Confident that Rainsford has drowned, Zaroff returns to his room. Rainsford, however, is already there. Zaroff is killed by his prey.

**Resumen** Este espeluznante relato ocurre en una isla del mar Caribe. Rainsford, un experto cazador, viaja en bote en busca de caza mayor, cuando accidentalmente cae al agua. Rainsford nada hasta una misteriosa isla, donde encuentra un palacio que es propiedad de un tal general Zaroff. En la cena, Zaroff le explica que para él la caza mayor ya no es un reto y que por eso, ahora se dedica a cazar náufragos. Sorprendido, Rainsford se rehusa a cazar seres humanos. Pronto, Rainsford se da cuenta de que él será la presa y que sólo podrá dejar la isla si consigue eludir a Zaroff por tres días. En la tarde del tercer día, Rainsford está acorralado y se arroja al mar. Creyendo que su presa se ha ahogado, Zaroff vuelve a su cuarto. Allí lo espera Rainsford y Zaroff es muerto por su presa.

**Identify Chain of Events** Part of the fun of a good story is finding out what happens next and what happens in the end. As you read a story or as you watch a movie, you probably anticipate, or think about, what will happen next. As you read "The Most Dangerous Game," use a Chain of Events organizer like the one below to keep track of what happens.

Begin with the conversation between Whitney and Rainsford on board the boat. Then draw boxes joined by arrows to mark each event in the story. The first two boxes have been modeled for you.

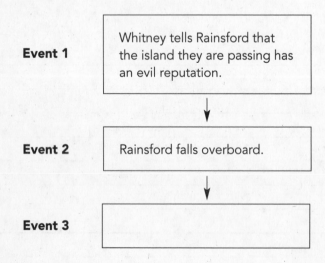

**Event 1**  Whitney tells Rainsford that the island they are passing has an evil reputation.

**Event 2**  Rainsford falls overboard.

**Event 3**

## "Casey at the Bat" by Ernest Lawrence Thayer

**Summary** A classic narrative poem about baseball, "Casey at the Bat" captures the sights, sounds, and excitement of a game in only a few lines of verse. With the score two to four in the bottom of the ninth, the Mudville baseball team seems sure to lose. Two men are out; then two batters get on base. That brings star player Casey to bat as the crowd cheers. A cocky Casey entertains the fans and sneers at the pitcher. Casey lets the first two pitches go by, and the fans object to the umpire calling them strikes. At the third pitch, Casey finally makes a mighty swing—and strikes out.

**Resumen** Éste clásico poema de béisbol, *Casey at the Bat*, captura en unos pocos versos el espectáculo, los sonidos y la emoción de un partido de béisbol. El anotador está dos a cuatro, es el fin de la novena entrada y parece casi seguro que el equipo de Mudville va a perder. Hay dos hombres afuera y dos bateadores en base. Es entonces cuando Casey, la estrella del equipo, va a batear, en medio de la ovación de la multitud. Muy seguro de sí mismo, Casey entretiene a los aficionados y se burla del lanzador. Casey deja pasar las dos primeras bolas, y los aficionados protestan la decisión del árbitro que las considera *strikes*. Cuando lanzan la tercera bola, Casey batea con toda su fuera, y no conecta.

**Translate Baseball Phrases** This poem uses many words and phrases in unusual, colorful expressions that characterize the language of baseball. In order to understand what is happening, you need to "translate" these expressions into plain English. Sometimes a dictionary will tell you what these words mean. Sometimes you may need to ask someone familiar with the language of baseball to explain the phrases to you.

Look for these colorful words and phrases in the poem. Figure out what the underlined words mean, and write a translation in the second column. Add more words and phrases to the first column as you read.

| Baseball Phrases | Translation |
|---|---|
| 1. It looked rocky for the Mudville nine. | Rough, difficult—as it would be to travel on a road covered with rocks |
| 2. Cooney died at second. | |
| 3. Blakey tore the cover off the ball. | |
| 4. Flynn was a-huggin' third. | |
| 5. Five thousand tongues applauded. | |
| 6. The pitcher ground the ball into his hip. | |

## "The Birds" by Daphne du Maurier

**Summary** In a terrifying tale of the random violence of nature, the peace and beauty of an isolated English farm are shattered by hundreds of murderous birds. Nat Hocke, his wife, and their two children first notice that the birds seem restless. That night a small flock bangs against the outside of the cottage. As Nat rushes to bolt the windows, dozens of birds attack his eyes and arms. He then charges upstairs to discover fifty birds in his children's bedroom. In daylight, the birds grow quiet; Nat prepares to protect his family from another attack. After another night of terror, Nat and his family awake to find their neighbors pecked to death and carcasses of dead birds strewn across the farm. The story ends with Nat shoring up the cottage as still larger birds splinter the doors.

**Resumen** Este relato muestra un aspecto siniestro de la naturaleza cuando cientos de pájaros homicidas destruyen la paz y belleza de un remota granja inglesa. Nat Hocke, su esposa y sus dos niños, notan primero un nerviosismo en los pájaros. Luego, una pequeña bandada se arroja contra las ventanas de la casa. Nat corre a cerrarlas y los pájaros lo picotean en los ojos y brazos. Nat luego corre al piso alto, donde descubre cincuenta pájaros en el cuarto de los niños. En el día, los pájaros se calman y Nat se prepara para proteger a su familia de otro ataque. Después de otra noche de terror, Nat y su familia descubren a sus vecinos muertos a picotazos, y a pájaros muertos por toda la granja. El relato termina con Nat reforzando la casa mientras los pájaros más grandes comienzan a astillar las puertas.

**Use a Timeline** This story builds in suspense from day to day. Work with a partner to divide the story into days. Use a chart like the one below to record the events of each day in the order in which they happen.

**Timeline**

| Day 1 Events | Day 2 Events | Day 3 Events |
| --- | --- | --- |
| | | |
| | | |
| | | |
| | | |
| | | |
| | | |
| | | |
| | | |
| | | |
| | | |

# "The Red-headed League" by Sir Arthur Conan Doyle

**Summary** In this spine-tingler, Sherlock Holmes uses his powers of observation and deductive reasoning to solve the mystery of an elaborate deception. Jabez Wilson, the red-haired owner of a small pawnshop, was employed by a group called "The Red-headed League" for four hours a day for eight weeks, after which his job was mysteriously eliminated. Wilson had learned of the job from his assistant, who volunteered to watch the pawnshop while the owner was away. Piecing the clues together, Holmes quickly suspects that the assistant is a notorious thief named John Clay who, Holmes surmises, set Wilson up with the phony job so that he could dig a tunnel from the shop cellar to a nearby bank. That night, Holmes and his trusted colleague Dr. Watson catch the criminals red-handed.

**Resumen** En esta selección, Sherlock Holmes usa sus poderes de observación y de deducción para resolver el misterio de un engaño. Jabez Wilson, un pelirrojo dueño de una casa de empeños, trabajaba cuatro horas por día para el grupo *The Red-headed League,* cuando su trabajo es misteriosamente eliminado. Wilson se había enterado del trabajo por su asistente, quien había ofrecido encargarse del negocio cuando Wilson estuviera trabajando. Usando las pistas, Holmes sospecha que el asistente es John Clay, un ladrón famoso, y que éste había engañado a Wilson con un trabajo falso, y así poder hacer un túnel desde el sótano del negocio hasta un banco vecino. Esa noche, Holmes y su colega, el Dr. Watson, capturan a los criminales *in fraganti.*

**Break Down Sentences** Many of the sentences in this story are four or five lines long—or even longer. To help you understand the long sentences, break them down into parts. For example:

**Sentence:** I had called upon my friend, Mr. Sherlock Holmes, one day in the autumn of last year and found him in deep conversation with a very stout, florid-faced, elderly gentleman with fiery red hair.

**Sentence broken into parts:** Last autumn I had called upon my friend, Mr. Sherlock Holmes. I found him in deep conversation with an elderly gentleman. The elderly gentleman was very stout and florid-faced. He had fiery red hair.

Find at least four more sentences that are four or more lines long. Break them into parts. Compare your sentences with those of your classmates.

1. _____

_____

_____

2. _____

_____

_____

3. _____

_____

_____

4. _____

_____

_____

**"The Listeners"** by Walter de la Mare
**"Beware: Do Not Read This Poem"** by Ishmael Reed
**"Echo"** by Henriqueta Lisboa

**Summary** These three poems begin and end in mystery, with images that hint at possibilities, not solutions. In "The Listeners," a man knocks on the moonlit door of a house. Inside, phantoms hear his voice but they do not answer. He senses their presence, shouts that he has kept his word, and then rides off on his horse. "Beware: Do Not Read This Poem" tells two stories. In the first story, a woman and other people disappear into a mirror. The second story is the tale of what happens to the reader who disappears into the poem. "Echo" describes parrots screaming in the jungle, their screams echoing off the rocks, but concludes that despite the blood-chilling sound, "no one died."

**Resumen** Éstos tres poemas comienzan y terminan en un misterio, y sus imágenes sugieren posibilidades, no soluciones. En *The Listeners,* un hombre llama a la puerta de una casa, iluminada por la luna. Adentro, fantasmas escuchan su voz pero no le responden. El hombre siente la presencia de los fantasmas, les grita que él ha mantenido su palabra y se aleja galopando. *Beware: Do Not Read This Poem,* trata de dos historias. Primero, una mujer y otras personas desaparecen en un espejo. Segundo, el poema cuenta qué le sucede al lector que desaparece en el poema. *Echo,* describe a loros gritando en la selva, el eco de sus gritos que rebota en las rocas y termina diciendo que, a pesar del escalofriante sonido, "nadie murió."

**Restate Poetry as Prose** Some poets write without punctuation or capital letters and use unusual symbols and spellings. Only the lines and their placement on the page help you follow the meaning. "Beware: Do Not Read This Poem" is written this way. In order to understand the poem better, you could rewrite the text of the poem as if it were prose. For each stanza of the poem, add capital letters, punctuation, and standard spelling to help you follow the meaning. For example, the first stanza would look like this:

Tonight, *Thriller* was about an old woman, so vain she surrounded herself with many mirrors. It got so bad that finally she locked herself indoors and her whole life became the mirrors.

Choose one poem to rewrite as prose. If you choose "Echo," rewrite the entire poem. If you choose "Beware: Do Not Read This Poem," rewrite a stanza. If you choose "The Listeners," Rewrite from lines 8–10.

_____

_____

_____

_____

_____

_____

_____

_____

_____

Name _____ Date _____

## "Caucasian Mummies Mystify Chinese" by Keay Davidson

**Summary** What's mysterious about mummies? This news article reports the discovery of more than 100 mummified bodies in a desert in northwestern China—Caucasian, not Asian, mummies. With their blond hair and white skin, these 4,000-year-old mummies alter the traditional view of Chinese history and suggest that China has been influenced by other civilizations throughout its long history. Remarkably, these bodies are preserved well enough to allow scientists to conduct DNA testing to discover who the mummies were and where they came from. The article reports that the discovery so baffled Chinese scholars that they kept the news to themselves for several years. According to the report, "It just didn't make sense to them."

**Resumen** ¿Cuál es el misterio de las momias? Este artículo nos estremece con la noticia de que, en un desierto del noroeste de China se han descubierto 100 cuerpos momificados. Las momias no son de asiáticos, sino de caucásicos. Con su pelo rubio y piel blanca, estas momias de 4,000 años cambian completamente la interpretación tradicional de la historia de China y sugieren la influencia de otras civilizaciones. Las momias están suficientemente bien preservadas como para que se puedan realizar pruebas de ADN y establecer quiénes eran y de dónde venían. El artículo afirma que el descubrimiento desconcertó tanto a los estudiosos chinos que por años fue un secreto. Según el artículo, "Simplemente, no tenía sentido para ellos."

**Analyze Sources** Newspaper reporters write about many subjects, but they're not experts on all of them. Reporters rely on authorities whom they interview for information. "Caucasian Mummies Mystify Chinese" refers to many such authorities. The one most often quoted is Victor Mair. As you read the article, look for the reporter's use of Mair's exact words—those words inside quotation marks with Mair's name before or after. Make a list of at least five important details provided by Mair or other authorities in the article.

| Quotation | Details |
|---|---|
|  |  |
|  |  |
|  |  |
|  |  |
|  |  |
|  |  |
|  |  |
|  |  |
|  |  |
|  |  |
|  |  |

## from *A Lincoln Preface* by Carl Sandburg

**Summary** This selection reflects the admiration Sandburg felt for the president who led the nation through the Civil War and afterward was assassinated. The author brings Abraham Lincoln's contradictory character to life through stories, recollections, and quotations. During the war, Lincoln held near dictatorial powers and brought about tremendous social and economic changes. When he died in April 1865, the nation, which had been reluctant to reelect him, mourned deeply. Sandburg shows Lincoln to be a man of contrasts—possessing a great sense of humor and insight into people, sometimes cunning and manipulative, often gracious and merciful. Sandburg crafts a portrait of a man determined to save the Union at all costs.

**Resumen** Esta selección refleja la admiración que Sandburg sintió por el presidente que condujo a la nación durante la Guerra Civil y que murió asesinado. El autor muestra el complejo carácter de Lincoln a través de historias, recuerdos y citas. Durante la guerra, Abraham Lincoln tuvo poderes casi dictatoriales e introdujo tremendos cambios sociales y económicos. Cuando murió, en abril de 1865, la nación que se había mostrado reacia a reelegirlo, sintió un dolor profundo. Sandburg muestra a Lincoln como a un hombre de contrastes, con gran sentido del humor y una gran intuición, a veces astuto y manipulador, con frecuencia cortés y misericordioso. Sandburg crea el retrato de un hombre determinado a salvar la Unión a toda costa.

**Summarize** This excerpt from *A Lincoln Preface* is made up of many little stories, or anecdotes. Most (but not all) paragraphs begin a new story. Choose ten of the anecdotes and write a one-sentence summary of each. Two have been modeled for you. When you finish, compare your summaries to those of your classmates.

1. A guard left his watch at the door, and Lincoln was shot and killed.

2. During Lincoln's presidency, the bloody Civil War brought much loss of property.

3. _____

4. _____

5. _____

6. _____

7. _____

8. _____

9. _____

10. _____

## "I Have a Dream" by Martin Luther King, Jr.
### from *Rosa Parks: My Story* by Rosa Parks with Jim Haskins
### "There Is a Longing . . ." by Chief Dan George
### "I Hear America Singing" by Walt Whitman

**Summary** Persuasive, exhilarating, and inspiring, these four selections describe the struggle for civil rights and the authors' visions of the United States. Martin Luther King, Jr., dreams that blacks and whites will join in brotherhood, with equal opportunity for all. Rosa Parks tells firsthand about her refusal to move to the back of a bus to allow white people to sit down. Her act sparked the civil rights movement of the 1960's. Chief Dan George longs to see his fellow Native Americans freed from the hardships and mistakes of the past, and living in dignity with a sense of worth and purpose. Walt Whitman captures the spirit of the United States by celebrating the diversity of voices in the workplace—from the mechanic to the mason.

**Resumen** Persuasivas, vívidas e inspiradoras, éstas selecciones describen la lucha por los derechos civiles y la visión de Estados Únidos de cada autor. Martin Luther King, Jr. sueña con negros y blancos unidos como hermanos, y con igualdad de oportunidades para todos. Rosa Parks cuenta de cuando se rehusó a ceder su asiento e ir a la parte posterior de un autobús. Esta acción inició el Movimiento por los derechos civiles de la década 1960–1970. El Jefe Dan George anhela ver a sus hermanos, los indígenas americanos, libres de las penurias y errores del pasado, viviendo con dignidad, con autoestima y propósito en sus vidas. Walt Whitman captura el espíritu de Estados Únidos al celebrar la diversidad de voces en el lugar de trabajo, desde el mecánico hasta el albañil.

**Identify Key Ideas** The writers of these selections talk about civil rights and their vision of the United States. In a small group, take turns reading the selections aloud. Read each prose selection one paragraph at a time, and each poem one stanza at a time. As you read, make a list of the rights or dreams each writer names or suggests. When you are finished, compare your list with those of your classmates. The first entry has been done for you.

### "I Have a Dream"

1. All created equal
2. Brotherhood
3. Freedom
4. Justice

5. Judge people by character, not color
6. Walk as equals
7. Land of liberty

### from *Rosa Parks: My Story*


### "There Is a Longing"


### "I Hear America Singing"

## "The Golden Kite, the Silver Wind" by Ray Bradbury

**Summary** In this fable, two cities are locked in a rivalry. Messengers bring word to each ruler, or Mandarin, about the wall of the rival town. Each time the Mandarin of one city changes his wall, the Mandarin of the other city changes his. One wall is shaped like a pig; the other, an orange. Since pigs eat oranges, the orange-shaped wall is changed to a club. Clubs beat pigs, so another wall is changed. And so it goes until the effort to alter the walls makes the people of both cities exhausted and sick. The two leaders finally meet and agree to make one wall in the shape of the wind, the other in the shape of a kite. Without wind, kites cannot fly; without kites, the sky is dull. The message is clear: Cooperation helps everyone involved.

**Resumen** En esta fábula hay dos ciudades rivales. Los mensajeros llevan noticias a los gobernantes, o mandarines, acerca de las murallas de la ciudad rival. Cada vez que un mandarín cambia sus murallas, el otro cambia las suyas. Una muralla tiene forma de cerdo; la otra de naranja. Como los cerdos comen naranjas, la muralla en forma de naranja es cambiada por la de un garrote. Los garrotes golpean a los cerdos. Y así continúa todo hasta que el trabajo de cambiar las murallas hace que la gente de ambas ciudades se enferme y empiece a morir. Los dos líderes se encuentran y acuerdan hacer una muralla en forma de viento y la otra en forma de cometa. Sin viento las cometas no pueden volar, sin cometas el cielo es aburrido. El mensaje es claro: la cooperación es mejor para todos.

**Recognize Cause and Effect** Listen to the audiocassette recording of the story. Make a cause-and-effect chart like the one below to show how each city wall changes as a result of the change in the other city's wall. The first line of the chart has been done for you.

**Walls of First City (Cause)**          **Other City's Response (Effect)**

| First Shape: orange | → | Response: pig to eat orange |

| Next Shape: | → | Response: |

| Next Shape: | → | Response: |

| Next Shape: | → | Response: |

| Next Shape: | → | Response: |

**"The Road Not Taken"** by Robert Frost
**"New Directions"** by Maya Angelou
**"To be of use"** by Marge Piercy

**Summary** These three selections celebrate the strength of the human spirit, as characters make choices at decisive points in their lives. In "The Road Not Taken," the speaker chooses a road that few people have traveled and reflects on how that choice has affected his life. In "New Directions," a poor woman left alone to take care of her small children is offered few opportunities. She decides to start a business of her own. With hard work and commitment, she turns the business into a success and finds the fulfillment she is seeking. In "To be of use," the speaker celebrates people who work hard, find meaning in their work, and give themselves wholly to the task at hand.

**Resumen** Éstos tres poemas celebran la fuerza del espíritu humano representado por tres personajes que toman decisiones en momentos determinados de sus vidas. En *The Road Not Taken,* el narrador elige un camino que poca gente recorre y reflexiona sobre cómo esa decisión ha afectado su vida. En *New Directions,* a una mujer pobre, que debe criar sola a sus niños, se le presentan muy pocas oportunidades. Ella decide empezar su propio negocio. Con dedicación, y mucho trabajo, la mujer logra que su negocio sea un éxito y halla la satisfacción que buscaba. En *To be of use,* la narradora elogia a la gente que trabaja duro, halla satisfacción en su trabajo y se entrega por completo a lo que hace.

**Paraphrase** Sometimes poetry seems hard to understand, the ideas hard to find. Sometimes, the best way to tackle poetry is to read it a sentence, or phrase, at a time, pausing at punctuation marks rather than at the end of each line. In a small group, take turns reading aloud "The Road Not Taken" and "To be of use." When you get to the end of a sentence—that is, to a period or semicolon—restate, or paraphrase, that part in your own words. For example, the first sentence in "The Road Not Taken" is the first five lines, up to the semicolon. Your paraphrase of that sentence might be something like this:

When I came to a fork in the road, I knew I couldn't go both ways, so I just looked down one way as far as I could see.

Take turns reading one of the poems and writing the sentences in your own words. When you finish, compare your sentences with those of your classmates.

_____
_____
_____
_____
_____
_____
_____
_____
_____
_____
_____

Name _____  Date _____

## "Old Man of the Temple" by R. K. Narayan

**Summary** In this fantasy tale set in India, the reader must decide what is fantasy and what is real. The story opens with a man and his driver on a lonely rural road at night. Doss, the driver, suddenly swerves the car, shouting at an old man. The narrator, however, sees no one. Doss claims to see the old man at the temple door, then in the car. The narrator, wondering about Doss's condition, sees Doss pass out. When awakened, Doss assumes an old man's personality. As he talks with the narrator, Doss claims to be Krishna Battar, a temple builder. The narrator tells Battar that he is dead and that he should join his deceased wife, Seetha. Battar falls, and Doss awakens as his old self. They learn that a strange knocking at the temple door had for years disturbed neighbors and animals. It occurred no more.

**Resumen** En este cuento fantástico que ocurre en la India, el lector debe decidir qué es fantasía y qué es real. Empieza con el narrador y Doss, su chófer, viajando de noche por una carretera rural. Doss repentinamente desvía el coche, y grita a un hombre viejo. El narrador no ve a nadie. Doss dice ver al viejo en la puerta de un templo y después en el coche. Luego, Doss pierde el conocimiento y cuando se recupera, tiene la personalidad del viejo. Doss le dice al narrador que su nombre es Krishna Battar, constructor de templos. El narrador le dice a Battar que está muerto, que debería reunirse con Sheeta, su mujer, también muerta. Cuando Battar se cae, Doss se despierta con su antigua personalidad. El narrador y Doss se enteran de que, por años, extraños golpes en la puerta del templo habían inquietado a los vecinos. Los golpes no ocurrieron más.

**Prepare a Readers Theater** This story contains narration and dialogue. With three classmates, plan a Readers Theater presentation of this story. Assign the four parts as follows:

One of you should read the narrator's thoughts.

Another should read the narrator's spoken words.

The third should be Doss.

The fourth should be Krishna Battar.

Practice reading your parts as a group. Battar should sound like an old man with "a thin, piping voice." The narrator and Doss should sound younger but mature. When you have practiced, present your Readers Theater to the class, or tape it to play for the class. Then ask your classmates to evaluate your performances.

Use the lines below to assign roles and jot down ideas about your performance.

| Role | Student |
| --- | --- |
| 1. Narrator's thoughts | _____ |
| 2. Narrator's spoken words | _____ |
| 3. Doss | _____ |
| 4. Krishna Battar | _____ |

**Performance Ideas** _____

_____

_____

_____

Name _____ Date _____

## "Perseus" by Edith Hamilton

**Summary** This Greek myth is a tale of adventure. It begins with a god telling King Acrisius that his grandson will kill him. Alarmed, the king casts his daughter Danaë and her son, Perseus, into the sea. They are rescued by Dictys. They live with him and his wife for many years until Polydectes, the ruler of the island, plots to marry Danaë and get rid of Perseus. Unaware of the ruler's intentions, Perseus promises the head of the monster Medusa as a wedding gift. After years of travel, and help from the gods, Perseus returns with Medusa's head. He kills Polydectes. Then he and his mother search for the old king. They find him quite by accident at an athletic contest. When Perseus throws a discus, he hits a spectator—the old king. The king dies. The prophecy comes true.

**Resumen** En este mito griego, un dios le dice al viejo rey Acrisius que su nieto lo matará. Alarmado, el rey abandona a su hija Danaë y a su nieto Perseus en el mar. Danaë y Perseus son rescatados por Dictys, y viven con él y su mujer varios años hasta que Polydectes, el gobernante de la isla, planea casarse con Danaë y deshacerse de Perseus. Sin conocer los planes del gobernante, Perseus le promete la cabeza de Medusa como regalo de bodas. Luego de viajar por años, y con la ayuda de los dioses, Perseus regresa con la cabeza de Medusa. Mata a Polydectes y luego, él y su madre buscan al viejo rey. Lo encuentran por accidente en un torneo deportivo. Cuando Perseus lanza el disco, éste golpea a un espectador: el viejo rey Acrisius. El rey muere, y se cumple así la profecía.

**Identify Characters** Keeping track of who's who in a story like "Perseus" aids understanding. Make your own "Who's Who" chart like the one below. First, name a character. Then, define the relationship between that character and other characters. Finally, list an important idea to identify him or her. The character Medusa has been done for you as an example.
Include these characters in your "Who's Who" list:

| | | | |
|---|---|---|---|
| Acrisius | Polydectes | Athena | Cepheus |
| Danaë | Gorgons | Gray Women | Apollo |
| Zeus | Medusa | Hyperboreans | Electryon |
| Perseus | Selli | Andromeda | Hercules |
| Dictys | Hermes | Cassiopeia | |

| Character | Relationship to Other Characters | Important Idea About Character |
|---|---|---|
| Medusa | one of the three ugly Gorgons | turned to stone anyone who looked at her |
| | | |
| | | |
| | | |
| | | |

Name _____     Date _____

## "Slam, Dunk, & Hook" by Yusef Komunyakaa
## "The Spearthrower" by Lillian Morrison
## "Shoulders" by Naomi Shihab Nye

**Summary** In these three poems, the characters face physical challenges. In "Slam, Dunk, & Hook," basketball players use their strength and skill in stiff competition. "The Spearthrower" honors women who compete in track with crowds cheering the heroines. "Shoulders" reminds readers that we must look out for one another in the same way that a man protectively carries his son asleep on his shoulder. Not all challenges are found in sports contests; everyday life has its challenges as well.

**Resumen** Los personajes de éstos tres poemas se enfrentan a desafíos físicos. En *Slam, Dunk, & Hook*, unos basquetbolistas se exigen al extremo usando fuerza física y habilidad en reñida competición. *The Spearthrower*, honra a las mujeres que compiten en eventos de pista, con multitudes que las alientan. *Shoulders*, nos recuerda que debemos protegernos unos a otros, de la misma manera en que un padre protege a su hijo cuando lo lleva dormido sobre sus hombros. Porque el exigirse al extremo no ocurre sólo en los deportes; la vida diaria es también un desafío.

**Explain Poetic Phrases** Some groups of words in these poems may be confusing. One way to understand unfamiliar phrases is to explain or restate the words and phrases in everyday language. Get together with two or three of your classmates, and determine how the following excerpts from "Slam, Dunk, & Hook," might be restated in everyday language. Two explanations have been given. Restate other lines from the poem at the end of the list.

| Confusing Phrases | Translation |
| --- | --- |
| 1. Mercury's insignia on our sneakers | 1. Mercury was a winged messenger; the sneakers are so marked by their manufacturer to make the players feel that they're flying. |
| 2. Hot swish of strings | 2. Sound of the ball going fast through the net; "hot" suggests the friction generated by the speed of the shot. |
| 3. Roundhouse labyrinth our bodies created | 3. _____ |
| 4. High note hung there a long second | 4. _____ |
| 5. Corkscrew up | 5. _____ |
| 6. Metaphysical when girls cheered | 6. _____ |
| 7. Muscles were a bright motor | 7. _____ |
| 8. Metal hoop nailed to our oak | 8. _____ |
| 9. _____ | 9. _____ |
| 10. _____ | 10. _____ |

### "Children in the Woods" by Barry Lopez

**Summary** In this poetic work of nonfiction, the author shares his thoughts on how to help children make the discoveries that enable them to understand their world. On a walk in the Cascade Mountain forest that surrounds his house, he and a group of children find a fragment of a raccoon's jaw. With this find, the children learn how different aspects of the natural world fit together. The author learns the importance of fostering the process of discovery rather than teaching the technical names for skeletal parts, plants, and animals. Understanding the relationships among parts of the whole in nature becomes a metaphor for how we can understand our own place in the world.

**Resumen** En este poético ensayo, el autor comparte sus pensamientos sobre cómo ayudar a los niños a hacer descubrimientos que los ayuden a entender su mundo. Durante una caminata por los bosques que rodean su casa, el autor y un grupo de niños encuentran un fragmento de la mandíbula de un mapache. Con este hallazgo, los niños aprenden cómo están relacionados distintos aspectos de la naturaleza. Por su parte, el autor aprende la importancia de alentar el proceso de descubrimiento en vez de simplemente enseñar los nombres de las partes del esqueleto, de las plantas y los animales. Entender las relaciones entre las partes de un todo en la naturaleza se convierte así en una metáfora sobre cómo entender nuestro propio lugar en el mundo.

**Outline Author's Argument** "Children in the Woods" is a nonfiction essay in which the author presents his ideas about how children should be taught to appreciate and understand the natural world. To help you follow the author's reasoning, make an outline that lists the main ideas and supporting details for each paragraph. Use the lines below to make notes on the main ideas and supporting details as you read.

_____

_____

_____

_____

_____

_____

_____

_____

_____

_____

_____

_____

_____

_____

_____

## "Rules of the Game" by Amy Tan

**Summary** In this story set in San Francisco's Chinatown, a generational tug-of-war is complicated by a conflict between Chinese and American cultures. As a young person of Chinese parentage who is growing up in the United States, nine-year-old Waverly is learning the unwritten and often unspoken rules of life while she learns the rules of chess. After her brother Vincent gets a used chess set, Waverly's fascination with the game blossoms. She challenges her brothers, the men at the park, and finally tournament players, eventually beating them all. Frustrated by her mother's tendency to "show her off," Waverly rebels and faces the toughest game of her life: how to deal with generational and cultural differences.

**Resumen** En este cuento ambientado en el barrio chino de San Francisco, las tensiones entre generaciones se complican aún más por el conflicto entre las culturas china y estadounidense. Waverly, una niña estadounidense de nueve años e hija de padres chinos, está aprendiendo las reglas no escritas, y muchas veces no mencionadas de la vida, al mismo tiempo que aprende las reglas del ajedrez. Después de que su hermano obtiene un juego usado de ajedrez, su fascinación por este juego florece. Waverly desafía a sus hermanos, a los hombres del parque y hasta a jugadores expertos, derrotando a todos. Frustrada por la tendencia de su madre a "exhibirla", Waverly se rebela y enfrenta el juego más difícil de su vida: cómo resolver las diferencias entre generaciones y culturas.

**Respond to Characters' Actions** In "Rules of the Game," the narrator explains how her actions conflict with her mother's wishes. As you read, you may agree or disagree with what the narrator says and does. To record your responses to her actions and those of other characters, make a chart like the one below. In the first column, list the character's name. In the second, tell what the character does. In the third, tell what you think about each character's actions. Share your chart with your classmates. The first example has been modeled for you.

| Character | What the Character Does | Your Reaction to What He/She Does |
|---|---|---|
| Mrs. Jong | She tells Waverly not to nag her to buy plums. | She sounds like a typical mother. |
|  |  |  |
|  |  |  |
|  |  |  |
|  |  |  |
|  |  |  |
|  |  |  |
|  |  |  |
|  |  |  |
|  |  |  |

Name _____ Date _____

## "Checkouts" by Cynthia Rylant
## "Fifteen" by William Stafford

**Summary** In these two selections, characters learn something about themselves as they experience lost opportunities. In "Checkouts," a teenage girl and a bag boy in the supermarket are attracted to each other, and yet they never act on those feelings. In "Fifteen," a boy chances upon a riderless motorcycle with the engine still running. Although he thinks about how thrilling it would be to take the motorcycle for a spin, the boy instead helps the injured owner. In both of these selections, the authors use irony, or a discrepancy between what the reader expects and what really happens, to capture the contradictory impulses of young people.

**Resumen** En éstas dos selecciones, los personajes pierden oportunidades pero aprenden algo sobre sí mismos. En *Checkouts*, una adolescente y un muchacho que trabaja en un supermercado se sienten atraídos pero nunca hacen nada para investigar esos sentimientos. En *Fifteen*, un muchacho encuentra una motocicleta con el motor en marcha y sin conductor. El muchacho admira la motocicleta e imagina lo apasionante que sería montarse en ella y andar por las rutas, pero en vez de hacerlo ayuda al conductor que está herido. En ambas selecciones, los autores usan la ironía, o una discrepancia entre lo que el lector espera que ocurra y lo que en realidad sucede, para capturar los impulsos contradictorios de los jóvenes.

**Analyze Characters' Behavior** Read "Checkouts" with a partner, one or two paragraphs at a time. As you read, make a character analysis chart like the one below. In the first column of the chart, write what the girl in the story does. In the second column, write why she does what she does. Then add the checkout boy to the chart, and list his actions and why he does what he does. The first entry has been done for you.

Use the same kind of character analysis chart for "Fifteen." Compare your explanations with those of your classmates.

### "Checkouts"

| Character | What the Character Does | Why the Character Does It |
|---|---|---|
| The girl | She spends days going through old pictures. | She misses her old life. |
| | | |
| | | |
| | | |
| | | |
| | | |
| | | |
| | | |
| | | |
| | | |
| | | |

**"Sympathy"** by Paul Laurence Dunbar
**"Caged Bird"** by Maya Angelou
**"We never know how high we are"** by Emily Dickinson
**from *In My Place*** by Charlayne Hunter-Gault

**Summary** These four selections tell about the way that dreams drive our secret lives, and suggest that a dream is part of our identity. In "Sympathy," the poet sympathizes with a caged bird that so wants to escape that it beats its wings bloody against the bars. It sings a plea for freedom. In "Caged Bird," the poet compares the caged bird with the free bird, lyrically describing how the caged bird sings for freedom. "We never know how high we are" celebrates people's accomplishments and our ability to rise to an occasion. In the excerpt from *In My Place*, the author shares her experience in 1961 of being the first African American to enroll at the University of Georgia. She and a fellow student suffered threats and physical danger, but their dreams held fast.

**Resumen** Estas cuatro selecciones sugieren que nuestros sueños manejan nuestros anhelos más secretos y son parte de nuestra identidad. En *Sympathy*, el poeta sabe qué siente un pájaro enjaulado que anhela tanto escapar que golpea sus alas contra las rejas hasta ensangrentarlas. En *Caged Bird*, la autora compara al pájaro enjaulado con el pájaro libre, describiendo líricamente su canto por la libertad. *We never know how high we are*, elogia los logros de la gente y su habilidad para hacer frente a todo. En el pasaje de *In My Place*, la autora describe su experiencia como la primera estudiante afroamericana matriculada en la Universidad de Georgia en 1961. Ella y otro estudiante recibieron amenazas y corrieron peligro físico, pero mantuvieron sus sueños con firmeza.

**Compare and Contrast Images** One way to compare themes in different works of literature is to compare and contrast the images that writers use to express their theme. The poets of "Sympathy" and "Caged Bird" both use the same image—a bird in a cage. Using a Venn Diagram like the one below, compare and contrast the image in these poems. Write the differences in the outer sections of the circles. Write the similarities in the overlapping part of the circles.

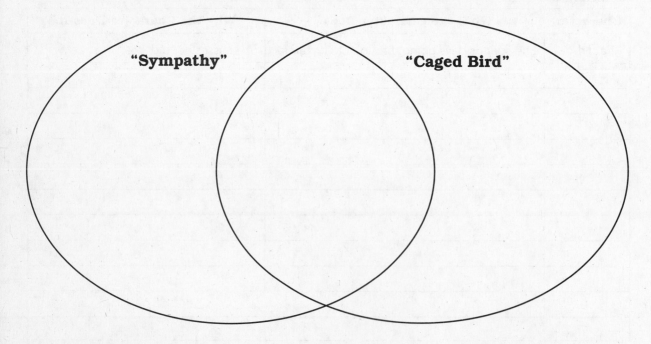

## "The Interlopers" by Saki (H. H. Munro)

**Summary** In this story, a catastrophe helps people discover what's truly important in life. Two men meet in a forest, prepared to kill each other because of a long-standing dispute over a piece of land. Before they can act, however, a storm knocks down a tree, pinning the pair to the ground. Badly hurt and unable to move, they continue to quarrel, vowing to fight until death. After threatening one another, they lie silently waiting to be rescued. One man, Ulrich, manages to open his flask, and he offers the other, Georg, a sip of wine. Georg refuses, but Ulrich makes an effort to end the feud. Georg agrees. Together they shout for help and soon hear the sound of movement in the woods. Ulrich can make out nine or ten figures approaching. Unfortunately, the figures are not men but wolves.

**Resumen** En este cuento una catástrofe ayuda a dos hombres a descubrir qué es realmente importante en la vida. Los hombres se encuentran en un bosque para matarse uno al otro de por una antigua disputa sobre tierras. Sin embargo, antes de que puedan hacerlo, un árbol cae sobre ellos y los inmoviliza. Malheridos y sin poder moverse, continúan peleando, y prometen hacerlo hasta la muerte. Luego se callan y esperan por ayuda. Uno de ellos, Ulrich, le ofrece al otro, Georg, un trago de vino. Georg lo rehusa, pero Ulrich continúa su esfuerzo para terminar la disputa. Al fin, Georg acepta. Juntos gritan para lograr socorro y pronto escuchan movimientos en el bosque. Ulrich ve nueve o diez figuras que se acercan. Desgraciadamente, no son hombres sino lobos.

**Follow Dialogue** Most of this story consists of dialogue between the two characters, Georg, the poacher, and Ulrich von Gradwitz, the landowner. Play the audiocassette recording of the story as you follow along in your book. Listen carefully to the dialogue between Ulrich and Georg. Then make a dialogue flow chart like the one below to follow the conversation between the two characters. The first few bits of conversation have been charted for you. When you finish, compare your flow chart with those of your classmates.

| Poacher Georg | Landowner Ulrich |
|---|---|
| "So you're not killed . . . but you're caught, anyway. . . . there's real justice for you!" | "I'm caught in my own forest land. . . . you will wish, perhaps, you weren't caught poaching on a neighbor's land." |
| | |

## "The Rug Merchant" by James A. Michener

**Summary** In this nonfiction work, the author makes discoveries about other people that help him see himself in a new way. The setting is a hotel in the Middle East. A thin, toothy man with an irresistible smile rides up on a camel, walks into a room, and throws dozens of beautiful carpets on the floor. The author protests that he doesn't have any money. For four days, the rug merchant persists. Finally, he persuades the author to make a purchase by offering to ship four rugs to the United States and accepting only a hand-written check as payment. It takes five years before the author's check clears and the rugs arrive. Why? As it turns out, the rug merchant used the author's improvised check (and his good name) as an advertisement to customers around the world.

**Resumen** El autor de este relato de no ficción descubre cosas sobre otra gente que lo ayudan a verse a sí mismo desde una nueva perspectiva. Un hombre delgado, de dientes grandes y sonrisa irresistible llega a un hotel del Medio Oriente montado en un camello, entra en un cuarto y arroja al suelo docenas de hermosas alfombras. El autor dice que no tiene dinero pero el vendedor de alfombras insiste por cuatro días. Finalmente, persuade al autor de hacer una compra con la asombrosa oferta de enviar cuatro alfombras a Estados Unidos y aceptando un cheque como pago. Toma cinco años para que el cheque se cobre y lleguen las alfombras. ¿Por qué? Resulta que el vendedor de alfombras usó el cheque del autor como un anuncio para otros clientes en otras partes del mundo.

**Question Author's Purpose** As you read a nonfiction work you should ask yourself why the writer gives you the information in the way that he or she does. Make a record of "The Rug Merchant" by asking a question for each paragraph and writing an answer to your question. A sample question and answer for the first three paragraphs have been modeled below.

1. **Q:** Why does Michener tell about the mosque and the man with the rugs?

   **A:** Michener introduces the reader to his subject with the story of how he first met the rug merchant.

2. **Q:** Who is this man with the rugs?

   **A:** He is a salesman.

3. **Q:** What does the man want Michener to do?

   **A:** He wants him to examine the rugs.

Name _____ Date _____

### "Combing" by Gladys Cardiff
### "Women" by Alice Walker
### "maggie and milly and molly and may" by E. E. Cummings
### "Astonishment" by Wisława Szymborska

**Summary** In these four poems, the speakers explore their identities through family connections, nature, and an appreciation of the world around us. "Combing" describes how women in different generations discover who they are as they fix each other's hair. "Women" addresses the strength of the women who paved the way for future generations. In "maggie and milly and molly and may," four girls identify with the treasures of the sea—shells, starfish, crabs, and stones. In "Astonishment," the poet explores some fundamental questions about life: why she is here at this particular time in this particular place.

**Resumen** Las mujeres en estos cuatro poemas exploran sus identidades a través de conexiones familiares, la naturaleza y una apreciación del mundo que nos rodea. *Combing* describe cómo mujeres de distintas generaciones descubren quiénes son mientras se ayudan a peinarse. *Women* se refiere la fortaleza de las mujeres que abrieron senderos para futuras generaciones. En *maggie and milly and molly and may,* cuatro niñas se identifican con los tesoros del mar: caracolas, estrellas de mar, cangrejos y piedras. En *Astonishment,* la poeta explora algunas preguntas fundamentales sobre la vida: ¿por qué está aquí, en este momento y lugar específicos?

**Connect** In these poems, the characters explore their identities by making connections to family, other generations, nature, or their place in the universe. For each poem, list a character, whom or what that character connects with, and what is discovered through this connection. The first one has been modeled for you.

| Character | Connects with Whom or What? | What is discovered? |
| --- | --- | --- |
| Speaker in "Combing" | other generations of women in her family | Combing hair is something that connects the generations of women in her family. |
| | | |
| | | |
| | | |
| | | |

Name _____ Date _____

## "The Secret Life of Walter Mitty" by James Thurber

**Summary** In this story, Walter Mitty, an ordinary man, leaves his tiresome day-to-day existence behind as he imagines himself a hero in a number of bold and exciting situations. His daydreams are triggered by common events on a shopping trip with his wife. Driving to town, he sees himself as a navy officer leading his ship through a hurricane. Passing a hospital, he imagines himself as a world-famous surgeon saving the life of a multimillionaire. Intermittently, events bring him back to reality—his wife nags him about his driving and, later, he nearly has an accident in the parking lot. As Mitty continues his shopping expedition, each errand triggers another daydream. The contrast between his secret life and his real life provides some genuinely comic moments.

**Resumen** En esta historia, Walter Mitty, un hombre común, escapa de su aburrida vida diaria imaginándose que es el héroe de situaciones emocionantes y audaces. Sus sueños son activados por sucesos comunes mientras va de compras con su mujer. Conduciendo hacia la ciudad, Mitty imagina que es un capitán navegando su barco durante un huracán. Al pasar frente a un hospital, Mitty imagina que es un cirujano de fama mundial, salvándole la vida a un multimillonario. Por momentos, distintos sucesos lo vuelven a la realidad: su mujer critica su manera de conducir y, más tarde, está a punto de tener un accidente en el estacionamiento. Y así, cada situación produce otro sueño. El contraste entre su vida secreta y su vida real ofrece algunos momentos verdaderamente cómicos.

**Distinguish Between Fantasy and Reality** In order to understand this story, you need to recognize when Mitty is daydreaming and when he is not. To help you distinguish between reality and the character's daydream fantasies, look for signals in the story that mark the shifts. Pause at the end of each page and fill in a chart like the following. For each page of the story, list examples of fantasy in the first column and examples of reality in the other. The first entry has been done for you.

| Fantasy | Reality |
|---|---|
| Mitty is a Commander in full-dress uniform. | Mrs. Mitty complains he is driving too fast. |

## "The Inspector-General" by Anton Chekhov

**Summary** In this play, set in Russia in the nineteenth century, a traveler begins asking his driver questions about the newly-appointed inspector-general, a government official appointed by the ruling czar to keep an eye on local affairs. The driver responds with detailed information provided, he says, by gossip from the inspector-general's servants. He tells of the inspector-general's failed attempts to disguise himself, his strange wheezing when he talks, and even his drinking habits. By the end of the story, the reader realizes that the traveler is, in fact, the inspector-general. Although the traveler feels humiliated when his charade backfires, the situation is humorous because he seems to be getting what he deserves.

**Resumen** Esta obra tiene lugar en Rusia, en el siglo XIX. Un viajero le hace preguntas a su conductor acerca del inspector general, un nuevo funcionario del gobierno designado por el zar para supervisar los asuntos locales. El conductor responde con información detallada, que proviene según él, de los mismos sirvientes del inspector general. El conductor cuenta los fallidos intentos del funcionario para hacerse pasar por otra persona, de su respiración dificultosa al hablar, y hasta de su costumbre de beber. Hacia el fin del cuento, el lector se da cuenta de que el viajero es en realidad el inspector general. Si bien el viajero se siente humillado cuando su estratagema le sale mal, la situación es cómica porque parece ser que él recibe lo que se merece.

**Prepare a Readers Theater** Plays are written to be performed. Reading a play aloud is more rewarding than reading it silently. With two other classmates, plan a Readers Theater presentation of this play. Each should take one of these three parts:

    The Storyteller

    The Traveler

    The Driver

Practice reading your parts as a group. When you have practiced, present your Readers Theater to the class or record it to play for the class. Then ask your classmates to evaluate your performances.

    Use the lines below to assign roles and to jot down ideas about your performance.

| **Role** | **Student** |
| --- | --- |
| 1. Storyteller | _____ |
| 2. Traveler | _____ |
| 3. Driver | _____ |

**Performance Ideas** _____

_____

_____

_____

_____

_____

_____

_____

Name _____     Date _____

## "Go Deep to the Sewer" by Bill Cosby
## "Fly Away" by Ralph Helfer

**Summary** These two selections focus on finding the humor in difficult personal situations. In "Go Deep to the Sewer," comedian Bill Cosby uses sports jargon to describe how he and his boyhood friends used the city streets as ball fields. Sewer covers served as stickball bases. Parked cars made good linebackers. With his humor, Cosby draws parallels between the obstacles on the urban playing fields and the obstacles in life. In "Fly Away," a famous animal trainer, known for his work with dangerous beasts, tells about one of his greatest challenges. He trained 5,000 flies to sit, stay, and then fly away on command for the glory of a Hollywood film. In this humorous remembrance, the author tells his secret early on to allow the reader to sit back and watch the fun.

**Resumen** Estas selecciones muestran cómo la gente halla humor aun en situaciones difíciles. En *Go Deep to the Sewer,* Bill Cosby cuenta cómo él y sus amigos usaban las calles de la ciudad como campos de béisbol, las tapas del alcantarillado servían como bases de *stickball* y los carros estacionados eran buenas líneas de defensas. Cosby traza paralelos entre los obstáculos de los campos de juego urbanos y los de la vida. En *Fly Away,* un famoso adiestrador de animales cuenta uno de sus mayores retos. Adiestró a 5,000 moscas para que aterrízaran, se quedaran quietas y luego, siguieran volando bajo sus órdenes, en una película de Hollywood. En esta humorística remembranza, el autor revela su secreto al comienzo para permitir que el lector disfrute más de la lectura.

**Translate Jargon** Much of the humor in these selections comes from the vocabulary. For instance, Cosby uses professional sports jargon to describe street games. To understand unfamiliar jargon from sports or elsewhere, work with a partner to examine the meaning of words or phrases individually. Then translate the jargon into plain English. Practice this strategy on the following phrases. The first two have been done for you. When you finish, add other examples from the stories and translate them as well.

1. Asphalt fields  These are the city streets where they played.

2. Allowed almost no lateral movement  They couldn't run to either side on the narrow streets.

3. Taking a handoff and sweeping to glory _____

4. Quarterback could diagram plays with trash _____

5. You can hit me at the fender. _____

6. Zig out to the bakery _____

7. You fake goin' in deep and then buttonhook at the DeSoto. _____

8. _____

9. _____

10. _____

# "An Entomological Study of Apartment 4A" by Patricia Volk

**Summary** In this feature article, natural curiosity drives the author to collect the bugs found in her apartment and to take them to an expert for identification. Entomologist Louis Sorkin not only identifies each bug but also explains their habits. As the author and the expert trade humorous remarks, the reader learns a lot about these creatures. By making light of the problem of insects in her home, the author is able to pass on new and interesting details about these unwelcome guests.

**Resumen** La curiosidad de la autora de este ensayo, la impulsa a coleccionar los insectos que encuentra en su departamento y llevarlos a un experto para que los identifique. El entomólogo Louis Sorkin no sólo identifica cada insecto sino que también explica sus costumbres. Mientras la autora y el experto intercambian bromas, el lector aprende mucho sobre estos seres. Al tratar con humor el problema de tener insectos en su casa, la autora logra hacer conocer nuevos e interesantes detalles sobre estos inoportunos visitantes.

**Recognize Puns and Word Play** Much of the humor in this selection comes from the clever way the writer uses language. For example, describing the entomologist Louis Sorkin as if he were a bug—"has a prominent forehead, gently rounded abdomen and powerful bandy legs"— sets the tone of amusement for the article. Figure out what is amusing about each of the following phrases from the article, and write your explanation on the back of this page. The first has been modeled for you. Add other words and phrases to your list.

1. A black crawly thing with more legs than the Rockettes The Rockettes are a dancing group that perform at Radio City Music Hall in New York. Their routine is famous for its chorus line of perfectly timed high kicks.

2. We scuttle into a room crammed with journals, papers and boxes of stoppered vials.

3. On the wall, a sign reads, "Feeling Lousy?"

4. Sorkin is the 911 of insect emergencies.

5. Maybe moisturizer kills [certain follicle mites around the nose and forehead].

6. I head home thinking about the high drama that goes on behind the kitchen pegboard.

7. When I put in the chili powder it started to move.

8. Sorkin's personal favorite is grubs over easy.

9. Sorkin is encyclopedic.

10. Sorkin and I nod goodbye and shake hands, a Homo sapiens-specific ritual.

Name _____ Date _____

**"Macavity: The Mystery Cat"** by T. S. Eliot
**"Problems With Hurricanes"** by Victor Hernández Cruz
**"Jabberwocky"** by Lewis Carroll

**Summary** In these poems, the clever use of language and the depiction of amusing characters and events make you laugh out loud. In "Macavity: The Mystery Cat," a criminal cat breaks human laws and laws of gravity. He is suspected of many crimes but is never caught. In "Problems With Hurricanes," the poet combines the serious with the ridiculous for comic effect. An out-of-the-ordinary description of death by flying fruit makes this image of hurricanes hilarious. In "Jabberwocky," the poet uses made-up words to describe a hero battling fearsome beasts. The reader needs to guess at the meaning of these made-up words, which contrast humorously with this tale of daring.

**Resumen** El ingenioso uso del lenguaje y la descripción de personajes y sucesos cómicos de estos poemas logran despertar las carcajadas del lector. En *Macavity: The Mystery Cat*, un gato criminal rompe no sólo las leyes humanas sino también las de la gravedad. Lo sospechan culpable de muchos delitos pero no lo atrapan nunca. En *Problems with Hurricanes*, el poeta combina lo serio con lo ridículo para lograr un efecto cómico. La descripción de un hecho extraordinario: la muerte causada por fruta que vuela pinta una imagen absurda de los huracanes. En *Jabberwocky*, el autor inventa palabras para describir a un héroe en batalla con bestias terroríficas. El lector necesita adivinar el significado de estas palabras, lo que contrasta humorísticamente con esta historia de valor.

**Identify Incongruity** Often, the basis for humor is incongruity—the difference between what is expected and what is being described. For example, in "Problems With Hurricanes," the poet describes a serious topic—death—but uses unexpected comical details—death from flying fruit. Read or listen to audiocassette recordings of "Macavity: The Mystery Cat" and "Problems With Hurricanes" and list two or three places in each where the humor comes from the difference between what is expected and what is actually described.

"Macavity: The Mystery Cat" _____

_____

_____

_____

_____

_____

"Problems With Hurricanes" _____

_____

_____

_____

_____

_____

_____

## "Talk" Retold by Harold Courlander and George Herzog

**Summary** A strange and funny folk tale, "Talk" tells about people's reactions when objects speak out, revealing minds of their own. The tale, set in western Africa, begins as a farmer is digging yams. One yam, which has felt neglected all year, tells the farmer to go away and leave him alone. Next, the dog speaks up, the palm tree responds, and a stone talks. Frightened, the farmer runs toward the village. As he meets others along the way, they, too, hear objects talking: a fish trap, a bundle of cloth, the river, and finally the chief's stool. The last line of the story, spoken to the chief by the stool, adds the final bit of humor: "Imagine, a talking yam."

**Resumen** Esta original y divertido cuento popular, *Talk,* trata de las reacciones de la gente cuando los objetos comienzan a hablar y demuestran tener su propia personalidad. El cuento, ambientado en el oeste de África, comienza con una familia escarbando la tierra en busca de batatas. Una batata, que se ha sentido abandonada todo el año, le dice al granjero que se vaya y la deje tranquila. Luego, el perro comienza a hablar, la palmera le responde y una piedra también habla. Asustado, el granjero sale corriendo hacia el pueblo. A medida que encuentra a otra gente en su camino, ellos también escuchan hablar a las cosas: una trampa para peces, un atado de tela, el río y finalmente, el asiento del jefe. El cuento con un toque de humor: el jefe dice, "Imagínense, una batata que habla."

**Read Aloud** Folk tales are usually stories that are handed down from generation to generation by being told and retold. In "Talk," the read-aloud quality is particularly strong. Prepare to read the tale aloud. Make a list of the objects that speak, beginning with the yam. Then, with your classmates, choose parts and read the selection aloud. One person should be the narrator. Others should read the parts of the farmer, fisherman, weaver, bather, and chief. Still others should read the parts of the objects that speak. Use this page to assign roles and to jot down ideas about what kind of voice you might use to bring your character to life.

## "One Ordinary Day, With Peanuts" by Shirley Jackson

**Summary** An out-of-the-ordinary man, Mr. John Philip Johnson, seems to have as his goal helping people enjoy life. He entertains the child of a frustrated woman who is busy moving out of her apartment. He helps two people to enjoy a day off together. He gives a man money for lunch. He even gives birds and dogs peanuts. When he arrives home and talks about his work day with his wife, however, she tells about opposite experiences. She has caused people misery by filing complaints and having them arrested. The surprise comes when they agree that the next day they will trade jobs.

**Resumen** Mr. Philip Johnson parece ser una persona especial, cuya meta es ayudar a la gente a disfrutar de la vida. Entretiene al hijo de una mujer que se está mudando de su departamento. Ayuda a dos personas a disfrutar juntas de un día libre. Da dinero a un hombre para su almuerzo. Hasta le da cacahuates a los perros y los pájaros. Sin embargo, cuando Mr. Johnson llega a su casa y habla con su mujer sobre cómo les fue en el trabajo, ella le cuenta experiencias opuestas. Ella creó problemas a la gente presentando demandas contra ellos y haciéndolos arrestar. La sorpresa llega cuando los esposos acuerdan intercambiar trabajos al día siguiente.

**Use a Chain-of-Events Organizer** To appreciate a good story, readers should anticipate the events of a story as they unfold. Sometimes a storyteller will intentionally put a twist into a story that the reader could not anticipate.

Use a Chain-of-Events organizer like the following to list the events of the plot in the story as they unfold. Then label each event as predictable or not predictable. For example, it is *not* predictable that Mr. Johnson will give a carnation to the small child in the carriage.

**Event 1**
Mr. Johnson buys a carnation for his buttonhole and then gives it to a small child.

not predictable

↓

**Event 2**

↓

Name _____ Date _____

## from *The Road Ahead* by Bill Gates

**Summary** A nonfiction vision of the future, this excerpt from *The Road Ahead* tells about the direction Bill Gates sees for technology in the home. As a child, Gates remembers the frustration of missing a television show on the day and time it was broadcast. Today, video tape recorders (VCRs) allow viewing whenever one wishes, although there is the inconvenience of timers and tapes. In the future, however, movies, television shows, and other kinds of digital information will be stored on servers. Computers will then access video-on-demand for home televisions connected to the broadband network. It will become the money-making venture of the near future.

**Resumen** Este pasaje de *The Road Ahead*, un ensayo futurista, presenta la visión de Bill Gates sobre la función de la tecnología en el hogar. Gates recuerda la frustración que sufría de niño cuando no podía ver un programa de televisión en el día y hora en que se transmitía. Hoy en día, las videograbadoras (VCR's) permiten ver cualquier programa cuando uno lo desea, si bien todavía tenemos que lidiar con cintas y programadores. Sin embargo, en el futuro, los programas de televisión, y otros tipos de información digitalizada, estarán almacenados en bases de datos. Las computadoras tendrán acceso en todo momento a los videos que se verán en los televisores del hogar conectados a una amplia red de programación. Éste será el negocio más lucrativo del futuro inmediato.

**Outline Main Idea and Supporting Details** To understand nonfiction, you must find the main ideas and study the details that tell about them. Working with a partner, list the main ideas and supporting details in this excerpt from *The Road Ahead*. Name the main idea for each paragraph. Then list the details that tell about it. The first paragraph has been modeled for you.

**Main Idea:** When Gates was a child, the only way to see *The Ed Sullivan Show* was to tune in on Sunday night at 8:00.

**Details about the Main Idea:**

1. Could see famous musicians and other acts
2. If away from TV, too bad
3. If missed show, not part of conversation later

Name _____ Date _____

## "The Machine That Won the War" by Isaac Asimov

**Summary** In this futuristic story, a giant computer named Multivac is credited with winning a war against a rival planet named Deneb. As the three main characters discuss the victory, they reveal their own wartime activities. Henderson admits that he was forced to "correct" computer data that had become meaningless. Jablonsky admits that he knew Multivac was unreliable but did nothing about it. To protect his job, he, too, adjusted data until it looked right. Finally, Swift admits that he hadn't taken the data seriously anyway. In fact, he used the oldest computer available to make his war decisions: the flip of a coin.

**Resumen** En este cuento sobre el futuro, se dice que la victoria contra Deneb, un planeta rival, ha sido posible gracias a una supercomputadora llamada Multivac. Mientras los tres personajes principales hablan sobre la victoria, cada uno revela lo que hizo durante la guerra. Henderson admite que se vio forzado a "corregir" información que no tenía sentido. Jablonsky admite que él sabía que Multivac no era fiable pero que no había hecho nada al respecto. Para proteger su trabajo, él también había corregido información. Finalmente, Swift admite que él no había creído en la información de cualquier manera. De hecho, él había usado el método más antiguo que existe para tomar decisiones durante la guerra: tirar una moneda.

**Paraphrase Conversations** Some of the conversations in this story are hard to read because they seem to have so many ideas. One way to make them clear is to paraphrase, or restate, the main idea of the conversation. Choose one sentence spoken by each character—Henderson, Jablonsky, and Swift—and restate the idea of their conversation. Use the example as a guide.

**Example:**

Henderson: "Do you know to what extent data concerning our production capacity, our resource potential, our trained manpower—everything of importance to the war effort, in fact—had become unreliable and untrustworthy during the last half of the war?"

Paraphrase: Do you realize how inaccurate our information had become in recent years?

Sentence 1 Paraphrase

_____

_____

Sentence 2 Paraphrase

_____

_____

Sentence 3 Paraphrase

_____

_____

_____

Name _____ Date _____

### "Fire and Ice" by Robert Frost
### "There Will Come Soft Rains (War Time)" by Sara Teasdale
### "The Horses" by Edwin Muir
### "All Watched Over by Machines of Loving Grace" by Richard Brautigan

**Summary** In each of these selections, the poets warn readers to consider the possible impact of present events and developments on the future. In "Fire and Ice," the poet considers how the world may be destroyed by either desire or hate, as he considers death by fire or ice. In "All Watched Over by Machines of Loving Grace," the poet believes that machines will free us from labor, improve the quality of our lives, and allow us to appreciate the natural world. In "There Will Come Soft Rains," the poet warns that nothing in the natural world will know or care if people wipe themselves out through war. In "The Horses," a seven days' war brings silence to the earth. The arrival of a herd of horses signals rebirth and renewal as the powerful animals help people cultivate the fields.

**Resumen** Estos poemas tratan del posible impacto que sucesos y adelantos actuales téndrán en el futuro. En *Fire and Ice*, el poeta considera cómo el mundo podría ser destruido por el deseo o el odio, así como él considera la muerte por fuego o hielo. En *All Watched Over by Machines of Loving Grace*, el autor cree que las máquinas nos librarán del trabajo, mejorarán la calidad de la vida y nos permitirán apreciar al mundo natural. En *There Will Come Soft Rains*, el poeta nos advierte que la naturaleza no se enterará, ni le importará, si la humanidad se autodestruye. Una guerra de siete días trae el silencio a la Tierra en *The Horses*. La llegada de una manada de caballos significa renacimiento y renovación: estos poderosos animales ayudan a la gente a cultivar los campos.

**Interpret Poetic Images** Poets use images or word pictures to express ideas and feelings. In order to understand what these images express, you must first form a mental picture of them and then decide how that picture makes you feel.

Following are some of the images, or word pictures, from the poems. On the back of this paper, describe the picture that forms in your mind when you read each of these images, and then tell how it makes you feel. The first one has been modeled for you.

### "All Watched Over by Machines of Loving Grace"

1. cybernetic meadow
   a grassy field with computers scattered among the flowers—feels like an advertisement for the benefit of computers
2. all watched over/by machines of loving grace

### "There Will Come Soft Rains"

1. wild plum trees in tremulous white
2. Robins will wear their feathery fire

### "The Horses"

1. old bad world that swallowed its children quick/At one great gulp
2. nations lying asleep/Curled blindly in impenetrable sorrow

Name _____  Date _____

## "If I Forget Thee, Oh Earth . . ." by Arthur C. Clarke
## from *Silent Spring* by Rachel Carson
## "To the Residents of A.D. 2029" by Bryan Woolley

**Summary** These selections examine the future by studying the problems we face today. "If I Forget Thee, Oh Earth. . ." warns about the threat of nuclear destruction, as a small colony of survivors endure a bleak existence on the Moon. Their only hope is that distant descendants might one day return to Earth. In the excerpt from *Silent Spring*, the author warns that environmental disasters might one day destroy the world. In "To the Residents of A.D. 2029," the author writes for future readers about present-day wastefulness and a sense of decline. He remains optimistic, however, and wishes future generations four things: an understanding of history, a better relationship between man and nature, an appreciation of beauty, and a sense of humor.

**Resumen** Estas selecciones examinan el futuro estudiando los problemas actuales. *If I Forget Thee, Oh Earth* nos alerta sobre el peligro de destrucción nuclear relatando la historia de una pequeña colonia de sobrevivientes en la Luna. Su única esperanza es que un día sus descendientes puedan regresar a la Tierra. En el pasaje de *Silent Spring*, la autora dice que los desastres ecológicos podrían destruir el mundo. En *To the Residents of A.D. 2029*, el autor escribe para futuros lectores sobre el derroche y sentido de declinación actuales. Sin embargo, se mantiene optimista, y desea cuatro cosas para las futuras generaciones: comprensión de la historia, una mejor relación entre la gente y la naturaleza, apreciación de la belleza y sentido del humor.

**Identify Predictions** Each of the writers in these selections talks about what is happening in an imagined present time in order to show us what they predict will happen in the future. To keep track of the predictions, make a chart like the one below listing details for "Now" and "In the Future." (Remember that "Now" can be a past time or a future time; it need not be "today.")

| Selection Title | Now | In the Future (Prediction) |
|---|---|---|
| "If I Forget Thee, Oh Earth . . ." | Marvin and father in dome; take vehicle through Outside to see the destroyed Earth. |  |

## "Gifts" by Shu Ting
## "Glory and Hope" by Nelson Mandela

**Summary** These two selections look to the future with hope for peace among the world's people. "Gifts" asserts that Earth's gifts are simple but profound: ponds, sky, plants, sunlight, children, birds, everything. "Glory and Hope" reflects the author's hope for the future of a beautiful, bountiful South Africa. In a speech delivered at his presidential inauguration, Mandela thanks all who helped, pledges the protection of freedom for all, and vows to work toward amnesty for those still in prison. He pleads for all to work together to prevent future oppression.

**Resumen** Éstas dos selecciones miran hacia el futuro con la esperanza de paz entre los pueblos del mundo. *Gifts* reflexiona sobre los regalos de la Tierra, que, de tan simples, son profundos: agua, cielo, plantas, sol, niños, pájaros, todo. *Glory and Hope* refleja la esperanza de su autor sobre el futuro de una hermosa y rica África del Sur. Éste es el discurso que Nelson Mandela pronunció el día en que asumió el poder y, en él, Mandela agradece a todos los que ayudaron, promete proteger la libertad para todos y se compromete a trabajar por la amnistía de todos aquéllos que todavía están en prisión. Mandela ruega a todos que trabajen juntos para evitar cualquier intento de opresión en el futuro.

**Break Down Long Sentences** Breaking sentences into their parts helps you understand long and complicated sentences. Listen to the audiocassette recording of Nelson Mandela's speech. Then work with a partner to break down any sentence that is more than five lines long. Use the example as a model.

**Example:**

**Mandela's Sentence:** That spiritual and physical oneness we all share with this common homeland explains the depth of the pain we all carried in our hearts as we saw our country tear itself apart in terrible conflict, and as we saw it spurned, outlawed and isolated by the peoples of the world, precisely because it has become the universal base of the pernicious ideology and practice of racism and racial oppression.

**Sentence in Parts:** We all share spiritual and physical oneness with this common homeland. That [shared oneness] explains the depth of the pain we all carried in our hearts as we saw our country tear itself apart in terrible conflict. That [shared oneness] also explains the depth of pain we carried as we saw our country spurned, outlawed and isolated by the peoples of the world. [Our country was spurned, outlawed and isolated by the people of the world] because it has become the universal base of the pernicious ideology and practice of racism and racial oppression.

Name _____  Date _____

## "The Gift of the Magi" by O. Henry

**Summary** On Christmas Eve, Della realizes that she has only $1.87, a grossly inadequate sum, to buy a present for her husband Jim. Money is a problem for the couple, whose income has just been reduced from $30 to $20 per week. Impetuously, Della decides to sell her prize possession—her hair—in order to buy Jim a platinum fob chain for his prize possession—his watch. When Jim arrives home, he is shocked by Della's appearance, not only because her hair is gone, but also because he has just sold his watch in order to buy his Christmas present for Della—combs for her hair. Such sacrifices, the narrator concludes, are wise. They are the gifts of the magi.

**Resumen** Una Nochebuena, Della se da cuenta que sólo tiene $1.87, una suma realmente muy pequeña, para comprar un regalo a Jim, su esposo. El dinero es un problema para la pareja, cuyos ingresos se habían visto reducidos de $30 a $20 por semana. Impetuosamente, Della decide vender su más preciada posesión, su cabello, para comprar a Jim una cadena de platino para el reloj que él tanto quiere. Cuando Jim llega a casa, lo sorprende la apariencia de Della, no sólo porque ya no tiene su hermoso cabello, sino porque él acaba de vender su reloj para comprarle su regalo de Navidad, un juego de peines. Estos sacrificios, concluye el narrador, son sabios. Son regalos de los Reyes Magos.

**Simplify Word Order** Several of the sentences in "The Gift of the Magi" contain unusual words in an unexpected order. For each sentence or sentence part in the following paragraph, restate the sentence in a way that makes sense to you. Change the word order and use more familiar words. The first part of the paragraph has been done for you.

> In the vestibule below was a letter-box into which no letter would go, and an electric button from which no mortal finger could coax a ring. Also appertaining thereunto was a card bearing the name "Mr. James Dillingham Young."

1. In the vestibule below was a letter-box into which no letter would go.

   The mailbox in the hall below was too small for letters.

2. and an electric button from which no mortal finger could coax a ring.

   _____

3. Also appertaining thereunto was a card bearing the name "Mr. James Dillingham Young."

   _____

Choose another paragraph from the story, and practice the strategy of simplifying the word order.

_____

_____

_____

_____

_____

_____

Name _____ Date _____

## "Sonata for Harp and Bicycle" by Joan Aiken

**Summary** Jason wonders why employees must leave the office at 5:00 P.M., so he sneaks into the building at night. Inside he encounters a presence asking for Daisy. In the morning Berenice, a co-worker, explains that years ago, Heron, the night watchman, mistakenly thought Daisy had betrayed him when she failed to show up the night he planned to propose. However, she had simply overslept. Distraught, Heron jumped from the fire escape, and Daisy died soon after. Their ghosts have been searching for each other in the office every night since—he riding his bicycle, she playing the harp. That night Jason and Berenice reunite the ghosts by waking Daisy and summoning Heron. Jason and Berenice parachute to the ground and kiss in midair.

**Resumen** Jason se pregunta por qué los empleados deben salir de la oficina a las 5:00 P.M. Para averiguarlo, una noche se cuela en el edificio. Dentro, Jason encuentra una "presencia" preguntando por Daisy. Por la mañana, Berenice, otra empleada, le explica a Jason que años atrás, Heron, el sereno, pensó que Daisy lo había traicionado porque no había ido la noche que él iba a proponerle matrimonio. Pero Daisy simplemente se había quedado dormida. Enloquecido, Heron se había arrojado de la escalera de emergencia, y Daisy había muerto poco después. Desde entonces, sus espíritus se habían buscado por la oficina. Esa noche, Jason y Berenice reúnen a los espíritus despertando a Daisy y llamando a Heron. Jason y Berenice se arrojan en paracaídas y se besan en el aire.

**Explain Comparisons** The author of "Sonata for Harp and Bicycle" uses fresh and interesting comparisons to describe the people and places in the story. As you read this selection, write the comparisons you find and tell what you think the author intends by the comparison. Use a chart like the following. Two comparisons from the first few paragraphs of the story have been modeled for you.

| Person or thing being described | It is compared to | This comparison suggests |
|---|---|---|
| a room | the inside of a parcel | It is a very small room. |
| darkness | a flight of bats | It is very dark and somewhat frightening. |
| _____ | _____ | _____ |
| _____ | _____ | _____ |
| _____ | _____ | _____ |
| _____ | _____ | _____ |
| _____ | _____ | _____ |
| _____ | _____ | _____ |
| _____ | _____ | _____ |
| _____ | _____ | _____ |

Name _____   Date _____

## "The Scarlet Ibis" by James Hurst

**Summary** The narrator remembers his boyhood with his brother, Doodle. Doodle was different from other children and a disappointment to his brother, who resented the responsibility of caring for him and was sometimes cruel to him. Still, a bond developed between them. Pride drove the narrator to teach Doodle to walk—a feat others had deemed impossible—and to set other physical goals for him. One day Doodle noticed a dying scarlet ibis that had been blown far from its normal range by a storm. Later that day, in the same storm, and only moments after the narrator had cruelly abandoned him, Doodle was struck by lightning and died.

**Resumen** El narrador recuerda la niñez, compartida con su hermano Doodle. Diferente de otros niños, Doodle fue una desilusión para su hermano, quién resintió tener la responsabilidad de cuidarlo y a veces fue cruel con él. Sin embargo, se formó un vínculo entre ellos. Una cuestión de orgullo hizo que el narrador enseñara a Doodle a caminar, una hazaña que otros creían imposible, y también a establecer otras metas físicas para él. Un día, Doodle halla un ibis carmesí moribundo, que había perdido su camino durante una tormenta. Más tarde, durante la misma tormenta, y sólo unos momentos después de haber sido cruelmente abandonado por su hermano, Doodle muere al ser alcanzado por un rayo.

**Classify Descriptive Details** "The Scarlet Ibis" is full of descriptive details that appeal to the senses. Read the following passage. Use the chart to tell what you see and hear. List movements, colors, positions, sounds, and other details. One example has been provided in each category. Complete this passage, and then practice the strategy by doing this exercise with another passage from the story.

At that moment the bird began to flutter, but the wings were uncoordinated, and amid much flapping and a spray of flying feathers, it tumbled down, bumping through the limbs of the bleeding tree and landing at our feet with a thud. Its long, graceful neck jerked twice into an S, then straightened out and the bird was still. A white veil came over the eyes and the long white beak unhinged. Its legs were crossed and its clawlike feet were delicately curved at rest.

| Movements | fluttering, _____ |
| --- | --- |
| | _____ |
| Colors | white, _____ |
| | _____ |
| Positions | neck in S-shape, _____ |
| | _____ |
| Sounds | flapping, _____ |
| | _____ |
| Other Details | limbs of the bleeding tree, _____ |
| | _____ |

# "Blues Ain't No Mockin Bird" by Toni Cade Bambara
# "Uncle Marcos" by Isabel Allende

**Summary** These stories offer two views of memorable people and events from the authors' childhoods. In "Blues Ain't No Mockin Bird," the author recalls a day when two men from the county food-stamp program approached her Granny's home and began filming. Quietly, Granny refused them the right to film but was ignored. She then called for Granddaddy, who—with a show of his physical power—sent the men away. "Uncle Marcos" opens with Uncle Marcos lying in his coffin. A frequent visitor to his sister Nivea's home, Marcos had been a worldly adventurer and the first to bring an airplane to town. Most of all, he had been a friend and soulmate to his niece, Clara.

**Resumen** En esto relatos los autores recuerdan a gente y sucesos memorables de su niñez. La primera trata del día en que dos hombres del programa de cupones para comida se acercaron a la casa de Granny y comenzaron a filmar. Calmadamente, Granny les dijo que no podían filmar, pero los hombres no le prestaron atención. Granny llamó a Granddaddy, quien, haciendo muestra de su poder físico y mental, logró que los hombres se fueran. La segunda historia comienza con el tío Marcos en su ataúd. Marcos, quién visitaba a menudo la casa de su hermana Nivea, había sido un gran aventurero y el primero en traer un avión a la ciudad. Pero, por sobre todo, había sido el amigo y compañero del alma de su sobrina Clara.

**Understand Dialect** "Blues Ain't No Mockin Bird" is written in dialect, a way of speaking that is unique to certain people and places. Choose a passage that uses dialect and rewrite it the way you would state it, using your own words and sentences. An example from the story has been done for you. Complete this passage, and then practice the strategy by rewriting another passage from the story.

(1) I'm looking to Cathy to finish the story (2) cause she knows Granny's whole story before me even. (3) Like she knew how come we move so much and (4) Cathy ain't but a third cousin we picked up last Thanksgivin visitin. (5) But she knew it was on account of people driving Granny crazy (6) till she'd get up in the night and start packin. (7) Mumblin and packin and wakin everybody up (8) sayin, "Let's get on away from here before I kill me somebody."

1. I'm waiting for Cathy to finish the story. _____

2. _____

3. _____

4. _____

5. _____

6. _____

7. _____

8. _____

## "The Man to Send Rain Clouds" by Leslie Marmon Silko
## "The Invalid's Story" by Mark Twain

**Summary** In these two stories, setting is a key element; it affects the characters and the outcomes. In the first story, an old Indian dies in New Mexico. Leon, a relative, asks the Indian's spirit for much-needed rain. Then just before the burial, he asks the priest to sprinkle holy water on the body. Though upset that no Last Rites were performed, the priest agrees. Leon is happy; now that the spirit has water, perhaps rain will come. In "The Invalid's Story," the narrator tells of a time he accompanied a dead friend's body to Wisconsin. As the trip begins, however, he mistakenly loads the wrong box onto the train. Then someone leaves behind a smelly cheese. He and a train worker think the smell is from the decaying body. The smell grows so bad in the closed car that both men jump from the train into an icy storm. The experience has left the narrator's health ruined.

**Resumen** En estos dos cuentos, la ambientación es un elemento clave, que afecta tanto a los personajes como al desenlace. En el primero, un indio viejo muere en Nuev Mexico. Leon, un pariente, pide a su espíritu que envíe lluvia. Luego, Leon pide al cura que rocíe el cuerpo con agua bendita. El cura, aunque molesto porque el indio no recibió extremaunción, lo hace. Ahora que el espíritu tiene agua, tal vez llueva. En *The Invalid's Story*, el narrador cuenta de un viaje que hizo a Wisconsin llevando el cadáver de un amigo. Pero sube al tren una caja equivocada y alguien se olvida un queso muy oloroso. Tanta el como un ferroviario creen que el olor viene del muerto. El olor se hace tan fuerte que los dos saltan del tren, en una tormenta de hielo. La experiencia arruinó la salud del narrador.

**Identify Cause and Effect** In stories, one event often causes another, which in turns causes another event. Identifying these causes and effects will help you understand the story.

Ask yourself why characters do things. What causes them to act? What is the effect? Sometimes a word, such as *because*, signals a cause-and-effect relationship. At other times, you must infer the cause and effect from the facts you are given. Choose one story, find the causes and effects, and list them on a chart like the following. One example from "The Ivalid's Story" has been provided.

| Cause | Effect |
|---|---|
| Hackett's death | → the narrator's initial misery |
| | → |
| | → |
| | → |
| | → |
| | → |
| | → |

Name _____ Date _____

## "The Necklace" by Guy de Maupassant
## "The Harvest" by Tomás Rivera

**Summary** These two stories are about people who make discoveries that profoundly affect their lives. In "The Necklace," Madame Loisel borrows a diamond necklace and loses it. Quietly, the Loisels buy a replacement for the necklace by taking a huge loan and sacrificing for ten years to repay it. When Madame Loisel finally admits to the owner what happened, she learns that the necklace did not contain real diamonds. In "The Harvest," Don Trine is seen taking mysterious walks alone at harvest time. Suspicious that money is involved, some youngsters follow him. When Don Trine is discovered "planting" his arms in the earth, everyone thinks he is crazy except one boy. The boy, who copies Don Trine's behavior, feels the power of the sleeping earth just as Don Trine does.

**Resumen** Los personajes de estos descubren algo que influye profundamente en sus vidas. En *The Necklace*, Madame Loisel toma prestado, y pierde, un collar de diamantes. Los Loisels se sacrifican económicamente por diez años y reemplazan el collar. Cuando Madame Loisel finalmente cuenta lo que ha ocurrido, descubre que los diamantes del collar eran falsos. En *The Harvest*, se ve a Don Trine haciendo solo misteriosas caminatas en época de cosecha. Sospechando que todo eso tiene que ver con dinero, unos jóvenes lo siguen. Cuando descubren a Don Trine "plantando" sus brazos en la tierra, todos creen que está loco. Todos, excepto un joven, quien hace lo mismo que había hecho Don Trine e, igual que Don, siente el poder de la tierra dormida.

**Sequence Events** Use the following sequence organizer to record the main events in "The Harvest." Some information has already been provided. When you are finished, make your own sequence organizer for "The Necklace."

| |
|---|
|  |

↓

| |
|---|
| Rumors get started about Don Trine. |

↓

| |
|---|
|  |

↓

| |
|---|
| The boys investigate the ditch. |

↓

| |
|---|
| The following Monday, the boys see Don Trine _____ |

↓

| |
|---|
| The next day, _____ |

↓

| |
|---|
| After that, the boy _____ |

## "Single Room, Earth View" by Sally Ride

**Summary** In this selection, Sally Ride gives an account of her experiences and those of other astronauts in space. For example, astronauts are amazed that the Hawaiian islands look just as they do on maps. At orbiting speed, continents zip by, but geological features stand out. Although they are too low to view the entire globe at once, astronauts can see a surprising amount of detail. Signs of civilization are clear, including pollution, but especially, astronauts see the oceans, with intricate patterns from different currents and water colors. Among the most spectacular sights are lighting seen from above and a sunrise seen every ninety minutes.

**Resumen** Sally Ryde nos ofrece una descripción de sus experiencias y de las de otros astronautas, en el espacio. Por ejemplo, ellos se maravillan de que las islas de Hawai sean iguales a las de los mapas. A esa velocidad, los continentes no se ven bien, pero las formaciones geológicas se destacan. Si bien los astronautas no viajan a suficiente altura para ver toda la Tierra, sí pueden ver una sorprendente cantidad de detalles. Los signos de la civilización son claros, incluyendo la contaminación, pero más que nada, los astronautas pueden ver aguas azules, con intrincados diseños, causados por las diferentes corrientes y aguas de colores. Entre las vistas más espectaculares se encuentran los relámpagos vistos desde arriba y una salida de sol cada 90 minutos.

**Identify Main Idea and Supporting Details** Paragraphs contain one main idea and details that support that idea. When you read nonfiction, first identify the main idea of a paragraph, and then look for details that tell about the main idea.

The main idea and one detail in the following paragraph have been underlined and listed below. Add two more details that tell about the main idea. Then practice this strategy, using other paragraphs from the story.

Since the space shuttle flies fairly low (at least by orbital standards; it's more than 22,000 miles lower than a typical TV satellite), we can make out both natural and manmade features in surprising detail. Familiar geographic features like San Francisco Bay, Long Island, and Lake Michigan are easy to recognize, as are many cities, bridges, and airports. The Great Wall of China is *not* the only manmade object visible from space.

Main Idea: The space shuttle flies fairly low. _____

Detail: We can make out both natural and manmade features in surprising detail. ___

Detail: _____

Detail: _____

Main Idea: _____

Detail: _____

Detail: _____

Detail: _____

**"The Washwoman"** by Isaac Bashevis Singer
**"On Summer"** by Lorraine Hansberry
**"A Celebration of Grandfathers"** by Rudolfo A. Anaya

**Summary** Each of these first-person accounts tells how the author's view of the world was molded by one or more remarkable people. In "The Washwoman," the narrator recalls an old woman who washed his family's clothes when he was a boy. He remembers her hard work, her struggle to endure, and her last visits to his home. In "On Summer," the author explains that she once disliked summer but, over time, came to associate it with people of indomitable will and, therefore, with life lived fully. In "A Celebration of Grandfathers," the author remembers the quiet ways of the "old ones" of his grandfather's generation, who understood the seasons and appreciated the land in which they lived. He urges understanding of, and respect for, grandfathers.

**Resumen** En cada uno de estos relatos en primera persona, sus autores nos cuentan cómo su visión del mundo fue moldeada por una o más personas extraordinarias. En *The Washwoman*, el autor recuerda a una anciana, que no era judía que lavaba la ropa de su familia cuando él era un niño. Recuerda el duro trabajo de la mujer, su lucha y perseverancia, y sus últimas visitas a la casa del autor. En *On Summer*, la autora nos dice que en una época no le gustaba el verano, pero, con el tiempo, comenzó a asociarlo a gente de voluntad inquebrantable y, por consiguiente, con la vida vivida plenamente. En *A Celebration of Grandfathers*, el autor recuerda la mancra tranquila y silenciosa en que los ancianos de la generación de su abuelo entendían las estaciones y el valle donde vivían. Finalmente, nos exorta a respetary comprender a los abuelos.

**Summarize Main Idea** To follow the ideas of a nonfiction article, you should pause occasionally and summarize the main ideas you have read so far. For example, the paragraph below from "On Summer" can be summarized in one sentence.

It also seemed to me, esthetically speaking, that nature had got inexcusably carried away on the summer question and let the whole thing get to be rather much. By duration alone, for instance, a summer's day seemed maddeningly excessive; an utter overstatement. Except for those few hours at either end of it, objects always appeared too sharp a relief against backgrounds; shadows too pronounced and light too blinding. It always gave me a feeling of walking around in a motion picture which had been too artsily-craftsily exposed. Sound also had a way of coming to the ear without that muting influence, marvelously common to winter, across patios or beaches or through the woods. I suppose I found it too stark and yet too intimate a season.

Main Idea: The author finds summer to be a very long, uncomfortable season.

Supporting Details: to be rather much, a summer's day seemed maddeningly excessive, objects appeared too sharp, light too blinding

Apply this strategy to other paragraphs from "The Washwoman," "On Summer," or "A Celebration of Grandfathers." Summarize the main idea and list some supporting details.

### from *A White House Diary* by Lady Bird Johnson
### "Arthur Ashe Remembered" by John McPhee
### "Georgia O'Keeffe" by Joan Didion

**Summary** These three selections offer insights into memorable people and events from three distinct points of view—a first-person account, a personal remembrance, and a biographical essay. In the first selection, Lady Bird Johnson relates in intimate, personal detail the tragic events of the day President Kennedy was assassinated and her husband assumed the presidency. In the second, John McPhee reveals the mixture of mental control and aggressive play that characterized the life and career of professional tennis player Arthur Ashe. The third selection is an essay paying tribute to artist Georgia O'Keeffe, whom the author describes as an independent woman who rejected convention and created astonishing paintings.

**Resumen** Estas tres selecciones, nos recuerdan gente y sucesos memorables desde tres puntos de vista distintos: un relato en primera persona, una remembranza y un ensayo autobiográfico. En la primera selección, Lady Bird Johnson ofrece detalles íntimos y personales del día en que el presidente Kennedy fue asesinado y su esposo, Lyndon Johnson, asumió la presidencia. En el segundo, John McPhee revela la mezcla de control mental y juego agresivo que caracterizaron la vida y carrera de Arthur Ashe. La tercera selección es un ensayo que rinde homenaje a la artista Georgia O'Keeffe, a quien el autor describe como a una mujer independiente y fuerte que rechazó las reglas convencionales para dar al mundo sus increíbles pinturas.

**Interpret Direct Quotations** The authors of these selections often quote the exact words someone spoke to give the reader some special insight into the person or the event. As you read these selections, write the quotations the author provides and interpret, or explain, the insights of each. Use a chart like the one below. Two entries have been made for you.

| Quotation | Insight It Provides |
|---|---|
| Mr. Kilduff entered and said to Lyndon, "Mr. President." | This statement indicates that the burdens of the presidency have suddenly passed to Lyndon Johnson. |
| I heard a Secret Service man say . . . "We never lost a President in the Service." | Those responsible for guarding President Kennedy felt a deep sense of responsibility for his death. |
| | |
| | |
| | |
| | |

## "Understanding Comics" by Scott McCloud

**Summary** Artist Scott McCloud uses comics in this visual essay, in which he himself appears as a comic-book character. McCloud explains that he did not like comics at first, but later became obsessed with them and began making them himself. He says that many people look down on comics, thinking they are all bad art or stupid stories. Scott, though, thinks comics are exciting and powerful, and he feels we need a better definition for them. He illustrates the concept of sequential art and uses it to create this new definition. He and an imaginary audience decide that comics is a medium whose pictures and sequence can not only give information, but can also produce an aesthetic response in viewers.

**Resumen** El artista Scott McCloud presenta este ensayo como una tira cómica, en la que él mismo es un personaje. McCloud nos dice que al principio no le gustaban las tiras cómicas, pero que luego se obsesionó con ellas y comenzó a crearlas. Él sabe que mucha gente menosprecia a las tiras cómicas y las considera un arte inferior o historias estúpidas. Sin embargo, Scott piensa que las tiras cómicas son apasionantes y poderosas y que necesitamos una mejor definición para ellas. Scott explica el concepto de arte secuencial y lo usa para crear esta nueva definición. Él, y una audiencia imaginaria, deciden que las tiras cómicas son un medio en el que las ilustraciones y la secuencia no sólo dan información, sino que también pueden producir una reacción estética en los lectores.

**Translate Cartoon Images** If a picture is worth a thousand words, how many words is a cartoon image worth? Work with a partner to restate in words the ideas expressed in the cartoon boxes. Use a chart like the one below. An example has been provided to get you started.

| Cartoon Image | Ideas Expressed |
| --- | --- |
| First frame: writer/cartoonist at his drawing board | The narrator of the cartoon is the writer himself; his work is done at an easel with lots of helpful equipment around him—a globe, pictures, posters, paints, reference books, and so on. |
|  |  |

Name _____ Date _____

**"Earhart Redux"** by Alex Chadwick

***In These Girls, Hope Is a Muscle*** by Madeleine Blais,
a book review by Steve Gietschier

***In These Girls, Hope Is a Muscle*** by Madeleine Blais,
book jacket

**Summary** These examples of workplace writing reflect three distinct purposes. In "Earhart Redux," the author mixes references of sound effects and skillfully framed questions to capture the inside story of Linda Finch's re-creation of Amelia Earhart's attempt in 1937 to fly around the world. His interview covers Finch's motives, the flight's technical and mechanical similarity to the original flight, and Earhart's legacy. In the book review of *In These Girls, Hope Is a Muscle*, the reviewer applauds Blais's heartfelt, yet gently humorous account of the championship season of a girl's basketball team. Finally, the book jacket promotes the book by quoting reviews, presenting an overview of the story, and commenting on the story's broader significance for the women's movement.

**Resumen** Cada uno de estos trabajos cumple un propósito diferente. En *Earhart Redux*, el autor combina sonidos, películas y preguntas para capturar la historia verídica del vuelo en que Linda Finch siguió la misma ruta tomada por Amelia Earhart en su intento de volar alrededor del mundo en 1937. Su entrevista considera los motivos de Finch para hacer esto, las similitudes técnicas entre ambos vuelos y el legado histórico de Earhart. En *In These Girls, Hope Is a Muscle*, el autor aplaude el sentido y el humor del relato de Blais sobre la temporada de un equipo femenino de básquetbol. Finalmente, la cubierta del libro promociona al libro citando reseñas y presentando una vista panorámica de la historia y comentando sobre su más amplio significado para el movimiento feminista.

**Propose Headlines** Newspapers generate interest in their articles with headlines. A good headline states the main idea of the article in as few words as possible. Writing a headline requires a solid understanding of the information in the article.

Check your understanding of these three selections by writing one or more headlines for each selection. Each headline should pinpoint a key idea in the article. Several good headlines are possible for each story. A sample headline has been provided.

| Story | Headline |
|---|---|
| "Earhart Redux" | Earhart's Flight: Can It Really Be Duplicated? |
| *In These Girls, Hope Is a Muscle* Book Review | _____ <br> _____ |
| *In These Girls, Hope Is a Muscle* Book Jacket | _____ <br> _____ |

Name _____ Date _____

### *The Dancers* by Horton Foote

**Summary** In this play, set in the 1950's, the characters face some common interpersonal problems: conflicts between a mother and a daughter, friends, and acquaintances. The conflicts begin when Elizabeth Crews arranges a date for her daughter, Emily, with a boy from out of town—without consulting her. A popular girl with a steady boyfriend, Emily is furious about it and refuses to leave her room when Horace comes to pick her up. Dejected, Horace wanders downtown for something to eat. There, he meets a friend of Emily's who agrees to be his date for the dance. Mother and daughter make up, friends reunite, and Horace gains new self-confidence.

**Resumen** Los personajes de esta obra, que tiene lugar durante la década de 1950, se enfrentan a problemas de relaciones muy comunes: conflictos entre madre e hija, amigos y conocidos. Los conflictos comienzan cuando Elizabeth Crews hace una cita, sin consultarla, entre su hija Emily y un muchacho que no es del pueblo. Emily una chica muy popular, y que ya tiene novio, se enoja y rehusa salir de su cuarto cuando Horace, el muchacho, pasa a buscarla para ir al baile. Descorazonado, Horace camina sin rumbo en busca de un lugar para comer. Allí, se encuentra con una amiga de Emily, que acepta acompañarlo al baile. Madre e hija hacen las paces, los amigos se juntan y Horace gana confianza en sí mismo.

**Prepare a Readers Theater** With your classmates, plan a reading of the play. Divide the play into scenes, and assign parts for each scene. Students may play more than one part. If you play more than one part, be sure the voice you use for each character is different. Practice your role, listening to the audiocassette recording as you follow your part in your book. Rehearse your part, giving your character an identifiable voice. Then, with your classmates, do a Readers Theater reading of the play. After the presentation, ask your classmates to evaluate your performances.

Use the lines below to assign roles and to jot down ideas about your performance.

| Role | Student |
|------|---------|
| Emily | _____ |
| Horace | _____ |
| Mrs. Crews | _____ |
| _____ | _____ |
| _____ | _____ |
| _____ | _____ |

**Performance Ideas:** _____

_____

_____

_____

_____

_____

### *The Tragedy of Romeo and Juliet,* Act I, by William Shakespeare

| Summary | Resumen |
|---|---|
| **The Prologue** informs the audience of the tragedy to come. | **El Prólogo** informa al público sobre la tragedia que va a ocurrir. |
| **Scene i** A fight between the supporters of rival families, the Capulets and the Montagues, angers the Prince of Verona, who vows to execute Capulet and Montague if it happens again. Romeo, a Montague, is told by a friend to give up his love for a woman we learn is named Rosaline. | **Escena 1** Una pelea entre partidarios de dos familias rivales, los Capulets y los Montagues, enoja al Prince of Verona, que jura hacer ejecutar Capulets y Montagues si hay más peleas. Un amigo le dice a Romeo, un Montague, que renuncie a su amor por Rosaline. |
| **Scene ii** Paris wants to marry Capulet's daughter, Juliet. Capulet says that this will happen only if she agrees. He invites Paris to a feast. Seeing that Rosaline is invited, Romeo decides to go as an uninvited masked guest. | **Escena 2** Paris quiere casarse con la hija de Capulet, Juliet, y el padre dice que sí sólo si Juliet consiente. Capulet invita a Paris a una fiesta. Al enterarse que Roseline está invitada, Romeo decide ir a la fiesta enmascarado. |
| **Scene iii** Juliet agrees to *consider* marrying Paris to please her mother. | **Escena 3** Juliet acepta *considerar* casarse con Paris para alegrar a su madre. |
| **Scene iv** Romeo predicts something terrible will happen. | **Escena 4** Romeo predice que algo terrible va a suceder. |
| **Scene v** Romeo and Juliet fall in love. Each learns the other's identity from the nurse. | **Escena 5** Romeo y Juliet se enamoran y se enteran quiénes son a través de la nana. |

**Summarize Plot** In order to follow the action of the play, you need to understand the events as they happen. Review the summary for each scene. With a partner, draw cartoon-strip characters and have them show the main action for each scene. Use simple stick figures for characters—you might add a skirt for Juliet, a hat for the nurse, a sword for Tybalt, a heart for Romeo, and so on, to distinguish one figure from another. Then add dialogue bubbles for each character. Put their words into modern English. When you finish, compare your cartoon strips with those of your classmates. Use this page to sketch some of your ideas.

## The Tragedy of Romeo and Juliet, Act II, by William Shakespeare

<table>
<tr><td>

**Summary**

**The Prologue** provides transition from Act I by confirming that Romeo and Juliet are in love.

**Scene i** Romeo hides in the Capulets' orchard, hoping to see Juliet.

**Scene ii** Juliet comes to a window. Unaware that Romeo is hiding, she declares her love for him and wishes he weren't a Montague. Romeo steps out and says that he loves her so much that he will give up his name. They plan to elope.

**Scene iii** Romeo goes to Friar Lawrence to ask him to marry them. The Friar agrees, hoping to bring peace to the families.

**Scene iv** Mercutio and Benvolio talk about Tybalt's challenge to duel Romeo. Romeo arrives and jokes with Mercutio. He gives Nurse a message for Juliet to meet him that afternoon at the friar's.

**Scene v** Nurse delivers the message.

**Scene vi** Friar leads them away to be married.

</td><td>

**Resumen**

**El Prólogo** presenta una transición del Primer acto y nos dice que Romeo y Juliet se han enamorado.

**Escena 1** Romeo se esconde en el jardín de los Capulets, esperando ver a Juliet.

**Escena 2** Juliet sale a la ventana y, sin saber que Romeo esta escondido declara su amor por él y dice que quisiera que no fuera un Montague. Romeo se hace ver y le dice que la ama tanto que abandonaría su nombre por ella. Los dos deciden huir juntos.

**Escena 3** Romeo pide a Friar Lawrence que los case. Friar acepta hacerlo para traer paz a las familias.

**Escena 4** Mercutio y Benvolio hablan sobre el desafío a duelo que Tybalt hizo a Romeo. Éste llega y bromea con Mercutio. Luego, Romeo le da a la nana un mensaje para que Juliet se encuentre con él esa tarde en lo de Friar Lawrence.

**Escena 5** La nana le da el mensaje a Juliet.

**Escena 6** Friar lleva a Romeo y Juliet para casarlos.

</td></tr>
</table>

**Analyze Characters** You understand characters by what they say, what they do, and what others say about them. Listen to the audiocassette recording of Act II as you follow along in your text. Listen for what characters do and say. Listen for what others say about them. With a partner, make a character chart like the following for these characters. You may not be able to fill in all the columns for each character.

| Character | What They Do | What They Say | What Others Say About Them |
|---|---|---|---|
| Romeo | | | |
| Juliet | | | |
| Nurse | | | |
| Benvolio | | | |
| Mercutio | | | |
| Friar Lawrence | | | |

### *The Tragedy of Romeo and Juliet, Act III,* by William Shakespeare

| Summary | Resumen |
|---|---|
| **Scene i** Mercutio baits Tybalt. Romeo arrives, knows Tybalt is Juliet's cousin, and ignores Tybalt's insults. Mercutio fights with Tybalt and is killed as Romeo tries to stop them. In turn, Romeo kills Tybalt, then flees. The Prince exiles Romeo.<br>**Scene ii** Nurse tells Juliet that Romeo has killed Tybalt and is hiding at Friar's. Juliet gives Nurse a ring for Romeo and asks that he visit her.<br>**Scene iii** Romeo tries to kill himself, but Friar suggests that Romeo see Juliet and then escape to Mantua.<br>**Scene iv** Capulet arranges for Juliet to marry Paris in three days.<br>**Scene v** Juliet and Romeo spend their wedding night together, parting at dawn. Juliet learns she is to marry Paris. She refuses, but her father vows to disown her if she doesn't comply. | **Escena 1** Mercutio provoca a Tybalt. Romeo sabe que Tybalt es primo de Juliet e ignora el insulto. Mercutio pelea en lugar de Romeo y Tybalt lo mata, cuando Romeo trata de separarlos. A su vez, Romeo mata a Tybalt, y huye. El Príncipe destierra a Romeo.<br>**Escena 2** La nana la cuenta a Juliet que Romeo ha matado a Tybalt y que está escondido en lo de Friar. Juliet le da un anillo para Romeo y pide que vaya a verla.<br>**Escena 3** Romeo trata de matarse, pero Friar le sugiere ir a ver a Juliet y que escapen juntos a Mantua.<br>**Escena 4** Capulet hace arreglos para que Juliet se case con Paris en tres días.<br>**Escena 5** Juliet y Romeo pasan juntos su noche de bodas y se separan al alba. Juliet se entera que deberá casarse con Paris. Juliet se rehusa pero su padre jura repudiarla si no lo hace. |

**Use a Story Map Organizer** Take stock of the events of the play that have unfolded before Act III opens. Use a Story Map to record the events that have built the plot so far. For example, you might include the following events: Romeo and Juliet's meeting; Capulet's arrangement for Paris to marry Juliet; Romeo and Juliet's secret marriage; Romeo's fight with Tybalt. Then add other events as you read Act IV. Decide which event should be considered the climax, or high point, of the plot. Compare your Story Map to those of your classmates and discuss the differences between them.

Setting:
> Place Verona, Italy _____
> Time _____

Problem:
> 

Event 1:      Romeo and Juliet meet
Event 2:      Capulet arranges for Paris to marry Juliet
Event 3:      Romeo and Juliet secretly marry
Event 4:
Event 5:

Climax:
(Turning Point)
>

Name _____ Date _____

## *The Tragedy of Romeo and Juliet*, Act IV, by William Shakespeare

| Summary | Resumen |
|---|---|
| **Scene i** Juliet seeks help from the Friar and finds Paris there planning their wedding. When Paris leaves, the Friar makes a plan to save Romeo and Juliet. He gives Juliet a trance-inducing drug to take the night before the wedding. Her parents, thinking she is dead, will put her in the crypt. Romeo will be told. He will be at the crypt to carry her to Mantua when she awakens. | **Escena 1** Juliet visita a Friar y encuentra allí a Paris haciendo planes para su casamiento. Cuando Paris se va, Friar piensa en un plan para salvar a Romeo y Juliet. Friar da a Juliet una droga para tomar la noche antes del casamiento. La droga la dormirá, sus padres pensarán que está muerta y la pondrán en la cripta. Le avisarán a Romeo y él estará en la cripta para llevar a Juliet a Mantua, cuando ella despierte. |
| **Scene ii** Juliet pretends to agree to marry Paris, apologizes to her father, and makes Capulet so happy that he moves the wedding up a day. | **Escena 2** Juliet finge aceptar casarse con Paris, pide disculpas a su padre y esto hace tan feliz a Capulet que adelanta la boda un día. |
| **Scene iii** Faced with marriage a day early, Juliet takes the drug a day earlier than planned despite her worries about possible mishaps. | **Escena 3** Frente al adelanto de la boda, Juliet toma la droga un día antes, pero se preocupa de que algo salga mal. |
| **Scene iv** The Capulets prepare for the wedding. | **Escena 4** Los Capulets se preparan para la boda. |
| **Scene v** Nurse finds Juliet, apparently dead. The wedding becomes a funeral. | **Escena 5** La nana halla a Juliet, aparentemente muerta. La boda se convierte en un funeral. |

**Recognize Dramatic Irony** It is important to recognize that Shakespeare's audience knows more than the characters know about what is happening to them. This creates an effect called *dramatic irony*. With a partner, tell the effect on the audience of each of the following situations. The first has been done for you.

| | |
|---|---|
| 1. Juliet speaks with Paris in Friar Lawrence's cell and gives him the impression she intends to marry him. | The audience knows that Juliet does not intend to marry Paris and, therefore, they may feel some pity for Paris while retaining compassion for Juliet. |
| 2. Juliet speaks with her father and mother giving them the impression that she intends to marry Paris. | |
| 3. On Tuesday evening, Juliet tells her mother to "let the nurse this night sit up with you:/ For I am sure you have your hands full all in this so sudden business." | |
| 4. Friar Lawrence consoles Juliet's parents, who believe that their daughter is dead. | |

## The Tragedy of Romeo and Juliet, Act V, by William Shakespeare

| Summary | Resumen |
|---|---|
| **Scene i** Romeo learns that Juliet is dead. Wanting only to be with her, he buys poison to commit suicide. | **Escena 1** Romeo se entera que Juliet está muerta. Queriendo unírsele, compra veneno para suicidarse. |
| **Scene ii** The friar learns that his message never reached Romeo. Horrified, he sends another message and rushes to the crypt to be with Juliet when she wakes up. | **Escena 2** Friar se entera que Romeo nunca recibió su mensaje. Horrorizado, le envía otro mensaje y va a la cripta para estar con Juliet cuando despierte. |
| **Scene iii** Paris comes to mourn; Romeo arrives soon after. They fight, and Paris is killed. Romeo lies next to Juliet, takes the poison, and dies. The friar arrives to find Paris and Romeo dead. Juliet wakes up. He tries to get her to go to a convent, but seeing Romeo dead, she no longer wants to live. Hearing a noise outside, the friar flees. Juliet kills herself with Romeo's dagger. The key characters gather, the whole story comes out, and in their grief, the rival families end their feud. | **Escena 3** Paris llega a lamentar la muerte de Juliet y Romeo llega poco después. Luchan y Paris es muerto. Romeo se tiende junto a Juliet, toma el veneno y muere. Friar llega y encuentra a Paris y Romeo muertos. Juliet se despierta. Friar trata de llevarla a un convento, pero al ver a Romeo muerto, Juliet ya no quiere vivir. Al escuchar un ruido, Friar huye y Juliet se mata con la daga de Romeo. Los personajes principales se reúnen, se enteran de todo, y, en su dolor, las dos familias terminan su rivalidad. |

**Recognize Metaphors** The drama in Shakespeare is supported by the metaphors, or comparisons, in the language he uses. For example, when Juliet grabs Romeo's dagger, she says, "This is thy sheath; there rust, and let me die." When she stabs herself, her body becomes the sheath for the dagger. She wants the dagger to stay there until it rusts.

With a partner, explain what things are being compared in the following passages. Then find three more metaphors in Act V. Write them on the back of this page, and explain what things are being compared.

1. PARIS (at the graveyard) Sweet flower, with flowers thy bridal bed I strew. . . .

_____

_____

2. ROMEO (at the graveyard) Thou detestable maw, thou womb of death,/Gorged with the dearest morsel of the earth . . .

_____

_____

3. ROMEO (at the graveyard) Thus I enforce thy rotten jaws to open,/And in despite I'll cram thee with more food.

_____

_____

# "I Wandered Lonely as a Cloud" by William Wordsworth

**Summary** In this poem, the speaker describes a time when, wandering alone, he suddenly came upon a field of yellow daffodils. The flowers, moving in the breeze, were under some trees near a lake. The speaker mentions how many flowers there were, how densely they grew, and how they formed a border around the bay. In the water, the small waves looked as if they were dancing, but the daffodils looked even more joyful; their delight made the speaker happy as well. At the time, he was not even aware of how much the sight affected him. Later, though, at times when he feels bored or thoughtful, he often finds himself picturing the scene again in his mind. Then the remembered vision of those golden daffodils raises his spirits, making him feel as happy as the flowers seem to be.

**Resumen** En este poema, el que habla, cuenta de una vez que caminaba sin rumbo cuando se encontró con un campo de lirios amarillos. Las flores estaban debajo de unos árboles y se movían en la brisa, cerca de un lago. El que habla dice que había muchas flores y que crecían muy juntas, bordeando la bahía. En el agua, pequeñas olas parecían danzar, pero los lirios se veían aún más felices, y esto hacía al que hablaba también feliz. En ese momento, él no se dio cuenta de cómo todo esto lo había afectado, pero más tarde, en momentos de aburrimiento o meditación, se encontraba volviendo a la imagen de los lirios. Esa visión le levantaba el espíritu y lo hacía tan feliz como las flores parecían serlo.

**Infer Feelings** In "I Wandered Lonely as a Cloud," the poet describes both what he sees and how he feels about what he sees. Sometimes his feelings are not stated directly. You have to infer his feelings from the tone and rhythms he uses to describe what he sees. In a double-column journal entry, record what the poet sees and how he feels. The first stanza has been modeled for you. Do the same with the other three stanzas of the poem.

| Stanzas | Feelings |
|---|---|
| **Stanza 1:** I wandered lonely as a cloud<br>That floats on high o'er vales and hills,<br>When all at once I saw a crowd,<br>A host, of golden daffodils;<br>Beside the lake, beneath the trees,<br>Fluttering and dancing in the breeze. | The poet feels as lonesome as a cloud floating high above the landscape.<br>He finds company in a field of daffodils that are blowing in the breeze. |
| **Stanza 2:** | |
| **Stanza 3:** | |
| **Stanza 4:** | |

**"Dream Deferred"** and **"Dreams"** by Langston Hughes
**"The Eagle"** by Alfred, Lord Tennyson
**"'Hope' is the thing with feathers—"** by Emily Dickinson

**Summary** These four poems use figurative language to express feelings, ideas, and experiences. In "The Eagle," the speaker describes an eagle high on an isolated mountaintop. The bird watches the waves move below and then suddenly drops towards the earth. "'Hope' is the thing with feathers—" describes hope as a feathered creature that lives within the human spirit. Even when life becomes difficult, hope keeps people's spirits up, and it does this anywhere and at no cost. In "Dream Deferred," the speaker wonders what happens to hopes and dreams that are postponed too long. He asks if they dry up, rot, change, lose energy, or explode. The poem "Dreams" expresses the idea that people must hold on to their dreams and goals. Otherwise, life is damaged; a life without dreams is an empty, cold existence.

**Resumen** Estos cuatro poemas usan un lenguaje figurativo para expresar sentimientos, ideas y experiencias. En *The Eagle*, se describe a un águila en la alto de una montaña. El ave observa las olas abajo y, súbitamente, se lanza hacia la tierra. "'Hope' is the thing with feathers—" describe a la esperanza como un ser emplumado que vive dentro del espíritu humano. Aun cuando la vida se vuelve difícil, la esperanza mantiene el espíritu de la gente, y lo hace en cualquier parte y sin ningún costo. *Dream Deferred*, se pregunta qué pasa con las esperanzas y los sueños pospuestos por mucho tiempo. Se pregunta si se secan, se pudren, cambian, pierden energía o estallan. *Dreams*, expresa la idea que la gente debe mantener sus sueños y anhelos. De otra manera, la vida se daña; una vida sin sueños es una existencia vacía y fría.

**Recognize Unusual Comparisons** These poems make some unusual comparisons in order to encourage the reader to see things in new and different ways. Look for these comparisons *as you read* the poems. Ask yourself what two things are being compared. Then decide why the poet thinks these two things are alike. Record your responses as shown below.

from "Dreams"

Hold fast to dreams/For if dreams die/Life is a broken-winged bird/
That cannot fly.

**The two things being compared:**
life without dreams
a broken-winged bird

**How they are alike:**
Both are damaged.
Both are in danger of dying.

Hold fast to dreams/For when dreams go/Life is a barren field/
Frozen with snow.

**The two things being compared:**

_____

_____

_____

**How they are alike:**

_____

_____

_____

Choose another poem from this section, and practice this strategy.

Name _____ Date _____

**"Blackberry Eating"** by Galway Kinnell

**"Memory"** by Margaret Walker

**"Eulogy for a Hermit Crab"** by Pattiann Rogers

**"Meciendo"** by Gabriela Mistral

**"Woman's Work"** by Julia Alvarez

**Summary** These poems use sensory language to share specific experiences. In "Blackberry Eating," the speaker decribes eating plump, cold, fall blackberries. His tongue plays with them just as it plays with certain words. "Memory" paints a picture of unhappy urban people; it uses vivid words to describe their appearance and feelings. In "Woman's Work," the speaker recalls disliking the housework that she did with her mother, who saw it as art. Still, she turned out like her mother, working at home, though now on paper. In "Meciendo," the speaker explains how natural elements cherish each other. She follows their example and cherishes her baby. The speaker in "Eulogy for a Hermit Crab" praises a dead hermit crab for its endurance, courage, and consistency despite all obstacles.

**Resumen** Estos poemas usan un lenguaje sensorial para compartir ciertas experiencias. En *Blackberry Eating*, alguien come moras jugosas y frías en otoño y su lengua juega con ellas al igual que juega con ciertas palabras. *Memory*, retrata a una pareja que no es feliz y describe su apariencia y sentimientos. En *Women's Work*, una mujer recuerda cuánto le desagradaban las tareas de la casa, y cómo su madre las veía como arte. Al fin, la mujer se vuelve como su madre, trabajando en la casa, pero sobre papel. En *Eulogy for a Hermit Crab*, una mujer elogia a un cangrejo ermitaño muerto por su perseverancia y valentía frente a todos los obstáculos. En *Meciendo*, una mujer explica cómo se cuidan entre sí las cosas en la naturaleza. Siguiendo su ejemplo, ella cuida de su bebé.

**Identify Speaker's Attitude** A speaker often has an attitude toward the subject of the poem. You can often describe that attitude quite simply in a word or two: *sympathetic, admiring,* or *critical.* The poet's choice of words will usually convey the attitude.

Look at the following underlined phrases. Some show admiration for the subject of the poem, a hermit crab. Others show sympathy—an understanding of the dangers that the crab faces. Decide which attitude each phrase shows. Then practice the strategy by identifying key phrases in another one of the poems.

| Key Words and Phrases | Attitude the Words Reveal |
|---|---|
| You were consistently brave | respectful |
| On these surf-drenched rocks, in and out of their salty | sympathetic |
| Slough holes around which the entire expanse | admiring |
| Of the glinting grey sea and the single spotlight | |
| Of the sun were spinning and spinning and spinning | |
| In a tangle of blinding spume and spray | _____ |
| And pistol-shot collisions your whole life long. | _____ |
| You stayed. Even with the wet icy wind of the moon | _____ |
| Circling your silver case night after night after night | |
| You were here. | _____ |

Part 2   **253**

Name _____ Date _____

**"Uphill"** by Christina Rossetti
**"Summer"** by Walter Dean Myers
**Ecclesiastes 3:1–8,** The King James Bible
**"The Bells"** by Edgar Allan Poe

**Summary** These poems are all examples of lyric poetry, a type of musical poetry in which a single speaker expresses personal thoughts and feelings. The poem "Uphill" is a series of questions and answers about a long uphill journey, which will end at a resting place filled with others who have completed the same journey. "Summer" describes many of the things that the speaker likes about summer days, including the heat and the activities. The selection taken from the Bible points out that there is a proper time for every human event—birth, death, silence, speech, love, and hate. In "The Bells," the speaker identifies four kinds of bells (happy sleigh bells, joyful wedding bells, scary alarm bells, and mournful church bells), their sounds and their effects on listeners.

**Resumen** Éstos son ejemplos de poesía lírica en la que se expresan pensamientos y sentimientos íntimos. *Uphill* es una serie de preguntas y respuestas acerca de un largo y arduo viaje cuesta arriba, que terminará en un lugar para descansar lleno de gente que ha completado el mismo viaje. En *Summer,* alguien describe muchas de las cosas que le gustan de los días de verano, incluyendo el calor y las actividades. La selección es de la Biblia y señala que hay un momento oportuno para cada evento de los seres humanos: nacimiento, muerte, silencio, comunicación, amor y odio. *The Bells,* identifica a cuatro tipos de campanas (alegres campanillas de un trineo, felices campanas de una boda, campanas de alarma que asustan y dolidas campanas de un funeral), sus sonidos y cómo afectan a quienes las escuchan.

**Identify Sensory Words** Lyric poetry is about someone's personal thoughts and feelings. Often the poet will use sensory language to share his or her feelings. That language helps readers to see, hear, feel, taste, and smell what the poet expresses.

Some of the following sensory words in "Summer" have been identified and classified. Look for additional sensory words, and record them in the proper column. You do not have to write a word in each column. Then choose another poem and practice this strategy.

I like hot days, hot days
Sweat is what you got days
Bugs buzzin from cousin to cousin
Juices dripping
Running and ripping
Catch the one you love days

Birds peeping
Old men sleeping
Lazy days, daisies lay
Beaming and dreaming
of hot days, hot days,
Sweat is what you got days

| Sight | Sound | Touch | Taste | Smell |
|---|---|---|---|---|
| sweat | buzzin | hot days sweat | | |

Name _____ Date _____

## "The Raven" by Edgar Allan Poe
## "The Seven Ages of Man" by William Shakespeare

**Summary** These poems are examples of narrative and dramatic poetry. In "The Raven," a speaker broods about his lost love, Lenore, late one night. He hears a noise at the door, and suddenly, in flies a raven. It speaks just one word: "Nevermore." The speaker asks the raven if he will ever feel better. The bird says only "Nevermore." Growing angry, the speaker tries to drive the raven away. But it stays, and so does the speaker's gloom. In Shakespeare's monologue taken from his play *As You Like It,* the speaker compares the world to a stage. People are just actors who play characters. Over time, the speaker says, a man plays many parts: a crying infant, a complaining schoolboy, a sighing lover, a quick-tempered soldier, a well-fed judge, a foolish aging man, and, finally, a feeble, childlike old man, without anything.

**Resumen** Éstos son ejemplos de poesía narrativa y dramática. En *The Raven,* un hombre medita de noche sobre Lenore, su amor perdido. Escucha un ruido a la puerta, y, súbitamente entra volando un cuervo que dice sólo una palabra: *Nevermore.* El hombre le pregunta al cuervo si alguna vez él se va a sentir mejor y sólo escucha *Nevermore.* El hombre se enoja y trata de ahuyentarlo pero el ave se queda, junto con la tristeza. En el monólogo tomado de *As You Like It,* de Shakespeare, se compara al mundo con un escenario. La gente son actores que representan papeles. Con el paso del tiempo, un hombre tiene muchos papeles: un bebé que llora, un alumno que se queja, un amante que suspira, un soldado de genio corto, un juez bien comido, un hombre tonto que envejece y, finalmente, un débil anciano, casi un niño, que no dice nada.

**Summarize Poetic Narrative** In "The Raven," Poe uses sentence patterns that may seem unusual to a modern reader, but the story is not difficult to follow if you think about it part by part. Poe also uses words that repeat certain sounds. In this way he creates the mood or feeling in this poem. Read and think about "The Raven" stanza by stanza, and summarize the story. Then read it again, listening for the words with sounds that seem to create a mood. Follow the example provided to apply this strategy with other stanzas. You may use the back of this paper.

Once upon a midnight dreary, while I pondered
   weak and weary,
Over many a quaint and curious volume of forgotten lore—
While I nodded, nearly napping, suddenly there
   came a tapping,
As of some one gently rapping, rapping at my
   chamber door.
"'Tis some visitor," I muttered, "tapping at my
   chamber door—
     Only this and nothing more."

**Summary:** Late one night, as I sat thinking about some material I had been reading, I heard a knock on the door.
**Words that create a mood:** dreary, weary, napping, tapping, rapping
**Mood:** dark and eerie

Name _____ Date _____

## "On the Grasshopper and the Cricket" by John Keats
## Sonnet 30 by William Shakespeare
## Three Haiku by Bashō and Chiyojo
## "Hokku Poems" by Richard Wright

**Summary** These poems all follow strict forms. Two are sonnets and seven are haikus. In Shakespeare's sonnet, the speaker describes how past memories often make him sad as he relives certain experiences. However, if he thinks about his dear friend, his sorrows end. Keats's speaker points out that earth always has poetry. When birds stop singing in summer's heat, the grasshopper sings. In winter, the cricket sings, reminding him of summer's song. The haikus by Basho and Chiyojo create three sharp images: a perfect evening, a wandering dragon-fly catcher, and a wildly swaying tree. In Wright's poems, the speaker comments on a half-exposed snail, a laughing boy changing color in the snow, a peach tree blooming in a city, and a drenching rain that travels from town to town.

**Resumen** Estos dos sonetos y siete haikus siguen formas estrictas. El soneto de Shakespeare, describe cómo una persona se entristece al revivir ciertas experiencias. Sin embargo, al pensar en sus buenos amigos, sus penas desaparecen. El soneto de Keats, dice que la tierra siempre tiene poesía. Cuando los pájaros dejan de cantar en el calor del verano, canta la cigarra. En invierno, el canto del grillo nos recuerda a la canción del verano. Los haiku de Basho y Chiyojo crean tres nítidas imágenes: un atardecer perfecto, un cazador de libélulas y un árbol que se mece violentamente. En los poemas de Wright, los temas son un caracol casi al descubierto, un niño que ríe y cambia de color en la nieve, un duraznero en flor en la ciudad y una lluvia torrencial que va de pueblo en pueblo.

**Restate Poetic Language** Sometimes poets use poetic language in place of more familiar language. This is especially true of the poets in Shakespeare's time. Read Shakespeare's Sonnet 30 to identify and list examples of poetic language. Then write more familiar words for the words you list. Create a chart like the one below. A few phrases have been modeled for you. Apply this strategy to one other poem.

### Sonnet 30

| Poetic Words | Familiar Words |
| --- | --- |
| sessions of sweet silent thought | periods of quiet thought |
| the lack of many a thing I sought | not getting what I want |
| weep afresh | cry again |
| The sad account | the unhappy story |

## The *Odyssey*, Part 1, by Homer

**Summary** This epic tells the story of the Greek hero Odysseus, who is trying to return home after a long war. In Part 1, Odysseus tells of his many adventures: his visit to the land of the Lotus Eaters; how he blinded, tricked, and escaped from a one-eyed Cyclops; his journey to Hades, the land of the dead; how he escaped from the Sirens, who lure men to their death; and how he avoided destruction by Scylla and Charybdis. He told of his men eating the Sun God's cattle, which resulted in a storm that killed the rest of his crew.

**Resumen** Esta épica narra la historia de Odysseus, quien vuelve a casa luego de una larga guerra. En la Primera parte, Odysseus habla de sus muchas aventuras: su visita a la tierra de los Lotus Eaters, de cómo enceguece y escapa de un Cyclop, de su viaje a Hades, la tierra de los muertos, de cómo había hecho para no oír el canto de las sirenas y cómo había escapado de Scylla y Charybdis. También narra cuando sus hombres comieron el ganado del Sun God, lo que causó una tormenta que mató al resto de la tripulación.

**Identify Story Elements** The *Odyssey* is really a series of adventures. It is easier to read and understand if you approach each adventure as you would approach any story—by identifying the setting, the characters, the problem or conflict, the main events, and the conclusion or outcome.

Practice this strategy on the adventure of the Lotus-Eaters, using the following worksheet. Then choose another adventure from the *Odyssey* and identify the same features.

> Upon the tenth
> we came to the coastline of the Lotus-Eaters,
> who live upon that flower. We landed there
> to take on water. All ship's companies
> mustered alongside for the midday meal.
> Then I sent out two picked men and a runner
> to learn what race of men that land sustained.
> They fell in, soon enough, with Lotus-Eaters,
> who showed no will to do us harm, only
> offering the sweet Lotus to our friends—
> but those who ate this honeyed plant, the Lotus,
> never cared to report, nor to return:
> they longed to stay forever, browsing on
> that native bloom, forgetful of their homeland.
> I drove them, all three wailing, to the ships,
> tied them down under their rowing benches,
> and called the rest: "All hands aboard;
> come, clear the beach and no one taste
> the Lotus, or you lose your hope of home."
> Filing in to their places by the rowlocks
> my oarsmen dipped their long oars in the surf,
> and we moved out again on our seafaring.

Setting: land of the Lotus-Eaters _____

Characters: Odysseus, his men, the Lotus Eaters _____

Problem: Those who eat Lotus never want to return home. _____

Main Events: _____

Conclusion: _____

## The *Odyssey*, Part 2, by Homer

**Summary** This epic tells the story of the Greek hero Odysseus, who is trying to return home after a long war. In Part 2, Odysseus returns home disguised as a beggar. His house is filled with men who are courting his wife, Penelope. She and his son, Telemachus, do not recognize him, but his old dog Argus does. Odysseus kills all the suitors, proves who he is, and is finally welcomed home by his wife.

**Resumen** Esta épica narra la historia de Odysseus, quien vuelve a casa luego de una larga guerra. En la Segunda parte, Odysseus llega a casa, disfrazado de mendigo. Su casa está llena de cortejantes de su mujer, Penelope. Ella y su hijo Telemacus, no reconocen a Odysseus, pero su viejo perro sí lo reconoce. Odysseus mata a todos los cortejantes, prueba quién es y finalmente es bienvenido por su esposa.

**Paraphrase Conversations** The *Odyssey* contains a number of conversations between characters. In order to follow the action of the story, you need to understand what is being said in these conversations. As you read, pause and paraphrase any conversation that may be confusing. See the example below. Use a chart like this one to paraphrase at least five other conversations.

| Conversation | Paraphrase |
|---|---|
| [Odysseus] "I'll tell you now. Suppose Athena's arm is over us, and Zeus her father's, must I rack my brains for more?<br><br>[Telemachus] "Those two are great defenders, no one doubts it, but throned in the serene clouds overhead; other affairs of men and gods they have to rule over." | If Athena and Zeus help us, isn't that enough?<br><br>They are powerful but we cannot depend on their help. They may have other things to do. |
|  |  |
|  |  |

Name _____ Date _____

## "An Ancient Gesture" by Edna St. Vincent Millay
## "Siren Song" by Margaret Atwood
## "Prologue" and "Epilogue" from *The Odyssey* by Derek Walcott
## "Ithaca" by Constantine Cavafy

**Summary** Each of these poems represents a modern interpretation of some part of the *Odyssey.* In "Siren Song," a siren seemingly asks to be set free from her tiresome role, but her flattery and plea for help is in fact the irresistible call that cannot be resisted. The speaker in "An Ancient Gesture" talks of wiping her teary eyes as she waits for a returning husband. She knows that Ulysses also shed tears, but his action was only a false gesture that he copied from his wife, whose tears were genuine. In Walcott's work, a blind blues singer sings of Odysseus, who battled both the sea and despair while his wife waited. He later returned to a happy home and a faithful wife. The speaker in "Ithaca" urges travelers not to fear dangers on a journey to Ithaca, but to enjoy the voyage. Experience gained, not the destination, is the real reward.

**Resumen** Éstas son reinterpretaciones actuales de partes de la *Odyssey.* En *Siren Song,* una sirena pide ser liberada de su papel, pero su pedido es en realidad su peligroso canto. En *Ancient Gestures,* una mujer habla de cómo secaba sus lágrimas mientras esperaba el regreso de su marido. Ella sabe que Ulysses hizo lo mismo, un gesto falso que él había copiado de su mujer, cuyas lágrimas sí eran genuinas. Walcott escribe de un cantor de *blues* ciego, que canta sobre Odysseus, quien combatió al mar y a la desesperanza, mientras su mujer lo esperaba. Él volvió más tarde a lo que todos realmente valoran: un hoga feliz y una mujer fiel. En *Ithaca,* se alienta a los viajeros no a temer los peligros de un viaje, sino a disfrutarlo. La experiencia ganada, no el destino, es el verdadero premio.

**Recognize Allusions** Many modern works of literature contain allusions, or references to classical literature like the *Odyssey.* An allusion is a casual or indirect reference. In order to understand the meanings of a piece of literature that contains allusions, you must be familiar with the subject of the allusion. As you read these poems, look for allusions to people or events in the *Odyssey.* Then briefly explain the allusion. An example has been provided.

| Allusion | Explanation |
| --- | --- |
| Siren Song | The sirens were sea nymphs whose sweet song lured men to their death on the rocks that surrounded their island. |
| | |

# Answers to Part 1

**The Cask of Amontillado
by Edgar Allan Poe**

**p. 6** **Reading Strategy** Fortunato has insulted Montresor. Montresor is determined to get revenge on Fortunato.

**p. 6** **Literary Analysis** The author creates an uncomfortable and mysterious feeling.

**p. 7** **Stop to Reflect** *Possible answer:* Yes. All burial places can feel frightening or eerie.

**p. 7** **Read for fluency** Fortunato speaks the following words:

*"Niter?" "Ugh! ugh! ugh!—ugh! ugh! ugh!—ugh! ugh! ugh!—ugh! ugh! ugh!—ugh! ugh! ugh!" "It is nothing."*

**p. 7** **Stop to Reflect** Possible answer: No. Montresor has already said that he wants to get revenge on Fortunato, so it seems unlikely that he cares about his health.

**p. 8** **Reading Check** Students should circle *skeletons* and *barrels of wine.*

**p. 8** **Literary Analysis** Any two of the following are answers:

*The niter hangs like moss.*

*We are below the river's bed.*

*Drops of moisture among the bones.*

**p. 8** **Reading Check** First, Fortunato tries to see into the niche.

Next, the narrator tells Fortunato to go in.

Then, the narrator chains Fortunato to the back wall.

Then, the narrator moves a pile of bones.

Finally, the narrator builds a wall.

**p. 9** **Literary Analysis** Any three of the following:

shrill, screams, bursting, chained, violently, or trembled.

**p. 9** **Reading Strategy** Students should cirlce *low laugh.*

A low laugh came out of the niche, and it made the hairs on my head stand up. (The saying "made the hair on my head stand up" means that the laugh startled and frightened him.)

**p. 10** **Stop to Reflect** No. It is obvious that Fortunato does not really find this funny because soon after he says "For the love of God, Montresor!"

**p. 10** **Reading Check** No. We know that no one found Fortunato alive, because the bones in front of the wall were not moved for fifty years.

## Review and Assess

1. Sample answer: Montresor wanted revenge because Fortunato had insulted him.

2. Montresor said he had wine, Amontillado, for Fortunato to taste.

3. Tier one: Fortunato moans.

   Tier two, three, and four: Fortunato vibrates his chains.

   Tiers five, six, seven: He screams loudly.

4. Students should circle the following: scary, disturbing, suspenseful
   *Possible answer:* An example of a disturbing moment in the story is when Montresor says "A succession of loud and shrill screams, bursting suddenly from the throat of the chained form, seemed to thrust me violently back."

5. *Subject:* I
   *What has the subject done?* paused; held the flambeaux (torch); threw rays (light) on the man inside

**The Most Dangerous Game
by Richard Connell**

**p. 15** **Reading Check** Rainsford and Whitney are going to hunt jaguars in South America.

**p. 15  Read Fluently** Students should try to read Rainsford's remarks in a scornful or indifferent tone and exclaim "Bah!" with exasperation. Students should circle answer (c).

**p. 15  Think Ahead** Students should circle *the hunters and the huntees* and label *the hunters* with Rainsford's name.

Predictions: He may be attacked by jaguars. Rainsford may become the "huntee," or hunted. He may have a change of heart about hunting.

**p. 16  Reading Strategy** Students should circle *For a seemingly endless time he fought the sea, began to count, and/or he could do possibly a hundred more.* The correct answer is (b) swimmer's movements.

**p. 16  Literary Analysis** Students might circle any three of these words: *darkness, screaming, anguish,* and *terror.* Possible answer: The high screaming sound could mean that an animal or possibly a person is in danger.

**p. 16  Read Fluently** Possible words include *polite* and *welcoming.*

**p.17  Stop to Reflect** Students should circle *I bought this island.*

**p.17  Reading Strategy** Students should circle *Rainsford does not immediatley realize that Zaroff hunts people* and *he realizes that Zaroff's ideal quarry is a person.* The correct answer is *(a) something hunted.*

**p. 17  Read Fluently** Rainsford is probably horrified and terrified because he realizes that Zaroff murders people.

**p. 18  Stop to Reflect** Zaroff hunts human beings. Students will probably say that Zaroff is a horrible person.

**p. 18  Reading Check** Students should circle *food and a knife.* The man has to avoid being found by Zaroff for three days.

**p. 18  Literary Analysis** It is suspensful because Zaroff has never lost, which means that Rainsford is in great danger.

**p. 19  Reading Check** If Rainsford does not agree to hunt with Zaroff, Zaroff will hand him over to Ivan.

**p. 19  Literary Analysis** Students should circle *Soon, Zaroff appears, following Rainsford's trail.* Some students may also circle *He calls out to Rainsford telling him he will be back.*

**p. 19  Literary Analysis** He hopes the tree will crash down on Zaroff.

**p. 20  Reading Check** Rainsford decides to jump into the sea.

**p. 20  Think Ahead** Some students may say Rainsford while others may say Zaroff. Accept all reasonable responses.

**p. 20  Reading Check** Rainsford wins in the end. Students should circle *He had never slept in a better bed, Rainsford decided.*

**Review and Assess**

1. Students should circle *competitive, rich,* and *sophisticated.*

2. Meaning 1: Zaroff plays a game with Rainsford—one so dangerous that they risk death.

   Meaning 2: Rainsford is the most dangerous of the hunted animals, or game, that Zaroff longs to hunt.

3. The correct answer is (c). Students should write *He had never slept in a better bed, Rainsford decided.*

4. *Possible responses:* Before the hunt with Zaroff, Rainsford thought that animals had no understanding of fear. Rainsford had no sympathy for the animals (jaguars) he hunted. After the hunt with Zaroff, Rainsford probably feels that he understands what the "huntees" face because he has been hunted down just like the animals he used to hunt.

5. Possible events include the following: Rainsford falling overboard—Rainsford in danger; when Zaroff returns with Ivan and the dog pack—Rainsford in danger; and Rainsford's confrontation with Zaroff at the end—Zaroff and Rainsford in danger

6. quarry: something that is hunted

   eludes: escapes; avoids

## Casey at the Bat
### by Ernest Lawrence Thayer

**p. 25** **Reading Check** It is the last inning of the baseball game.

**p. 25** **Reading Strategy** The score is 2 to 4. The Mudville players, Flynn and Blakey have just batted. Flynn is on third base.

Blakey is on second base.

**p. 25** **Stop to Reflect** Possible answer: Yes. Everyone seems confident in Casey, so he must have succeeded often in the past.

**p. 26** **Stop to Reflect** Students should underline *And when responding to the cheers he lightly doffed his hat.* Students should circle *proud* and *confident*.

**p. 26** **Literary Analysis** *Event:* pitcher holds the ball; *Event:* pitcher lets go of the ball; *Climax:* Casey swings his bat

**p. 26** **Literary Analysis** Students should circle *Mighty Casey has struck out.*

### Review and Assess

1. Their team is losing and the game is almost over.

2. Blakey: 2nd; Flynn: 3rd; Casey: home plate

3. Casey looks calm and proud when he first comes to bat. He also smiles when he is first at bat. Before his final swing, he looks angry with clenched teeth./Students should circle *a, c,* and *d.*

4. The pitcher throws the ball three times.

5. The climax is when Casey swings at the ball. The anticlimax is when Casey strikes out.

6. *Main Points:* Mudville is losing and it is the last inning. Casey is ready to bat. Casey strikes out.

   *Details:* Everyone cheers for Casey. He has a proud and calm manner. There is no joy in the town when Casey strikes out.

   *Summary:* Mudville is losing and it is the last inning. How Casey plays will determine if the team wins or loses. Casey swings three times, but gets three strikes. Casey has struck out. The fans in the town are very unhappy.

## Unit 2

### *from* A Lincoln Preface
### by Carl Sandburg

**p. 31** **Reading Strategy** *Possible answer:* What kind of a president was he? How did he feel about the American Civil War?

**p. 31** **Reading Strategy** Sample answer: Lincoln was killed in 1965. He was commander of the Union army.

**p. 31** **Literary Analysis** Yes. Students should circle the words *I do love an open fire: I always had one at home.*

**p. 32** **Reading Check**

1. Students should underline the words *The enemy was violating the Constitution to destroy the Union.*

2. Students should draw a box around the words *I will violate the Constitution, if necessary, to save the Union.*

**p. 32** **Stop to Reflect** (b) He thinks it is important.

**p. 32** **Reading Strategy** He writes about the railroad. Students should circle the words *the plans for railroad connection from coast to coast must be pushed through and the union Pacific realized.*

**Reading Check**

1. speeches
2. letters
3. telegrams
4. official messages

**p. 33** **Reading Strategy** Students should write the information they already knew about Lincoln. Then, they should write the most interesting point they learned about Lincoln.

**p. 34** **Literary Analysis** Students should circle the words *he liked best of all the stories told of him.* These words tell us that he Lincoln had a sense of humor.

**p. 34** **Read Fluently** Lincoln is saying that he is surprised that a peaceful man such as himself is heading such a violent war.

**p. 35** **Stop to Reflect** *Possible answer:* His life could be considered rich and full because he worked to end slavery. His life can also be considered rich and full because he was a friend to many people, he had a sense of humor, and he was a strong leader.

**p. 35** **Reading Strategy** Students should name one thing they learned about Lincoln in the passage.

**Review and Assess**

1. (b) one country/*Possible answer:* Since the southern states were fighting against the northern states, he was trying to express his desire for a more united country by saying that the Mississippi River should belong to only one country.

2. Students should circle the following: He defended the United States. He could tell a funny story. He was a powerful president.

3. (c) Lincoln did not like violence.

4. *Possible answer:* Lincoln was troubled by the awful war, but he felt the war was necessary to keep the Union together. He helped Nevada become a state so that Nevada's votes could help him free slaves. He had a sense of humor.

**I Have a Dream**
**by Martin Luther King, Jr.**

**p. 40** **Stop to Reflect** *Possible answer:* There were probably so many people at the March on Washington because the issue of equality for all people was an issue that affected Americans everywhere.

**p. 40** **Reading Check** Possible answer: He dreams that his children will live in a country that judges people by their actions rather than by their appearance or ethnicity.

**p. 40** **Reading Strategy** *Possible response:* I feel understanding and emotional. It makes me think more about how inequality affects children. Children are innocent and often have to live with the choices of adults. It makes me realize the responsibility adults have toward children to make the world a better place for all people.

**p. 41** **Read Fluently** *Possible answer:* all of God's children; new meaning; My country; sweet land of liberty; Land where my fathers died; land of the pilgrim's pride; every mountainside; let freedom ring.

**p. 41** **Literary Analysis** His purpose is (c) to persuade.

**Review and Assess**

1. (a) Students should write the following states: New Hampshire, New York, Pennsylvania, Colorado. (b) King is trying to show that equality for all people is an issue that affects everyone in every part of the country.

2. "The content of their character" means the way people act and think.

3. (c) to persuade—He uses one of the most important documents in U.S. history to show that our country is founded on the belief that all people are created equal, and therefore we should follow this American document and start treating all people equally.

6. Possible answer: *an oasis of freedom and justice:* optimistic, united with all people; *let freedom ring:* hopeful, inspired

### Old Man of the Temple
### by R.K. Narayan

**p. 46** **Reading Check** The two characters are the Talkative Man and Doss.

**p. 46** **Literary Analysis** (b) An old man comes out of locked doors.

**p. 47** **Reading Strategy** *Fantasy:* Doss awakens as an old man. *Reality:* Doss falls asleep

**p. 47** **Stop to Reflect** Students could select any of the following changes: Doss is like an old man. His hands shake. His voice is thin and high. Doss says he is 80 years old. This probably makes the narrator nervous.

**p. 47** **Read Fluently** 1. the old man 2. lonely, confused

**p. 48** **Reading Check** 1. The old man says everyone knows him. 2. He says he built the temple. 3. He says the name of a king.

**p. 48** **Reading Strategy** The fantasy is that one of the men talking is actually dead.

**p. 48** **Literary Analysis** (a) The old man is 500 years old.

**p. 49** **Background** The narrator helps the old man break the tie to his old life and move on to another level with his wife.

**p. 49** **Reading Check** The narrator has to walk back to his car and honk his horn to get the people to come to their door.

**p. 49** **Reading Check** The old man was bothering the villagers.

The knocking stopped because the old man went away.

### Review and Assess

1. 1. Doss changes into an old man.
2. The Talkative Man tells the old man he is dead.
3. The old man sees his dead wife.
4. The people in the village do not hear knocking anymore.

2. 1. His hands shake.
2. His voice is thin and high.
3. He says he is 80 years old.

3. The people of the village do not open their doors at night because they do not want to let the thing they call "it" into their homes.

4. (d) A man in the story is 500 years old. It is impossible for someone to live to 500 years of age.

5. *Real*—Talkative Man (Narrator): He is a businessman; Doss: He is a taxi driver; Old Man: He talks and has feelings. *Fantastic*—Talkative Man (Narrator): He sees and talks to a 500 year-old dead man; Doss: He changes into a very old man; Old Man: He is 500 years old. He seems to only appear to some people.

### Unit 3
### Rules of the Game
### by Amy Tan

**p. 54** **Reading Check** Students should circle *a bag of candy.*

**p. 54** **Stop to Reflect** *Possible answer:* Waverly is a quick learner, and she figures out what she needs to do in order to get what she wants.

**p. 54** **Reading Check** Students should circle *the chess set.*

**p. 55** **Literary Analysis** *Younger Generation:* They immediately line up the chess pieces and start reading the instruction book. *Older Generation:* When they get home, their mother immediately tells Vincent to throw away the chess set because it is used.

**p. 55** **Reading Check** 1. She read the rules and looked up the big words in the dictionary. 2. She borrowed books from the library. 3. She studied each chess piece.

**p. 56** **Reading Strategy** *Waverly:* She loved the game and studied it every night. *Brothers:* They grew tired of the game and preferred playing outside.

**p. 56** **Reading Check** The lifesavers are used for the two missing chess pieces

**p. 56** **Stop to Reflect** *Possible answer:* Yes. It is brave of Waverly to ask the old man to play chess with her because he probably has more experience playing chess.

**p. 57** **Stop to Reflect** 1. She learned to keep her pieces in neat rows. 2. She learned to not lose her temper.

**p. 57** **Read Fluently** The mother gave Waverly her chang. It was a small tablet of red jade. She gave it to Waverly for good luck.

**p. 58** **Literary Analysis** *Waverly:* She believes you may need to lose chess pieces to win the game. *Mother:* She believes you should lose fewer chess pieces to win the game.

**p. 58** **Reading Check** Students should underline the words *Waverly no longer needed to do house-hold chores. She spent her free time practicing to be a better chess player.*

**p. 58** **Stop to Reflect** *Possible Answer:* No. A special talent should not excuse someone from helping out around the house.

**p. 58** **Stop to Reflect** *Possible Answer:* The man probably felt nervous because of the possibility that a young child might win against him.

**p. 59** **Reading Check** Students should circle these words: *When she said her brothers were too noisy, she got her own bedroom. When she said she could not finish her dinner, she was permitted to leave the table.*

**p. 59** **Literary Analysis** Students should underline this sentence: *"I wish you wouldn't do that, telling everybody I'm your daughter."* Students should draw a box around these words: *"Aiii-ya. So shame be with mother?" She grasped my hand even tighter as she glared at me.*

**Stop to Reflect** (c) To win, do not let others know what you are going to do. Sample response: Waverly will not lose her temper again with her mother. She will remain calm and accept that her special talent has made her mother very proud of her.

### Review and Assess

1. Students should circle the following phrases: how to win; how to behave when playing chess.

2. (b) quietly beating an opponent at chess; *Possible response:* A strong wind is often quiet, but can also be very forceful, just as a chess player can be very quiet, but play with force to win the game.

3. *Waverly's Ideas:* Life in Chinatown provided everything she needed. Winning a chess game takes skill and practice. *Mother's Ideas:* Life in Chinatown was something to rise above. Winning a chess game takes luck.

4. *Waverly:* plays chess, born in the U.S., believes in skill; *Mother:* watches chess, born in China, believes in luck; *Similarities:* strong-willed, proud, secretive.

## Checkouts
### by Cynthia Rylant

**p. 65  Read Fluently** (a) happy

**p. 65  Literary Analysis** *Possible answer:* There are many people with carts, trying to get past each other. People wait in long lines, often with full carts. It is ironic that shopping makes her calm because grocery stores are often crowded and can be stressful if the lines are long.

**p. 65  Reading Strategy** *Possible answer:* I like to shop. There are so many choices. Sample answer: The girl liked shopping too. Her feelings are similar to mine.

**p. 66  Literary Analysis** Students should circle *he drops her jar of mayonnaise.* We are surprised that she falls in love because we would probably expect her to be frustrated or annoyed if the bag boy dropped and broke her groceries. We don't expect this action to cause her to fall in love.

**p. 66  Reading Check** 1. The girl smiled at the boy. He dropped the jar of mayonnaise. 2. She used a different checkout lane. He pretended that he did not see her.

**p. 66  Stop to Reflect** Students should circle *glancing toward the other, each smiled slightly, then looked away.* Sample answer: Yes. I was surprised that they smiled at each other. I thought they would pretend to not see each other.

### Review and Assess

1. (b) Her parents moved the family to a new town.

2. busy, nervous

3. Possible Answer: She may have liked him because he was nervous, which showed he was sensitive. It is also possible that she liked him because he worked in a grocery store, a place that makes her feel calm and happy.

4. (a) The correct answer is *(c) They smiled and looked away.* (b) *Possible answer:* I thought they would speak and become friends.

5. Possible Response: *Similar Event in My Life:* I saw my best friend with another person when my friend should have been with me. *How I Felt:* I was jealous. *How the Character Must Feel:* She might feel jealous, but if she likes her date, she might not mind very much.

## The Interlopers
### by Saki (H.H. Munro)

**p. 71  Reading Strategy** Students should underline the words *He is hunting on his own forest lands. But another family also claims this land.*

*Cause:* an argument over who owns the land

**p. 71  Reading Check** Georg

**p. 72  Reading Check** 1. a rifle 2. hate 3. murder

**p. 72  Literary Analysis** (a) Georg struggles against nature. This is an external conflict.

**p. 73  Reading Check** The tree has caught Ulrich.

**p. 73  Literary Analysis** The conflict is between Ulrich and Georg. It is an external conflict.

**p. 73  Stop to Reflect** Possible Response: Yes. They seem to hate each other so much that I cannot imagine the conflict ending.

**p. 74  Literary Analysis** This is internal conflict because Ulrich is struggling with feelings within himself.

**p. 74  Reading Check** Ulrich.

**p. 74  Reading Strategy** Students should underline *He says people in the town will be surprised if he and Ulrich become friends. He says their friendship will bring peace among people.*

**p. 74** **Reading Check** They think of the wonderful things their friendship will bring.

**p. 75** **Reading Check** The men want to show their respect for each other by saving the other man.

**p. 75** **Read Fluently** Students should circle *afraid*.

**p. 75** **Stop to Reflect** The interlopers were the wolves. Possible response: The wolves kill the men, and the men never get to show their friendship to others. The feud probably continued.

## Review and Assess

1. Both families claimed they owned the same land.

2. No, the men were not friends at the beginning of the story. They were hunting for each other.

3. Yes, the men were friends at the end of the story. They shared a flask of wine. The thought of the wonderful things their friendship will bring. They shouted for help together.

4. 1. (a) Ulrich hates Georg. Ulrich also feels sorry for Georg.
   2. (a) The two men are hunting for each other.

5. The answers are underlined : <u>Both families claimed they owned the same land.</u> The two men were enemies. <u>A tree fell.</u> The two men were trapped. Ulrich asks Georg to be his friend. <u>Georg consideres Ulrich's offer and decides to be his friend.</u> The men shout. <u>Wolves run toward the men.</u>

### Unit 4

### The Secret Life of Walter Mitty
### by James Thurber

**p. 80** **Reading Strategy** Students should underline the following: *The crew have faith in their brave Commander.*

**p. 80** **Literary Analysis** Students should circle the following: *She seemed grossly unfamiliar, like a strange woman who had yelled at him in a crowd.*

**p. 80** **Reading Check** He drives past the hospital.

**p. 81** **Stop to Reflect** He is daydreaming and not paying attention to his driving.

**p. 81** **Reading Strategy** A newsboy walks by, shouting about a trial in Waterbury.

**p. 81** **Stop to Reflect** He is speaking to himself but is overheard by a woman on the street.

**p. 81** **Literary Analysis** He stopped walking and the buildings of Waterbury rose up out of the misty courtroom and surrounded him again.

**p. 82** **Reading Check** He sees a magazine article titled "Can Germany Conquer the World Through the Air?"

**p. 82** **Read Fluently** She is annoyed because he was hard to find in the hotel lobby. Also, he isn't wearing his overshoes.

**p. 82** **Reading Strategy** The final paragraph of the paragraph should be circled.

## Review and Assess

1. She thinks he is driving too fast.

2. He has been hard to find, and he isn't wearing his overshoes.

3. In his daydreams, Mitty is brave and heroic. In real life, he is clumsy and quiet.

4. We wouldn't know that Mitty sees himself as a hero. We would know him only as a clumsy, quiet person.

5. a. He is a Commander flying a plane in a storm.

   b. He is a world-famous doctor performing an emergency operation.

   c. He is an expert shooter on the witness stand in court.

d. He is a war pilot flying through heavy gunfire to blow up a target.

e. He bravely faces death before a firing squad.

**Go Deep to the Sewer
by Bill Cosby**

**p. 87 Literary Analysis** The words *as a child* should be circled.

**p. 87 Reading Strategy** a. an orange peel b. gum c. a manhole

**p. 87 Stop to Reflect** Students may say that it shows they love to play.

**p. 87 Literary Analysis** Students should underline the following: *we kept looking for a football that could have been seen only on radar screens.*

**p. 88 Literary Analysis** He exaggerates the speed and height at which the rubber ball flies.

**p. 88 Reading Strategy** Students should circle the following: *Suddenly, the car that marked the base drove away.*

**p. 88 Read Fluently** Junior sounds more frustrated because he "cried in outrage."

**Review and Assess**

1. They play in the street.
2. The players can barely see the football
3. It bounces higher and moves faster
4. He recalls playing games as a child.
5. They use the trash to represent themselves.
6. a. second base

   b. The fenders of parked cars

   d. The car that represents third base drives away.

**Talk
retold by Harold Courlander
and George Herzog**

**p. 93 Literary Analysis** Students should circle the following: *one of the yams said to him, "Well, at last you're here. You never weeded me, but now you come around with your digging stick. Go away and leave me alone!"*

**p. 93 Reading Strategy** They are illogical because the dog, tree, branch, and stone can talk.

**p. 93 Reading Check** He becomes frightened when his fish trap speaks.

**p. 94 Reading Strategy** It's funny because a stool can't really talk either.

**p. 94 Stop to Reflect** He was probably scared when he realized that his stool was talking.

**Review and Assess**

1. He becomes frightened because all the items talk to him.
2. All the characters feel "Not Scared."
3. He thinks the story is too wild to be true.
4. It's funny because the stool says a talking yam is odd. In truth, a talking stool is also odd.
5. a. farmer: yam, dog, tree, branch, stone

   b. fisherman: fish trap

   c. weaver: cloth

   d. bather: river

   e. chief: stool
6. People do not always believe something until it happens to them.

**Unit 5**

*from* **The Road Ahead
by Bill Gates**

**p. 99 Literary Analysis** Students should cite the following details: You had to watch the program at the same time it was shown on TV. Otherwise you missed the show.

**p. 99 Reading Strategy** luxury

**p. 99 Reading Check** asynchronous: not happening at the same time

**p. 99 Literary Analysis** Students should cite the following reasons: It gives them more control over their schedule. It also gives them more choices of movies to watch on TV.

p. 100 **Stop to Reflect** Students may say they agree because people are already used to paying for rented videos and for cable TV.

p. 100 **Reading Check** You'll be able to watch the program at any time.

p. 100 **Reading Strategy** Students should name start it, stop it, go to any earlier part, pause. Possible response: It is a very useful invention.

p. 100 **Literary Analysis** People will buy video-on-demand if it is affordable, and it will likely become something that everyone will feel he or she must have.

**Review and Assess**

1. a. synchronous; b. asynchronous

2. "Video-on-demand" means you can watch a movie that has been shown on TV at any time you like.

3. "Killer application" means an invention so popular that everyone feels they must have it.

4. It gives you more choices of movies to watch on TV.

5. He thinks it will be popular because it will let you watch movies whenever you want. It will offer you more movie choices.

6. Students should check the following:

   With video-on-demand, you'll be in absolute control.

   You could claim the freedom and luxury to serve as your own program scheduler.

   Video-on-demand is an obvious development.

### The Machine That Won the War
### by Isaac Asimov

p. 105 **Reading Strategy** Students may circle any of the details in the bracketed passage, since all of them are relevant to understanding the plot.

p. 105 **Reading Check** *director:* Swift; *data interpreter:* Jablonsky; *programmer:* Henderson

p. 105 **Stop to Reflect** A computer is run by humans. If they feed it data that isn't reliable, then the computer's results won't be reliable, either.

p. 105 **Literary Analysis** Details: *a hundred subsidiary computers here on Earth, on the Moon, on Mars, even on Titan.*

p. 106 **Read Fluently** Henderson corrected the data because he believed it was unreliable. He was afraid he would be fired if he told people that the data was unreliable.

p. 106 **Reading Check** At first he corrected only a little bit. Over time, he corrected much more.

p. 106 **Reading Strategy** Relevant details: *His best technicians weren't available to service the machine; he didn't trust the work that other technicians did on it.*

p. 106 **Reading Check** Jablonsky adjusted the information that came from Multivac.

p. 107 **Stop to Reflect** Swift's actions show that he cared a lot about winning the war. He didn't want to rely on a machine that he suspected was not reliable. He trusted his own instincts more than the machine's advice.

p. 107 **Read Fluently** The word *coin* should be circled.

**Review and Assess**

1. Henderson—chief programmer; supplied Multivac with data

   Jablonsky—chief interpreter; interpreted advice that Multivac gave

   Swift—director of Solar Federation; made final decisions about war

2. The three men were celebrating Earth's victory after a ten-year war against the planet of Deneb.

3. All three men confess that they made changes because they believed Multivac's data was unreliable.

4. At first, the "machine" refers to Multivac. Later, you realize the "machine" is a simple coin.

5. There are computers on the Moon, on Mars, and on Titan.

   There are no coins anymore because of a metal shortage.

6. Swift made decisions simply by tossing a coin. If it landed on heads, he would do one thing. If it landed on tails, he would do another.

### *from* Silent Spring
### by Rachel Carson

**p. 112 Reading Check** *Possible answers:* cattle and sheep died; patients got new sicknesses; birds couldn't fly; plants dried up; apple trees didn't grow fruit; fish died; white powder appeared on roofs.

**p. 112 Reading Strategy** Fact: *This town does not actually exist; every one of these disasters has actually happened somewhere, and many real communities have already suffered.* Opinion: *This imagined tragedy may easily become a stark reality we all shall know.*

**p. 112 Literary Analysis** The text causes me to worry about the careless use of chemicals that can lead to sickness and death in plants, animals, and people.

**Review and Assess**

1. *Possible answers:* trees, fields, streams, birds, fish, farm animals.

2. doctors' patients—get new sicknesses; birds—tremble violently, can't fly; plants—dry up, turn brown; apple trees—fail to grow fruit; fish—die.

3. A strange white powder appears.

4. Check *a, c, d.*

5. Sample answer: Yes, Carson convinced me. She explained how plants, animals, and people can get sick and die from chemicals. She explained that some of these things have already happened in real towns.

6. a—fact; b—fact; c—fact; d—opinion.

### Unit 6

### The Gift of the Magi
### by O. Henry

**p. 117 Literary Analysis** Della and Jim Young are a very poor couple. They live in a run-down apartment. Jim makes only twenty dollars a week.

**p. 117 Literary Analysis** Tomorrow would be Christmas Day, and she had only $1.87 with which to buy Jim a present.

**p. 117 Reading Strategy** Possible questions: Why does Della let down her hair? Why does the narrator mention Della's hair and Jim's watch? Why does Della enter Madame Sofronie's store?

**p. 118 Reading Check** Della wants to sell her hair.

**p. 118 Reading Check** She chooses a simple but handsome watch chain

**p. 118 Stop to Reflect** He will feel bad because she had to cut her beautiful hair for him.

**p. 118 Reading Strategy** *Possible questions:* Why does Jim stare so strangely at Della when he sees her? What is Jim thinking when he stares at Della?

**p. 119 Reading Check** She hopes that Jim will not be upset. She wants him to know that her hair will grow back the way he likes it.

**p. 119 Reading Strategy** Jim has bought Della a set of expensive combs for her long hair.

**p. 119 Literary Analysis** Jim has sold his watch to get the money to buy Della's combs.

**p. 119 Reading Check** They gave up the things they loved most to show their love for each other.

**Review and Assess**

1. Della sells her long hair to Madame.

2. a. a watch chain b. hair combs

3. Their gifts show their love for each other; They each give up what they love to please the other.

4. a. poor b. run-down

5. Della wants to buy Jim a Christmas present, but she has only $1.87 to spend.

6. a. What will Della do to get a present for Jim? Why does Jim look horrified when he sees Della?

   b. Both questions were answered. Della sells her hair for the money to buy Jim a watch chain. Jim looks horrified because he has sold his watch to buy Della hair combs.

### The Scarlet Ibis
### by James Hurst

**p. 124 Literary Analysis** The word is *I*.

**p. 124 Reading Check** She means that the child may not have a normal mind.

**p. 124 Reading Strategy** Students may say they would have more compassion than the narrator. Or, they may say they would share the narrator's bitterness about having a mentally-challenged brother.

**p. 125 Reading Check** He crawls backwards like a doodle-bug.

**p. 125 Literary Analysis** *He was a burden in many ways; all of which I ignored once we got out of the house; to discourage his coming with me.*

**p. 125 Stop to Reflect** The narrator becomes more patient and friendly with Doodle.

**p. 125 Reading Strategy** Students might say that they wouldn't give up, because they want their brother to succeed.

**p. 126 Literary Analysis** The sentence to be circled is the one beginning "They did not know. . . ."

**p. 126 Stop to Reflect** The narrator is not afraid of a challenge. He has confidence in his ability to succeed. He cares about Doodle's progress.

**p. 126 Read Fluently** The bird flaps its wings and falls through the tree. It lands dead on the ground.

**p. 127 Reading Strategy** Students might say they would not leave Doodle behind because it would be cruel and dangerous.

**p. 127 Stop to Reflect** Doodle, like the ibis, is now dead. His red blood resembles the red of the ibis. His limp body is like the bird's limp body.

**p. 127 Literary Analysis** Students should circle: *I began to weep; the tear-blurred vision; I screamed; threw my body to the earth above his; I lay there crying.*

**Review and Assess**

1. Descriptive words might be *tiny, weak,* or *sick.* Descriptive phrases used by the narrator include "a disappointment," "all head," "a tiny body which was red and shriveled like an old man's."

2. He is ashamed of having a crippled brother.

3. Doodle lays dead on the ground, just like the ibis. Doodle is covered in red blood, resembling the red bird. Doodle, like the ibis, has an exotic beauty, even in death.

4. He was born when I was six. I began to make plans to kill him. I did not know then that pride is a wonderful, terrible thing.

5. Students might say they would work Doodle hard because it's the only way he'll succeed. Students may say they would not work Doodle hard because he's too weak to handle it.

## The Necklace
## by Guy de Maupassant

**p. 132 Reading Strategy** *She had . . . not the slightest chance of being . . . married by a rich and distinguished man; so she slipped into marriage with a minor civil servant.*

**p. 132 Literary Analysis** *Possible answer:* Don't make money the most important thing in your life.

**p. 132 Reading Check** *Possible answers:* She wants a rich husband; money; a fancy house; fine foods; a nice wardrobe; jewelry; to charm; to be envied; to be admired; to be sought after

**p. 133 Reading Strategy** *Possible answer:* She is embarrassed and ashamed about the things she owns.

**p. 133 Read Fluently** "Why don't you go and see Madame Forestier and ask her to lend you some jewelry?"

**p. 133 Stop to Reflect** *Possible answers:* She looks very beautiful, because of her nice dress and jewelry. She looks very beautiful, because she is so happy.

**p. 133 Reading Check** She is happy because she is admired by others.

**p. 134 Reading Check** She is upset because the necklace is gone.

**p. 134 Reading Strategy** Students should circle *I didn't sell this necklace, madame. I only supplied the case.*

**p. 134 Stop to Reflect** *Possible answer:* Madame Loisel fears that Madame Forestier will think the new necklace is cheaper than the lost one."

**p. 135 Literary Analysis** *Possible answer:* Don't live a lifestyle that is more expensive than you can afford. Don't borrow things you can't afford to pay back.

**p. 135 Reading Check** It takes the Loisels ten years to pay their debt.

**p. 135 Literary Analysis** *How strange and fickle life is! How little it takes to make or break you!*

**p. 136 Reading Strategy** *Possible answer:* She is proud that she has worked off the debt. She feels there is nothing to fear or hide anymore.

**p. 136 Literary Analysis** *Possible answer:* Things aren't always worth what they seem.

### Review and Assess

1. She is unhappy because she is not rich. She feels that she deserved a better life.

2. a. a new dress  b. jewelry

3. a. maid; b. an attic under the roof; c. house chores herself; d. a second job at night

4. Madame Forestier's necklace was false and worth five hundred francs at most.

5. All sentences should be checked **except** *People in the Ministry of Education are not to be trusted.*

6. She is admired by everyone, which is one of her greatest desires.

## Unit 7
## Single Room, Earth View
## by Sally Ride

**p. 141 Reading Strategy** fast

**p. 141 Literary Analysis** typhoons, volcanoes, meteors

**p. 141 Reading Check** She must keep watching to know exactly what she is passing over.

**p. 141 Literary Analysis** Students should circle: *Africa, Antarctic, Ganges River, Indian Ocean, Caribbean*

**p. 142 Reading Strategy** slow

**p. 142 Reading Check** They were obscured by a huge dust storm.

**p. 142 Literary Analysis** Students should circle: *Some cities look out of focus, and their colors muted.*

**p. 142 Stop to Reflect** The photos from space are taken from much farther away, so they give a wider picture of the pollution problem.

**p. 143 Reading Check** Students should circle: *eddies* and *spirals*

**p. 143 Read Fluently** It was hard for her to tell the Earth from the sky. The twinkling lights might be stars or city lights.

**p. 143 Literary Analysis** Students should circle: *It looks like bursting balls of light, like a fireworks show. Students should underline: Blue and orange bands streak across the horizon.*

### Review and Assess

1. The view is so much different from far away than it is from close up.

2. The cities are covered by a haze of air pollution.

3. a. lightning b. sunrise

4. She describes her trip on a space shuttle.

5. a. the Antarctic b. the Caribbean c. Northern Africa (from Morocco to the Sudan) d. the Persian Gulf

6. You would read slowly.

### On Summer
### by Lorraine Hansberry

**p. 148 Literary Analysis** As a child, she liked the other seasons, but not summer.

**p. 148 Reading Strategy** Possible answers: *feeling very, very hot; I acutely disliked the feeling; too-grainy texture of sand; too-cold coldness of the various waters; the icky-perspiry feeling of bathing caps.*

**p. 148 Literary Analysis**

a. The days are too long.

b. The days are too sunny.

**p. 148 Reading Check** She likes to talk, and she makes delicious cupcakes.

**p. 149 Stop to Reflect** As an adult, she can travel to beautiful places. As a child, she had to stay home in the hot city.

**p. 149 Reading Strategy** Hansberry was amazed by the dying woman's courage.

**p. 149 Read Fluently** Students should circle: *that she might live to see at least one more summer.*

**p. 149 Literary Analysis** She has gone from liking summer least to liking it most of all seasons.

### Review and Assess

1. She wishes that the woman might live to see at least one more summer.

2. As an adult, she no longer associates summer with uncomfortable heat. Instead, she associates it with travel to beautiful places and being inspired by a dying woman.

3. *Possible answers:* She had to take naps in a hot, dark room in the summer. The sand was too grainy. The water was too cold. The bathing caps felt icky-perspiry. The days were too long. The days were too sunny.

4. She thought she looked very old, but she liked how she talked and made tasty cupcakes.

5. She admires the woman for her spirit and energy, despite her deadly illness.

6. a. winter—austere, silent; b. spring—frivolous; c. summer—life at the apex, gentlest nights, longest days, noblest of the seasons.

### A Celebration of Grandfathers
### by Rudolfo A. Anaya

**p. 154 Literary Analysis** strong in their beliefs; we learned a wise path of life to follow; They had something important to share with the young.

**p. 154 Stop to Reflect** They cared not just about themselves but about everyone else, too. They felt like part of a community.

**p. 154 Reading Strategy** He admires them. Possible sentences to circle: The old people had great faith, says Anaya. They prayed sincerely.

**p. 155 Literary Analysis** For Anaya, time seems to stand still when he meets the old people. He feels their strength. The experience affected him deeply.

**p. 155 Stop to Reflect** Anaya was bitten because he stood too close to an anthill. He didn't know that where he was standing was dangerous.

**p. 155 Reading Strategy** Students may circle the sentences starting "In his language..." until the end of the paragraph.

**p. 155 Reading Check** He says that today's children don't want to take part in their ancestors' ways of life.

**p. 156 Read Fluently** Possible answers: *We need to . . . know where we stand; speak softly; respect others; share what we have; pray not for material gain; pray for rain for the fields; pray for the sun; pray for peaceful nights; pray for an abundant harvest.*

**p. 156 Reading Check** TV ads show old people as healthy and lively, but that's not the way it really is with many of the elderly.

**p. 156 Literary Analysis** Possible answers: *vision blurs; health wanes; even the act of walking carries with it the painful reminder of the autumn of life.*

## Review and Assess

1. Possible answers: strong, sincere, caring, hard-working, giving, faithful, religious, wise, respectful.

2. Youth today are not connected to their ancestors' ways of life, while youth of the past were.

3. The topic of his essay is his grandfather and others like him. In his essay he celebrates their strength, spirit, and values.

4. Possible answers: a. hard-working: He drives his crops to market. b. wise: He knows how to treat ant bites. c. caring: He spends time on the farm with his grandson.

5. Young people should listen more to old people.

Young people need patience to deal with old people.

## Unit 8
### The Tragedy of Romeo and Juliet by William Shakespeare
### Act II Scene ii

**p. 161 Reading Check** They hate each other.

**p. 161 Literary Analysis** Stressed syllables are underlined.

*But soft! What light through yonder window breaks?*

*It is the East, and Juliet is the sun!*

*Arise, fair sun, and kill the envious moon,*

*Who is already sick and pale with grief*

*That thou her maid art far more fair than she.*

**p. 161 Reading Check** He has come to her home without telling her. He is hiding in the dark beneath her balcony.

**p. 161 Reading Strategy** Commas should be circled after the words *Romeo, or, not, love,* Punctuation marks should be underlined after *Romeo! Romeo? name; Capulet.*

**p. 162 Stop to Reflect** The lovers care for each other more than they care for their own families.

**p. 162 Reading Strategy** Students should circle *am.*

**p. 162 Reading Check** Juliet's family and Romeo's family hate each other. The Capulets might harm Romeo if they knew he was there to see their daughter.

**p. 163 Literary Analysis** *What shall I swear by? Do not swear at all;*

**p. 163 Reading Check** She loves talking with Romeo so much that it's hard for her to leave him.

**p. 163 Read Fluently** Where and what time thou wilt perform the rite

**p. 163 Reading Check** She asks what time tomorrow she should send her messenger. He tells her to do it by nine o'clock.

**p. 164 Literary Analysis** Stressed syllables are underlined:

*'Tis almost morning. I would have thee gone—*

*And yet no farther than a wanton's bird,*

*That lets it hop a little from his hand,*

*Like a poor prisoner in his twisted gyves,*

*And with a silken thread plucks it back again,*

*So loving-jealous of his liberty.*

**p. 164 Reading Strategy** No. There is no punctuation at the end of the line. The sentence makes no sense if you pause after *sorrow*.

**Review and Assess**

1. He knows it is dangerous to be seen with Juliet, since Juliet's family and his own family hate each other.

2. They are each willing to give up their family names.

3. She says that if he wants to marry her, she'll send a messenger to Romeo the next day. Romeo should tell the messenger where and when the marriage will take place.

4. Romeo goes to his priest.

5. Stressed syllables are underlined:

*Three words, dear Romeo, and good night indeed.*

*If that thy bent of love be honorable,*

*Thy purpose marriage, send me word tomorrow,*

*By one that I'll procure to come to thee,*

*Where and what time thou wilt perform the rite;*

*And all my fortunes at thy foot I'll lay*

*And follow thee my lord throughout the world.*

6. Punctuation to be circled after these words: *East, Arise, sun, moon,*

   Punctuation to be underlined after these words: *soft! breaks? sun! she.*

## Unit 9
### Memory
### by Margaret Walker

**p. 169 Stop to Reflect** They suggest that the people are poor, since they haven't replaced their worn-out hats and parasols with newer ones.

**p. 169 Reading Strategy** Possible words to be circled: hurt bewilderment on poor faces; a deep and sinister unrest; these brooding people; ghostly marching on pavement stone; closing fast around their squares of hate.

**p. 169 Literary Analysis** their muttering protests, their whispered oaths

**Review and Assess**

1. It is windy, cold, and rainy.

2. The hats and parasols are old and worn-out, which suggests that the owners are too poor to buy new ones

3. She sees a look of hurt bewilderment, or confusion.

4. Students will probably say no, since the people are poor, unhappy, and angry.

5. a. touch b. smell c. sound d. sight

6. angry; Possible words: a deep and sinister unrest; their squares of hate; their muttering protests; their whispered oaths

### Woman's Work
### by Julia Alvarez

**p. 174 Literary Analysis** Words to be circled: *she scrubbed the bathroom tiles.*

**p. 174 Reading Strategy** Words to be underlined: *the summer sun would bar the floor I swept till she was satisfied; She kept me prisoner in her housebound heart.* This image makes the daughter feel bad.

**p. 174 Stop to Reflect** Students might say that the daughter resented her mother for making her work indoors while her friends were outside. They might also say that the daughter loved her mother for training her so well in the art of woman's work.

**p. 174 Read Fluently** Words to be circled: *my mother's child; a woman working at home on her art, housekeeping paper as if it were her heart.*

## Review and Assess

1. Possible answers: scrubs the bathroom tiles; cleans the whole upstairs; cleans the downstairs; shines the tines of forks; shines the wheels of carts; cuts lacy lattices for pies.

2. She teaches her to keep a house much better than her heart.

3. She dislikes cleaning as a child because she can't go outside to play with her friends.

4. She grew up to be like her mother. The words "housekeeping paper" might suggest that she is a writer, and she feels as devoted to writing at home as her mother was about cleaning her home.

5. b. sound c. sight d. sight

6. Frowning, because her mother makes her stay inside to do housework while her friends are outside having fun.

## "The Raven"
## by Edgar Allan Poe

**p. 179 Literary Analysis** Time: midnight; Place: chamber

**p. 179 Reading Check** He is trying to find a magical way to bring back Lenore.

**p. 179 Reading Strategy** The speaker whispers the name "Lenore!" It shows that he thinks and hopes she is tapping at his door.

**p. 180 Reading Check** The raven has been making the tapping sound.

**p. 180 Stop to Reflect** He thinks the raven will leave tomorrow because "other friends" he left him in the past. The speaker is very depressed. He feels that happiness is impossible for him.

**p. 180 Reading Check** *She* is Lenore. It must be Lenore because she is the only person the speaker has been thinking about.

**p. 181 Reading Strategy** He asks the raven if his suffering will ever end. He asks if her will ever hold his lost Lenore again. His questions show that the speaker is very sad and desperately Lenore back with him.

**p. 181 Read Fluently** He is desperate to be rid of the raven.

**p. 181 Literary Analysis** The speaker: He is left fearing that his suffering will never end. The raven: He remains in the speaker's room and refuses to leave.

## Review and Assess

1. He hopes the books will describe a magical way to bring back Lenore.

2. The raven can speak. However, it only says the word "Nevermore."

3. The raven refuses to give any answer except "Nevermore."

4. Time: midnight; Place: the speaker's chamber

5. Possible answers:
   a. The speaker hears a tapping at his door.
   b. The speaker sees a raven above his door.
   c. The speaker asks the raven questions about Lenore.
   d. The raven repeats only the word "Nevermore."
   e. The speaker orders the raven to leave.
   f. The raven refuses to leave.

6. Possible answer:
   a. What he thinks: wants to bring back Lenore; is sad that she will never again press against his cushion
   b. What he says: whispers Lenore's name; begs the raven to tell him if Lenore will return to him
   c. What he does: reads books in an effort to bring back Lenore; angrily orders the bird to leave after it says only "Nevermore"
   d. Inferences: The speaker is very much in love with Lenore. He is very depressed that she is gone. He is angry because she is never coming back.

### The Seven Ages of Man
### by William Shakespeare

**p. 186 Literary Analysis** Words to be circled: *They have their exits and their entrances; one man in his time plays many parts; his acts being seven ages.*

**p. 186 Reading Strategy** Words to be underlined: *Sighing like furnace, with a woeful ballad/ Made to his mistress' eyebrow.* The speaker thinks lovers are foolish because they praise the tiniest details about those they love.

**p. 186 Reading Check** He desires honor and argues a lot.

**p. 186 Reading Strategy** He thinks it's a sad age to reach because you're helpless and unable to enjoy life.

### Review and Assess

1. He only desires honor, and he argues a lot.
2. Possible answers: memory, teeth, eyes, taste, everything
3. Life is a sad experience from birth to death.
4. b. schoolboy—whining, creeping like snail
   c. lover—sighing like furnace, with a woeful ballad/Made to his mistress' eyebrow

   d. soldier—only desires honor, argues a lot
   e. justice—fat man with mean eyes
   f. pantaloon—old, foolish; high-pitched voice sounds like a child's
   g. second childishness—without teeth, eyesight, or taste
5. The speaker views life and all of its stages negatively.

### Unit 10

### *from* the Odyssey, Book 1 by Homer
### Translated by Robert Fitzgerald
### The Cyclops

**p. 191 Reading Check** Words to be circled: *the island of the Cyclopes*

**p. 191 Literary Analysis** *a prodigious man; knowing none but savage ways, a brute/so huge, he seemed no man at all; he seemed rather a shaggy mountain reared in solitude.*

**p. 191 Think Ahead** Possible answer: No. I don't think that Odysseus would agree with stealing.

**p. 192 Reading Strategy** To be circled: commas and semicolons To be boxed: periods

**p. 192 Literary Analysis** Words that may be underlined: *Odysseus says they are Trojans returning from the war. Odysseus asks for help or gifts that the Cyclops might wish to offer them.*

**p. 192 Reading Check** The Cyclops picks up the men, beats them, tears them apart, and eats them.

**p. 193 Literary Analysis** *Possible answer:* Odysseus bravely faces danger when he jams a sharp pole into the Cyclops' eye.

**p. 193 Reading Strategy** Words to be circled: seared; broiling, Words to be underlined: bar; popped.

**p. 193 Reading Check** The other Cyclopes think the blind Cyclops means that nobody did him harm. The blind Cyclops means that Odysseus, whom he thinks is named 'Nohbdy,' did him harm.

**p. 194 Stop to Reflect** If the men rode on the sheep's backs, the Cyclops would probably see the men as he led the animals out of the cave.

**p. 194 Reading Strategy** Students should circle *going this way and that to untie the men. and drove them down to where the good ship lay.*

**p. 194 Reading Check** Students should draw a box around *They fear that the blind giant will figure out their sea position from his voice. The Cyclops may throw a huge rock at them.*

**p. 195 Reading Strategy** Students should circle all commas and colons, and they should underline the exclamation point.

**p. 195 Reading Check** The Cyclops hates Odysseus because Odysseus blinded him and stole his animals.

**p. 195 Literary Analysis** They give him the ram, the most prized of all the flock.

**Review and Assess**

1. Possible words: enormous, scary, violent, wild, savage, cruel

2. He eats two of Odysseus' men, and the next day he eats two more.

3. They steal his sheep and a ram.

4. *Possible answers:* a. clever; b. brave c. clever, cares for his men

5. Students should circle all commas and the hyphen, and they should underline the exclamation point and the period.

# Answers: Part 2

## "The Cask of Amontillado" by Edgar Allan Poe (p. 201)

### Form a Mental Picture

Suggested responses: Student sketches should accurately portray each scene by incorporating details from the selection. For example, sketches of Fortunato's costume should include: a clown outfit, tight-fitting parti-striped dress, conical cap and bells.

## "The Most Dangerous Game" by Richard Connell (p. 202)

### Identify Chain of Events

Sample responses:

**Event 3:** Rainsford hears a scream from the island and swims toward the sound.

**Event 4:** After a rough swim, Rainsford reaches the island and falls asleep.

**Event 5:** Rainsford follows a hunter's tracks to a palatial mansion.

(Student should continue presenting the events in order.)

## "Casey at the Bat" by Ernest Lawrence Thayer (p. 203)

### Translate Baseball Phrases

Sample responses: 2. was out at second base 3. hit the ball hard 4. was on third base 5. fans cheered 6. pressed the ball to his hip in preparation to pitch

## "The Birds" by Daphne du Maurier (p. 204)

### Use a Timeline

Sample responses:

**Day 1 Events:** At work Nat notices many more birds than usual and considers how bold they have become. That night, birds attack Nat when he opens the window. Answering a cry from his children's room, Nat finds birds attacking them. (Students should continue presenting the events in order.)

**Day 2 Events:** Nat notices the corpses of the birds in the children's room, but sees no sign of live birds. The sky turns hard and leaden, indicating a swift change in the weather to a cold, "black winter." Nat sees his daughter Jill off to school and goes to the farm, where people doubt his fantastic story. (Students should continue presenting the events in order.)

**Day 3 Events:** The broadcast from the wireless does not come on, leaving the family on its own. The birds watch as Nat and his family make their way to the farm. Nat finds the farm destroyed by the birds, and the farmer and his wife dead. (Students should continue presenting the events in order.)

### "The Red-headed League"
### by Sir Arthur Conan Doyle (p. 205)
**Break Down Sentences**

Sample response:

**Sentence:** You will remember that I remarked the other day, just before we went into the very simple problem presented by Miss Mary Sutherland, that for strange effects and extraordinary combinations we must go to life itself, which is always far more daring than any effort of the imagination.

**Sentence broken into parts:** You will remember that I made a remark the other day. I made it just before we went into the very simple problem presented by Miss Mary Sutherland. I remarked that, for strange effects and extraordinary combinations, we must go to life itself. Life is always far more daring than any effort of the imagination.

(Students should present four such sentences broken down into parts.)

### "The Listeners" by Walter de la Mare
### "Beware: Do Not Read This Poem"
### by Ishmael Reed
### "Echo" by Henriqueta Lisboa (p. 206)
**Restate Poetry as Prose**

Sample responses:

**"The Listeners" (lines 1–8):** "Is there anybody there?" said the Traveler, knocking on the moonlit door. And his horse in the silence clamped the grasses of the forest's ferny floor. And

a bird flew up out of the turret, above the Traveler's head. And he smote upon the door a second time. "Is there anybody there?" he said.

**"Beware: Do Not Read This Poem" (fourth stanza):** Do not resist this poem. This poem has your eyes. This poem has his head. This poem has his arms. This poem has his fingers. This poem has his fingertips. This poem is the reader and the reader this poem.

**"Echo":** The green parrot let out a shrill scream. The rock, in sudden anger, replied. A great uproar invaded the forest. Thousands of parrots screamed together and the rock echoed. From all sides strafing space steely screams rained and rained down. Very piercing screams! But no one died.

### "Caucasian Mummies Mystify Chinese"
### by Keay Davidson (p. 207)
**Analyze Sources**

Sample responses:

**Quotation:** "In the 1910s and 1920s, it was a game of the imperialist (Western) archaeologists to go in and take away important stuff—ancient manuscripts, artworks, painting, statues. . . (Chinese officials are) very sensitive to that and they don't want to make the same situation recur." (Students should continue to list Mair's quotations.)

**Details:** Chinese officials may have hidden the find because they didn't know how to put it into any of their schemes for history; mummies were in perfect condition; DNA analysis is being used to identify the mummies' place of origin; European features suggest the people came from Northern Europe; China has been significantly influenced by other civilizations throughout history and prehistory.

### from *A Lincoln Preface*
### by Carl Sandburg (p. 208)

**Summarize**

Sample responses: 3. Lincoln told Harriet Beecher Stowe that he would not last long after the Civil War ended. 4. When an Illinois Congressman expressed surprise that Lincoln was elected President, Lincoln replied that the times called for a man without a policy. 5. Lincoln told a Cabinet officer that he would violate the Constitution to save the Union.

(Students should continue to list summaries of the anecdotes.)

### "I Have a Dream"
### by Martin Luther King, Jr.
### from *Rosa Parks: My Story*
### by Rosa Parks with Jim Haskins
### "There Is a Longing . . ."
### by Chief Dan George
### "I Hear America Singing"
### by Walt Whitman (p. 209)

**Identify Key Ideas**

Sample responses:

**from *Rosa Parks: My Story*:**
1. Equality 2. Dignity 3. Freedom
4. Justice

**"There Is a Longing . . .":** 1. Sense of worth and purpose 2. Place in society 3. Courage 4. Harmony with environment 5. Education 6. Pride
7. Knowledge 8. Freedom

**"I Hear America Singing":** 1. Pride of workers 2. Individuality 3. Unity for common good

### "The Golden Kite, the Silver Wind"
### by Ray Bradbury (p. 210)

**Recognize Cause and Effect**

Sample responses:

**Cause:** club to beat pig

**Effect:** fire to burn club

**Cause:** lake to put out fire

**Effect:** mouth to drink lake

**Cause:** needle to sew up mouth

**Effect:** sword to break needle

**Cause:** scabbard to sheathe sword

**Effect:** lightning to destroy sheathe

### "The Road Not Taken" by Robert Frost
### "New Directions" by Maya Angelou
### "To Be of Use" by Marge Piercy (p. 211)

**Paraphrase**

Sample responses:

**"The Road Not Taken" (starting with second sentence):** I then took the other, which was just as attractive, and perhaps had the better claim because it looked grassy and fresh. Although, perhaps they were equally used as both were covered with fresh leaves. I hoped to explore the other path later. Yet I doubt I will ever be able to do so. Someday I shall recall this decision with regret. I chose the less-traveled road, and that has made all the difference in my life.

**"To Be of Use":** The people I love the best attack their work head-on. They seem to become part of their work. I love people who bond with the task and pursue it with patience and fortitude to see it through. I want to be with the people who actually do the difficult work, forming a common bond to get a job done. Much of the work people do is as common as mud. Not done well, it crumbles into dust. But work well done has a satisfying shape. Greek amphoras and Hopi vases are treasured in museums, but they were made to be of use. The pitcher's value is in the water it carries, and a person's value comes from doing work that is real.

### "Old Man of the Temple"
### by R. K. Narayan (p. 212)
**Prepare a Readers Theater**

Suggested responses: Students should assign the four roles and jot down details from the story that will help them with their performance.

### "Perseus" by Edith Hamilton (p. 213)
**Identify Characters**

Sample responses:

**Character:** Acrisius

**Relationship to Other Characters:** father of Danaë and grandfather of Perseus

**Important Idea About Character:** puts his daughter and grandson in a chest, which is cast into the sea

**Character:** Danaë

**Relationship to Other Characters:** mother of Perseus

**Important Idea About Character:** according to prophecy, her son will kill her father

(Students should complete the chart for all the characters.)

### "Slam, Dunk, & Hook"
### by Yusef Komunyakaa
### "The Spearthrower" by Lillian Morrison
### "Shoulders" by Naomi Shihab Nye (p. 214)
**Explain Poetic Phrases**

Sample responses: 3. The players' bodies were so intertwined while reaching for the ball that they formed what looked like a maze in the area of the court beneath the basket. 4. The ball hung in the air for what seemed like a long time, although it was only a second. 5. The players made a motion like a corkscrew, twisting as they rose in the air to dunk the ball. 6. Metaphysical means "beyond the physical"; when the girls cheered, the players were so immersed in the game that the experience was spiritual to them. 7. A motor makes a machine go; the players' muscles, shiny with sweat, were like a bright motor, powering their moves. 8. The metal hoop used to play basketball was nailed to what was once an oak tree.

(Students should continue listing phrases and restating them.)

### "Children in the Woods"
### by Barry Lopez (p. 215)
**Outline Author's Argument**

Sample responses:

I. Children notice small details about nature.

A. As a child, the author stopped to look at a pattern of sunlight in a windowpane.

B. A woman mentioned how remarkable it is that children notice these things.

II. The incident has had a lasting effect on the author.

A. He feels a sense of responsibility toward children when he remembers it.

B. He was acutely affected by the woman's words.

(Students should continue to complete the outline.)

### "Rules of the Game" by Amy Tan (p. 216)
**Respond to Characters' Actions**

Sample responses:

**Character:** Waverly

**What the Character Does:** She teases a tourist by telling him that guts, duck's feet, and octopus gizzards are served in a restaurant.

**Your Reaction to What He/She Does:** She is a bold girl.

**Character:** Mrs. Jong

**What the Character Does:** She tells Waverly that Chinese people do the best torture.

**Your Reaction to What He/She Does:** She seems like a proud woman.

(Students should continue to complete the chart.)

## "Checkouts" by Cynthia Rylant
## "Fifteen" by William Stafford (p. 217)

**Analyze Characters' Behavior**

Sample responses:

**"Checkouts"**

> **Character:** The girl
>
> **What the Character Does:** She goes to the grocery shop.
>
> **Why the Character Does It:** She can relax and wander.
>
> **Character:** The boy
>
> **What the Character Does:** He drops a jar of mayonnaise.
>
> **Why the Character Does It:** He is nervous because it is his first day at work and he is shaken when the girl he has been admiring smiles at him.
>
> (Students should continue to complete the chart.)

**"Fifteen"**

> **Character:** The speaker
>
> **What the Character Does:** He takes the motorcycle to the road and stands with it.
>
> **Why the Character Does It:** He admires the bike and wants to ride it.
>
> (Students should continue to complete the chart.)

## "Sympathy" by Paul Laurence Dunbar
## "Caged Bird" by Maya Angelou
## "We never know how high we are" by Emily Dickinson
## from *In My Place* by Charlayne Hunter-Gault (p. 218)

**Compare and Contrast Images**

Sample responses:

**"Sympathy"** and **"Caged Bird"**

> Similarities: not free; longs for freedom; sings; feels anger
>
> Differences: The bird in "Sympathy" sees what he cannot have, beats his wings bloody, and sings a prayer; the bird in "Caged Bird" can "seldom see through his bars of rage," stalks down his cage, and sings of freedom.

## "The Interlopers" by Saki (H. H. Munro) (p. 219)

**Follow Dialogue**

Sample responses:

> **Poacher Georg:** "Are you sure your men will find much to release? I have men, too. . . . When they drag me out . . . it won't need much clumsiness . . . to roll this mass of trunk right over the top of you. . . . I shall send my condolences to your family."
>
> **Landowner Ulrich:** "It is a useful hint. . . . My men had orders to follow . . . and when they get me out—I will remember the hint. Only as you will have met your death poaching on my lands I don't think I can decently send any message of condolence to your family."
>
> (Students should continue to chart the conversation.)

## "The Rug Merchant"
### by James A. Michener (p. 220)
### Question Author's Purpose

Sample responses: 4. Q: How will the man persuade Michener to buy a rug? A: He will wear him down. 5. Q: Of what is the man proud? A: He is proud that not one rug was woven in Afghanistan. 6. Q: What does the man tell Michener to entice him to buy a rug? A: He tells Michener that the rugs will look great in his place in Pennsylvania.

(Students should continue to write questions and answers for each paragraph.)

## "Combing" by Gladys Cardiff
## "Women" by Alice Walker
## "maggie and milly and molly and may" by E. E. Cummings
## "Astonishment" by Wisława Szymborska (p. 221)
### Connect

Sample responses:

**Character:** Speaker in "Women"

**Connects with Whom or What?** women of her mother's generation

**What Is Discovered?** These women made life better for the generations of women to follow.

**Character:** maggie, milly, molly, and may

**Connects with Whom or What?** nature

**What Is Discovered?** Nature can help us better get in touch with ourselves.

**Character:** Speaker in "Astonishment"

**Connects with Whom or What?** place in the universe

**What Is Discovered?** People will never really know their place in the universe.

## "The Secret Life of Walter Mitty"
### by James Thurber (p. 222)
### Distinguish Between Fantasy and Reality

Sample responses:

**Fantasy:** Mitty is a doctor caring for a millionaire banker; Mitty, as the doctor, fixes a complicated machine; Mitty is the defendant in a murder trial; Mitty is a captain ready to fly a bomber; Mitty is a man facing a firing squad.

**Reality:** Mrs. Mitty tells him to put on his gloves; The parking-lot attendant tells him to back up his car; He buys overshoes; He remembers that his wife told him to buy puppy biscuits; Mrs. Mitty finds him sitting in the hotel lobby.

## "The Inspector-General"
### by Anton Chekhov (p. 223)
### Prepare a Readers Theater

Suggested responses: Students should assign the three roles, jot down ideas about their performance, and finally present their performance to the class. The class should evaluate the performance.

## "Go Deep to the Sewer" by Bill Cosby
## "Fly Away" by Ralph Helfer (p. 224)
### Translate Jargon

Sample answers: 3. Cosby wanted to be handed the ball and then run for a touchdown. 4. The quarterback uses garbage to indicate the plays. 5. You can throw the ball to me at the fender of the car. 6. Make the first movement of a zigzag toward the bakery. 7. You pretend to go far out and then turn at the DeSoto.

(Students should continue to list and translate examples of jargon.)

## "An Entomological Study of Apartment 4A" by Patricia Volk (p. 225)

### Recognize Puns and Word Play

Sample responses: 2. *Scuttle* means "scurry"; an insect would make such a movement. 3. A louse is a small, wingless insect that infests the hair or skin of people and animals. 4. People dial 911 to get help in emergencies. 5. Moisturizer is a harmless cream. 6. One does not usually think of the lives of insects as being "high drama." 7. The insect was in the chili powder. 8. Eggs over easy is a favorite breakfast of many people. 9. Sorkin's mind is so full of facts that he is like an encyclopedia. 10. "Homo sapiens" refers to people. The ritual of nodding goodbye and shaking hands is contrasted with the insects' way of greeting each other.

## "Macavity: The Mystery Cat" by T. S. Eliot

## "Problems With Hurricanes" by Victor Hernández Cruz

## "Jabberwocky" by Lewis Carroll (p. 226)

### Identify Incongruity

Sample Responses:

"Macavity: The Mystery Cat": 1. It is not expected that a cat would be "the bafflement of Scotland Yard." 2. It is not expected that a cat would cheat at cards.

"Problems With Hurricanes": 1. It is not expected that a flying banana would kill someone. 2. It is not expected that a mango could smash someone's skull.

## "Talk" by Harold Courlander (p. 227)

### Read Aloud

Suggested responses: Students should assign the roles, jot down ideas about what kind of voice to use, and then read the selection aloud.

## "One Ordinary Day, With Peanuts" by Shirley Jackson (p. 228)

### Use a Chain-of-Events Organizer

Sample responses:

Event 2: Mr. Johnson stops to help a harried woman who is busy moving out of her apartment; predictable

Event 3: After a woman, who is late for work, crashes into Mr. Johnson, he pairs her up with a man in the same situation, pays them both for a days' work, and gives them money to go out on a date; not predictable

(Students should continue to list events and label each as predictable or not predictable.)

## from *The Road Ahead* by Bill Gates (p. 229)

### Outline Main Idea and Supporting Details

Sample responses:

### Paragraph 2

**Main Idea:** Conventional television allows us to decide what we watch but not when we watch it.

### Details about the Main Idea:

1. Synchronous broadcasting—viewers synchronize their schedule with the time of broadcast
2. How Gates watched *The Ed Sullivan Show* and how most will watch the news tonight

## Paragraph 3

**Main Idea:** Videocassette recorders gave us more flexibility in the early 1980s.

**Details about the Main Idea:**

1. If fuss with timer and tape, can watch program any time
2. Converts synchronous communication into "asynchronous" communication

(Students should continue listing the main idea and supporting details for each paragraph.)

## "The Machine That Won the War" by Isaac Asimov (p. 230)

### Paraphrase Conversations

Sample responses:

Sentence 1, Paraphrase:

Henderson: "What do you know of the data Multivac had to use: predigested from a hundred subsidiary computers here on Earth, on the moon, on Mars, even on Titan."

Paraphrase: What do you know of the information Multivac had to use from networked computers in different locations?

Sentence 2, Paraphrase:

Jabolonsky: "If it had mattered, I would have followed it up and spotted you, John, and found out what you were doing."

Paraphrase: If it had been important, I would have checked, noticed you, and discovered what you were doing.

Sentence 3, Paraphrase:

Swift: "Multivac is not the first computer, friends, not the best-known, nor the one that can most efficiently lift the load of decision from the shoulders of the executive."

Paraphrase: Multivac is not the first, best-known, or most efficient decision-making computer.

## "Fire and Ice" by Robert Frost
## "All Watched Over by Machines of Loving Grace" by Richard Brautigan
## "There Will Come Soft Rains" by Sara Teasdale
## "The Horses" by Edwin Muir (p. 231)

### Interpret Poetic Images

Sample responses:

**"All Watched Over by Machines of Loving Grace":** 2. friendly looking machines looking out over a group of happy people—feels uncomfortable, as if the machines have taken over

**"There Will Come Soft Rains":** 1. a line of plum trees quivering in the gentle wind—feels peaceful 2. robins showing their fine red feathers—feels happy and carefree

**"The Horses":** 1. a giant globe swallowing the people—feels frightening and upsetting 2. the people of every country asleep, curled up as if nothing will wake them—feels distressing

## "If I Forget Thee, Oh Earth . . ." by Arthur C. Clarke
## from *Silent Spring* by Rachel Carson
## "To the Residents of A.D. 2029" by Bryan Woolley (p. 232)

### Identify Predictions

Sample responses:

**Selection**: "If I Forget Thee, Oh Earth . . ." In the Future: Future generations will return to Earth.

**Selection:** from *Silent Spring*

**Now:** Nature is alive with all its wonders.

**In the Future:** Everything dies.

**Selection:** "To the Residents of A.D. 2029"

**Now:** We have polluted the waters and the air, used up valuable resources, put ourselves on the brink of war, and failed to solve social problems like poverty.

**In the Future:** Some problems will be solved but others will still exist.

## "Gifts" by Shu Ting
## "Glory and Hope"
### by Nelson Mandela (p. 233)
## Break Down Long Sentences

Sample responses:

**Mandela's Sentence:** We enter into a covenant that we shall build the society in which all South Africans, both black and white, will be able to walk tall, without any fear in their hearts, assured of their inalienable right to human dignity—a rainbow nation at peace with itself and the world.

**Sentence in Parts:** We enter into a covenant. It [the covenant] is that we shall build a society in which both black and white South Africans will be able to walk tall. They will walk without any fear in their hearts. They will be assured of their inalienable right to human dignity. It will be a rainbow nation at peace with itself and the world.

(Students should continue to break down any sentence longer than five lines.)

## "The Gift of the Magi"
### by O. Henry (p. 234)
## Simplify Word Order

Sample responses: 2. The electric button did not work 3. Near the letter-box was a card with the name "Mr. James Dillingham Young."

(Students should choose another paragraph and simplify the word order.)

## "Sonata for Harp and Bicycle"
### by Joan Aiken (p. 235)
## Explain Comparisons

Sample responses:

**Person or thing being described:** the staff

**It is compared to:** lemmings

**This comparison suggests:** They are moving quickly.

**Person or thing being described:** Miss Golden's eyes

**It is compared to:** peridots

**This comparison suggests:** Her eyes are a green color resembling the gems.

**Person or thing being described:** sound of traffic

**It is compared to:** a ninth wave

**This comparison suggests:** The sound of the traffic was very loud.

(Students should continue to complete the chart by identifying and explaining comparisons.)

## "The Scarlet Ibis" by James Hurst (p. 236)
## Classify Descriptive Details

Sample responses:

**Movements:** tumbling, bumping landing, jerking

**Colors:** (no additional colors)

**Positions:** neck straightening out, legs crossed, feet curved at rest

**Sounds:** thud

**Other Details:** wings uncoordinated, spray of flying feathers, veil over eyes, beak unhinged

(Students should complete the chart for another passage from the story.)

## "Blues Ain't No Mockin Bird"
### by Toni Cade Bambara
## "Uncle Marcos" by Isabel Allende (p. 237)
## Understand Dialect

Sample responses: (2) because she knows Granny's whole story better than I do. (3) For example, she knew why we move so much, and (4) Cathy is only a third cousin we picked up while visiting last Thanksgiving. (5) However, she knew we moved because people were driving Granny crazy (6) until she got up in the night and started packing. (7) She was mumbling, packing, and waking everybody up (8) saying, "Let's get away from here before I kill somebody."

(Students should rewrite the dialect from another passage from the story.)

**"The Man to Send Rain Clouds"**
**by Leslie Marmon Silko**

**"The Invalid's Story"**
**by Mark Twain (p. 238)**

**Identify Cause and Effect**

Sample responses:

> **Cause:** A stranger sets a package of Limburger cheese on the end of the coffin-box.
>
> **Effect:** A horrible odor comes from that area.
>
> **Cause:** A horrible odor comes from the box.
>
> **Effect:** The narrator is depressed by this reminder of his friend's death.
>
> **Cause:** A storm rages outside.
>
> **Effect:** Thompson makes the compartment airtight and starts a fire in the stove.
>
> **Cause:** Thompson makes the compartment airtight and starts a fire in the stove.
>
> **Effect:** The smell becomes even more overpowering.
>
> (Students should continue to list all the causes and effects for the chosen selection.)

**"The Necklace"**
**by Guy de Maupassant**

**"The Harvest" by Tomás Rivera (p. 239)**

**Sequence Events**

> **Event 1:** Don Trine takes walks by himself and does not want anyone coming with him.
>
> **Event 3:** The boys follow Don Trine to an irrigation ditch.
>
> **Event 5:** The following Monday, the boys see Don Trine dig holes, stick his arm in up to his elbow, and fill in the dirt around his arm.
>
> **Event 6:** The next day, one of the boys goes through the same procedure.

**Event 7:** After that, the boy keeps going to the field every afternoon to follow the procedure until a hard freeze prevents him from doing so.

(Students should make a sequence organizer for "The Necklace.")

**"Single Room, Earth View"**
**by Sally Ride (p. 240)**

**Identify Main Idea and Supporting Details**

Sample responses:

> Detail: Familiar geographical features, cities, bridges, and airports are easy to recognize.
>
> Detail: The Great Wall of China is not the only man-made object visible from space.
>
> (Students should list the main idea and supporting details from a few other paragraphs in the selection.)

**"The Washwoman"**
**by Isaac Bashevis Singer**

**"On Summer" by Lorraine Hansberry**

**"A Celebration of Grandfathers"**
**by Rudolfo A. Anaya (p. 241)**

**Summarize Main Idea**

Sample responses:

> Paragraph from "The Washwoman": Laundering was not easy in those days. The old woman had no faucet where she lived. She had to bring in the water from a pump. For the linens to come out so clean, they had to be scrubbed thoroughly in a washtub, rinsed with washing soda, soaked, boiled in an enormous pot, starched, then ironed. . . .
>
> Main Idea: Doing the laundry was a difficult task for the old woman to endure.
>
> Supporting Details: bring water from a pump; linens scrubbed in a washtub, rinsed with washing soda, soaked, boiled, starched, then ironed; pieces handled ten times or more; wrung-out

wash carried up to attic and hung on clotheslines; brittle in winter; fights with others for the attic clothesline.

(Students should summarize the main idea and supporting details for other paragraphs.)

### from *A White House Diary* by Lady Bird Johnson
### "Arthur Ashe Remembered" by John McPhee
### "Georgia O'Keeffe" by Joan Didion (p. 242)

**Interpret Direct Quotations**

Sample responses:

**Quotation:** "It was Lyndon who spoke of it first, although I knew I would not leave without doing it. He said, 'You had better try to see Jackie and Nellie.'"

**Insight It Provides:** Lyndon Johnson was calm, considering the things that should be attended to. He was also aware that the two women would need comfort.

**Quotation:** ". . . she [Mrs. Kennedy] said, 'I want them to see what they have done to Jack.'"

**Insight It Provides:** Jackie Kennedy was more concerned with showing what had been done to her husband than with her own comfort.

(Students should continue to write and interpret quotations from the selections.)

### "Understanding Comics" by Scott McCloud (p. 243)

**Translate Cartoon Images**

Sample responses:

**Cartoon Image:** Second frame: writer/cartoonist is still working on a cartoon at his drawing board while he remembers what he thought of comics when he was a kid.

**Ideas Expressed:** By continuing to work and talk, the writer/cartoonist sets a friendly, casual tone. By using bold capital letters, he suggests that he was very sure of what comics were when he was a little kid.

**Cartoon Image:** Second and third frames: The cartoonist has stopped working and is talking directly to the audience, telling about his low opinion of comics as a kid.

**Ideas Expressed:** By talking directly to the audience, the cartoonist gives weight to what he is saying.

(Students should continue to describe the cartoon image and then indicate the ideas expressed.)

### "Earhart Redux" by Alex Chadwick
### *In These Girls, Hope Is a Muscle* by Madeleine Blais (book review)
### *In These Girls, Hope Is a Muscle* by Madeleine Blais (book jacket) (p. 244)

**Propose Headlines**

Sample responses:

**Story:** *In These Girls, Hope Is a Muscle*
Book Review

**Headline:** The Lady Hurricanes: Quest for Excellence

**Story:** *In These Girls, Hope Is a Muscle*
Book Jacket

**Headline:** Blais's Moving Narrative Pays Homage to Women Athletes

### *The Dancers* by Horton Foote (p. 245)

**Prepare a Readers Theater**

Suggested responses: Students should divide the play into scenes, assign roles for each scene, and jot down details from the play that will help them with their performance. Then they should perform their play for the class. After the presentations, the class should evaluate each performance.

### The Tragedy of Romeo and Juliet, Act I
### by William Shakespeare (p. 246)

**Summarize Plot**

Suggested responses: Students should indicate all important characters with stick figures, adequately distinguishing one figure from another. The cartoon strips should indicate the main action of the scene, with the words in the dialogue bubbles appearing in modern English.

### The Tragedy of Romeo and Juliet, Act II
### by William Shakespeare (p. 247)

**Analyze Characters**

Sample Responses:

**Character:** Romeo

**What They Do:** Declares his love for Juliet; goes to Friar Lawrence to arrange an elopement.

**What They Say:** "Then plainly know my heart's dear love is set/On the fair daughter of rich Capulet."

**What Others Say About Them:** Mercutio says, "Alas, Poor Romeo, he is already dead: stabbed with a white wench's black eye; run through the ear with a love song. . . ."

**Character:** Juliet

**What They Do:** Declares her love for Romeo in the balcony scene; meets Romeo at Friar Lawrence's cell so they can wed.

**What Others Say About Them:** The Nurse says, ". . . my mistress is the sweetest lady. . . ."

(Students should continue to fill in the chart for the other characters.)

### The Tragedy of Romeo and Juliet, Act III
### by William Shakespeare (p. 248)

**Use a Story Map Organizer**

Sample responses:

Setting: Time—fourteenth century

Problem: Romeo and Juliet are in love, but their families are feuding.

Event 4: Romeo kills Tybalt and is banished by the Prince.

Event 5: The Capulets arrange for Juliet's speedy marriage to Paris, but she refuses.

Event 6: Friar Lawrence proposes that Juliet fake her death and then go to Mantua with Romeo.

Climax: Romeo kills Tybalt.

(Students should continue to list the main events from the play.)

### The Tragedy of Romeo and Juliet, Act IV
### by William Shakespeare (p. 249)

**Recognize Dramatic Irony**

Sample responses: 2. The audience might fear that Juliet's act is a little too convincing. Her father moves up the wedding day, causing potential problems for Juliet. 3. The audience, knowing that Juliet is trying to get rid of her mother so she can be alone to take the potion, might feel some anxiety for the girl. She not only cannot depend on her mother for support, but must deceive her. 4. The audience, knowing that Juliet is not dead, might feel some sympathy for the Capulets, who believe they have lost their daughter.

### The Tragedy of Romeo and Juliet, Act V
### by William Shakespeare (p. 250)

**Recognize Metaphors**

Sample responses: 1. Paris compares Juliet to a flower to suggest that she was taken in the full bloom of life. 2. Romeo compares the tomb with a stomach and a womb since, like those two, it contains something, in this case Juliet's body ("dearest morsel of earth"). 3. Romeo now compares the tomb with a monster whose jaws he is forcing open. When he says he will "cram thee with more food," he suggests that he wants to join Juliet in the tomb.

Sample response for the three new metaphors: 4. Romeo (at the graveyard) Death, that hath sucked the honey of thy breath,/ Hath had no power yet upon thy beauty. By comparing Juliet's life to honey sucked away by death, Romeo indirectly calls her a flower.

(Students should continue identifying and explaining metaphors.)

### "I Wandered Lonely as a Cloud" by William Wordsworth (p. 251)

**Infer Feelings**

Sample responses:

**Stanza 2:** (Students should write the stanza)
**Feelings:** The poet is awed by the fact that the daffodils are as continuous as the stars, stretching in a seemingly endless line.

**Stanza 3:** (Students should write the stanza)
**Feelings:** The poet feels the flowers outdo the sparkling waves in portraying cheer. He takes great joy in watching the daffodils flutter in the wind. The fact that they seem so cheerful makes him happy too.

**Stanza 4:** (Students should write the stanza)
**Feelings:** The poet remembers the flower with pleasure when he is at home on his couch. He feels grateful for a memory that can always bring him joy.

### "The Eagle" by Alfred, Lord Tennyson
### "'Hope' is the thing with feathers—" by Emily Dickinson
### "Dream Deferred" and "Dreams" by Langston Hughes (p. 252)

**Recognize Unusual Comparisons**

Sample responses:

**The two things being compared:** life without dreams; a barren field frozen with snow

**How they are alike:** Both are empty; both are lacking warmth

(Students should choose another poem and identify and explain the comparisons.)

### "Blackberry Eating" by Galway Kinnell
### "Memory" by Margaret Walker
### "Woman's Work" by Julia Alvarez
### "Meciendo" by Gabriela Mistral
### "Eulogy for a Hermit Crab" by Pattiann Rogers (p. 253)

**Identify Speaker's Attitude**

Sample responses: tangle of blinding spume and spray—sympathetic; pistol-shot collisions—sympathetic; You stayed, wet icy wind—admiring; You were here—respectful

(Student should identify the speaker's attitude in key phrases of one of the other poems.)

### "Uphill" by Christina Rossetti
### "Summer" by Walter Dean Myers
### Ecclesiastes 3:1–8, The King James Bible
### "The Bells" by Edgar Allan Poe (p. 254)

**Identify Sensory Words**

Sample responses:

**Sight:** old men sleeping, daisies lay, beaming
**Sound:** peeping
**Taste:** Juices dripping

(Students should identify sensory words in another poem.)

### "The Raven" by Edgar Allan Poe
### "The Seven Ages of Man" by William Shakespeare (p. 255)

**Summarize Poetic Narrative**

Sample responses:

**Stanza 2**
**Summary:** I remember it was December and I was trying to lose myself in my books to end my sorrow over the loss of Lenore.

**Words that create a mood:** bleak, dying, ghost, sorrow

**Mood:** mournful

**Stanza 3**

**Summary:** I was so frightened that each rustling of the curtains filled me with terror, and I rationalized that the sound was just a late visitor.

**Words that create a mood:** sad, uncertain, fantastic terrors

**Mood:** sad and frightening

(Students should continue to summarize each stanza, list the words creating a mood, and describe the mood.)

## "On the Grasshopper and the Cricket" by John Keats
## Sonnet 30 by William Shakespeare
## Three Haiku by Bashō and Chiyojo
## "Hokku Poems" by Richard Wright (p. 256)

### Restate Poetic Language

Sample responses:

**Sonnet 30**

**Poetic Words:** remembrance of things past

**Familiar Words:** memories of the past

**Poetic Words:** friends hid in death's dateless night

**Familiar Words:** friends who have died

(Students should continue to list poetic words and translate to familiar words for Sonnet 30 and one other poem.)

## The *Odyssey*, Part 1 by Homer (p. 257)

### Identify Story Elements

Sample responses:

**Main events:** 1. The Lotus-Eaters offer the sweet Lotus to Odysseus's men. 2. The men who eat the Lotus no longer want to return home. 3. Odysseus drives the men who ate the Lotus to the ships, ties them down, and warns the others not to eat the Lotus. 4. The ships take off.

**Conclusion:** Odysseus forces the men into the ships and takes off.

(Students should identify the story elements for another adventure from the *Odyssey*.)

## The *Odyssey*, Part 2 by Homer (p. 258)

### Paraphrase Conversations

Sample responses:

**Conversation:** [Odysseus] "A pity that you have more looks than heart. You'd grudge a pinch of salt from your own larder to your own handyman. You sit here, fat on others' meats and cannot bring yourself to rummage out a crust of bread for me!"

[Antinous] "You think you'll shuffle and get away after that impudence? Oh, no you don't."

**Paraphrase:** [Odysseus] You are a stingy person who will not help others even though you have plenty.

[Antinous] I won't let you get away with such disrespect.

(Students should paraphrase at least five conversations.)

**"An Ancient Gesture"
by Edna St. Vincent Millay**

**"Siren Song" by Margaret Atwood**

**"Prologue" and "Epilogue"
from The *Odyssey* by Derek Walcott**

**"Ithaca" by Constantine Cavafy (p. 259)**

**Recognize Allusions**

Sample responses:

**"An Ancient Gesture"**

**Allusion:** Penelope

**Explanation:** Penelope was the wife of Odysseus, who patiently and loyally awaited his return. She would weave all day and undo her work at night to stall her many suitors.

**"Prologue" and "Epilogue" from
The *Odyssey***

**Allusion:** God of the Sea

**Explanation:** This refers to Poseidon, who was angry with Odysseus for the blinding of his son, the Cyclops.

**Allusion:** long years after Troy

**Explanation:** Troy was the scene of the Trojan War, the ten-year war waged against Troy by the Greeks in order to rescue the abducted Helen.

(Students should continue to list allusions in the poems to people or events in the *Odyssey* and then explain each allusion.)